Books by M. A. Stoneridge

A HORSE OF YOUR OWN, new, revised edition

GREAT HORSES OF OUR TIME

Practical Horseman's
BOOK OF
HORSEKEEPING

Practical Horseman's
BOOK OF
HORSEKEEPING

Edited by

M. A. STONERIDGE

with a Foreword by William C. Steinkraus

Doubleday & Company, Inc.
Garden City, New York
1983

Library of Congress Cataloging in Publication Data

Main entry under title:

Practical horseman's book of horsekeeping.

   1. Horses.   I. Stoneridge, M. A.
SF285.3.P725   1983   636.1
ISBN 0-385-17788-7
Library of Congress Catalog Card Number 82–45150

FOREWORD

Considering the fact that *Practical Horseman* is not much more than a decade old, I have been looking forward to its appearance in hard covers for a long time. I read and admired its inaugural issue, in January 1973, having known its predecessor, *The Pennsylvania Horse,* and before long I started talking to Pam Goold, then as now the magazine's editor, about considering an eventual anthology as soon as there was enough material on hand to justify it. The idea was a "natural," right from the start, for it was obvious that much of the material the magazine was publishing had too much permanent value for it to be permitted to disappear or to drift inexorably to the bottom of the stack of magazines that are too good to throw away but never come to hand when you need to refer to them.

As it happens, the project has taken longer to be realized than I first expected. The *Practical Horseman* staff was too busy putting out new issues to find time to pore through the back ones, and it was not until the well-known equestrian journalist M. A. Stoneridge (who is, I can say with pardonable pride, also my sister) undertook the editing and enlisted the enthusiastic support of her publisher, that the idea became an actuality. By then it was apparent that a single volume would be inadequate to encompass the whole range of material that had appeared, and the project was divided into two parts: the present volume, and a second one, devoted to training, showing, and riding, which will appear later.

The origins of my enthusiasm for this kind of project go back a long way. Perhaps because I was born into a non-horsey family, and thus depended heavily on the printed word as a source of instruction, information, and entertainment about my growing passion, I have been addicted to horse magazines for as long as I can remember. I read everything I could get my hands on, from *Black Beauty* to the *American Racing Manual,* but my staple diet was hard-core "how-to" material, some in book form, but much also in periodicals. I especially favored articles by authors whose names I recognized from their exploits in the show-ring, hunting field, or racetrack, for I have always paid close attention to advice whose practical value had already been demonstrated in the crucible of competition. Because of this you can see that I was (and am) peculiarly susceptible to the *Practical Horseman*'s editorial approach.

The magazine's name—*Practical Horseman*—perfectly reflects its underlying concept, and I have a special feeling, too, about those two particular words. "Practical"—as opposed to speculative or theoretical—means derived from or capable of being put into practice or action, and in this case it means that the content is derived from the practical experience of the noted riders, trainers, and others involved, their ideas having been solicited because of their current level of accomplishment in equestrian sport. The ideas may differ, but all share the "practical" origin, having survived the acid test of day-to-day use in the barn or the saddle. And to me, what people do (or think they do) when they are "going good" competitively is *always* interesting, whether or not I completely agree with it.

"Horseman" is an even more special word, and the horse people use it much more restrictively than the dictionary definition suggests. As early as 1615, Gervase Markham was distinguishing between those who were "meerely riders, and no keepers" and those who not only could sit on a horse, but also knew how to train, breed, and care for them, and I was brought up to regard the designation "good horseman" as the highest praise a rider could merit. It implied a sound and comprehensive knowledge of virtually every aspect of horse care and training, on or off the horse, and it still applies only to a chosen few.

The following pages, then, constitute a virtual treasure trove for the horse enthusiast: a generous sampling of the opinions and practices of some of the best horsemen (and horsewomen) of our day, as their accomplishments attest, set forth in word and picture for the guidance of those of us who may have to depend largely on self-education for our equestrian progress. I can only hope that you find it as stimulating and as useful in hard covers, as I have reading it serially through the years.

WILLIAM STEINKRAUS

CONTENTS

Contents

Practical Horseman's
BOOK OF
HORSEKEEPING

Chapter 1

CHOOSING AND BUYING
A HORSE

THE RIDING HORSE BREEDS

By ALEXANDER MACKAY-SMITH, Virginia horseman and breeder who is also a prominent figure in American equestrian journalism as an author, editor, and publisher.

Arabian

It is from Arabian strains that most of the world's breeds derive the refinement known to horsemen as quality. Quality manifests itself especially in the head, with its large eyes set wide apart, small muzzle, small ears, and short span from poll to nose. Manes and tails have a special silkiness. The skin is supple, with short hairs and a natural gloss.

The Arabian has the shortest back, containing one less vertebra than other breeds. It has a moderately sloping shoulder, rather low withers, high, flat croup, and a very high-set tail. Not a heavy horse, the Arabian nevertheless is very sound, with prominent tendons and rather large, sound feet. Small (14.0 to 15.1 hands), it is active and tough, with knee action higher than the Thoroughbred's. Its temperament is kind, but it won't accept abuse in the patient manner of many Quarter Horses.

From roughly 1850 to 1950, the popularity of the Arabian horse in Europe and the Americas was based to a considerable extent on its beauty.

During the 1950s, Wendell Robie, an Arabian breeder in Auburn, California, opened a new chapter in Arabian history by founding the Western States 100-Miles-in-24-Hours Trail Ride, from Lake Tahoe to Auburn. This was the pioneer Endurance ride. Arabians and part-Arabians quickly established their superiority in Endurance competition, invariably filling a majority of the first ten places.

The ability of the Arabian to maintain its speed over long distances harks back to its desert origins. The Bedouins used horses primarily for long-distance tribal raids. They traveled aboard pacing camels, leading the war horses at their sides.

Modern Polish breeders maintain and refine quality by admitting to the stud book only those mares and stallions which have proved their ability on the racetrack.

Because of the Arabian's combination of quality, endurance, and soundness, its bloodlines appear in the pedigrees of virtually every breed of horse used in the world today for competitive sport. They are found not only in the Thoroughbred, but also, through the descendants of horses brought to America by the Spaniards, in the various breeds competing with stock saddles: Quarter Horses, Appaloosas, Palominos, Paints, Pintos, Paso Finos. Arabian blood also flows in the veins of Standardbred harness racehorses, and of our breeds competing in saddle-seat classes: the American Saddlebred Horse, the Tennessee Walking Horse, the Morgan. Even the dressage breeds, the Lippizaner, the Andalusian, and the heavy draft Percheron carry Arabian blood.

Of all the world's breeds, the blood of the Arabian has had the greatest influence.

Thoroughbred

Thoroughbreds today not only dominate running races on the flat and over fences, but also classes for hunters, both conformation and working, in our horse shows. Thoroughbreds and near-Thoroughbreds are dominant as field hunters, jumpers, event horses, and polo ponies.

The Thoroughbred was created in the late-seventeenth and early-eighteenth centuries by adding to the native British strain of sprinters (ancestors of the American Quarter Horse) the distance strains of the Arabian. Since that time, sires and dams have been selected on the basis of speed in running races. The Thoroughbred has developed galloping action superior to all other breeds in grace, smoothness, length of stride, closeness to the ground, and overall efficiency. Galloping ability, plus great stamina over middle distances and determination to beat opponents, makes Thoroughbred blood, in whole or nearly in whole, a necessity for all sports in which speed is a factor.

The Thoroughbred has the most extreme slope of shoulder and the most prominent withers of any breed. It has the deep and narrow heart girth typical of the horse that travels at speed. Beyond these characteristics, the saying among racing people that Thoroughbreds run in all shapes and sizes holds true. Breeding stock has always been selected on the basis of running ability, rather than for a specific conformation type.

Generally, the breed seems to divide into two broad types: The distance

An Arabian stallion, Serafix, who sired 450 foals during his lifetime, 80 of which became class A halter champions.

Wendell Robie and his Arabian gelding Nugget during the 100 Mile Western States Trail Ride, which Robie founded in the fifties. Since then, Arabians or part-Arabians have finished first in every ride but two. (Barieau photo)

Thoroughbreds participate in a wide range of equestrian sports, of which the most popular is flat racing.

Snowbound, a Thoroughbred-race-track discard, became an outstanding jumper. Ridden by Bill Steinkraus, he was an Olympic Gold Medal winner.

runner tends to be long-backed, well-coupled, and deep and narrow through the heart. The sprinters range toward the Quarter Horse in type. They are shorter-legged, with more powerful quarters, wider chests, and rounder barrels.

The Thoroughbred head has quality but not the extreme refinement of the Arabian head. It's longer from eye to muzzle, the eyes are not quite so prominent or wide-set, and the muzzle is not so tapering.

The Thoroughbred has a rather long neck, which is carried level. Its stride is long and low. Size ranges from 15.0 to 17.0 hands.

Because of the great variation in the breed, we are able to select individual Thoroughbreds to perform a range of tasks. The field hunter trots and canters at restrainable speeds for long distances, carrying heavy weights over rough ground, and has a quiet temperament. Other strains lend themselves to selection for steeplechasing, combined training, show jumping, dressage, and polo.

The Thoroughbred is not only the world's fastest breed of horse, but also the one most used in the various types of international equestrian sport.

Trakehner, Hanoverian, Holstein

Ever since the eighteenth century, the breeding of light and general-purpose horses has been a principal concern of the German Army, first under the monarchy, then under the republic. Between the two world wars, German Government horse breeding was headed by a civilian, Dr. Gustav Rau, also editor of the leading equestrian magazine *Sankt Georg*. In 1936, while heading a delegation of German officials touring U. S. Army remount depots and privately owned stud farms, Dr. Rau explained to the author that his government was endeavoring to increase rapidly the number of horses in Germany, "because we shall need them in Russia."

Three strains of horses were promoted for military purposes, each being bred in a different locale in the country. For officers' chargers, there was the Trakehner, named after the government stallion depot at Trakehnen, in East Prussia. Horses bred in Trakehnen were a result of the mating of Thoroughbreds and Arabians with the Schwaike, an unsightly little horse indigenous to the area. The result was the Trakehner, near-Thoroughbred in type but with more bone, quieter disposition, and more hock action. The Trakehner has a more horizontal frame than the Thoroughbred, with a long neck and a longer back. It's a big horse, 16 hands to 17.2, with prominent withers, rounded croup, and a medium tail set.

Trakehners were the leading German breed of sport horse before World War II and proved themselves in the 1936 Olympic Games, at which Nurmi won the Three-Day Event and Kronos the Grand Prix de Dressage.

The Hanoverian breed originated in Hanover. In general, the Hanoverian is a heavier horse than the Trakehner, with a shorter neck and less prominent withers. The hindquarters are broader and more muscular, the bone is heavier, the foot larger.

Holsteins, bred in Holstein as artillery and transport horses, were the heaviest of the three.

After World War II, the Cavalry was abolished and agriculture became mechanized. German horsemen altered their breeding plans to produce horses for sport and recreation. Outcrossing was encouraged. With the infusion of Thoroughbred and Arabian blood, as well as exchanges of blood across breed lines, breed distinctions blurred. Today the three stud books represent not so much differences in type as of origin. Breeders in Hanover register their horses in the Hanoverian Stud Book, and so forth. The aim of all German breeders is to produce a marketable type of sport horse.

It isn't unusual for a single stallion to be approved by more than one stud book. In 1960, the Anglo-Arab stallion Ramzes stood at the Vornholz Stud, of Baron von Nagel. His offspring the next year were registered in the Westphalian Stud Book, since the Vornholz Stud is in Westphalia. Later in the year, Ramzes stood in the province of Holstein. His resulting get were registered in the Holsteiner Stud Book.

The German breeding programs, backed by the skills of German riders and trainers, have paid handsome dividends in international competition. The program has emphasized a spectacular way of moving (particularly at the trot), an obedient temperament, and a powerful physique. German-breds lead the world in dressage. They are equaled only by Irish-bred horses as international show jumpers. They have also had great success in Com-

The Trakehner stallion Zauberklang, by Prince Conde out of Zauberspiel by Impuls, owned by Wonderland Farms, West Chester, Pennsylvania.

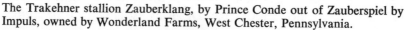

The German-bred Hanoverian Grande, ridden by Michael Matz, winners of the 1977 American Gold Cup.

bined Driving competitions run according to the rules of the Fédération Équestre Internationale (F.E.I.), the international governing body of the equestrian sports. These successes have led to a considerable export trade. Stallions have been brought to the United States and Canada, where they have been widely accepted and patronized.

Cleveland Bay

The Cleveland Bay originated in the Vale of Cleveland, in the North Riding, of Yorkshire, England. It was in the adjoining valley, the Vale of Bedale, that the Thoroughbred originated later, during the latter part of the seventeenth and the early-eighteenth centuries. Whereas the aim of the breeders in the Vale of Bedale was to breed a racehorse, the aim of breeders in the Vale of Cleveland was to breed an active general-purpose horse, one that could work steep hill farms, trot smartly to the nearest market town between shafts, and follow the local pack of foxhounds. Inevitably, the standards of the one group of breeders influenced the other. In consequence, the

Cleveland Bay is very similar to the Thoroughbred, but with more size, substance, and soundness of wind, limb, and temperament. Size ranges from 16 to 16.3 hands and weight from 1,250 to 1,500 pounds. The coat is always bay with black points at the mane, tail, and legs from the hocks and knees down.

Because of their native environment (Cleveland soils are thin), these horses need relatively little feed in relation to their size.

Cleveland Bays are a natural, not an extreme, outcross with Thoroughbred blood. Stallions were brought to Germany and France beginning in the late-eighteenth century to upgrade the Norman, the Oldenburger, the Hanoverian, and other strains, considerably before Thoroughbreds were imported for the same purpose.

Because there have been no outcrosses in the breed since 1883, registrations in the Cleveland Bay Stud Book are a guarantee of prepotency. Stallions can be relied on to stamp their get with the breed characteristics of size, substance, soundness, quiet temperament, good shoulders and withers, a well-attached head, a long neck, and a free way of moving with excellent hock action.

The Cleveland Bay stallion crossed with Thoroughbred and near-Thoroughbred mares consistently produces weight-carrying field hunters and successful show jumpers and event horses. Britain's famous jumper Foxhunter was part Cleveland Bay. Canada's top Three-Day horse, Sumatra, was also part Cleveland Bay.

The breed has been supported by Britain's royal family during this century. King George V maintained a stud of Cleveland Bays at Hampton Court; Queen Elizabeth owns the stallion Mulgrave Supreme; and Prince Philip uses Cleveland Bays in international Combined Driving events.

American Saddle Horse

Because of its extravagant action and because of the special style in which it is presented, many people think of the American Saddle Horse as a show animal. In fact, it is perhaps the most comfortable to ride of all our native breeds and is remarkable for its powers of endurance. The breed is distinguished for the rack, a lateral four-beat gait, which enables the rider to sit still without rising as the horse glides along, and which invariably inspires shouts and whistles of enthusiasm from the ringside.

The rack goes back to the seventeenth century, a hundred years before posting to the trot was invented, when virtually all horses used for travel were laterally gaited, either pacers or rackers. Even after trotting Thoroughbreds were imported from England, the southern planters kept their Saddle Horse strains and continued to use them for inspecting their broad acres until the advent of the automobile. This day-after-day and day-long work, carrying prosperous (and heavy) planters on their rounds, produced

Wing Commander, leading sire of champion Saddle Horses in the twentieth century. (Courtesy of American Saddle Horse Association)

horses that had great endurance and gave great comfort. The breed has remained popular in this country and has achieved popularity in a number of other countries with large farms and agricultural ranches, notably South Africa and Australia.

In the American show ring, it makes a spectacular appearance. The head exhibits extreme quality, reflecting the Arabian and Thoroughbred influence as well as the efforts of selective breeders. The neck comes out of the shoulder at a higher angle than the Thoroughbred and has good length. The withers have moderate height; the shoulder has moderate slope. The barrel is round, rather than deep, and the tail is high, an effect heightened by cutting and setting in show stock. The legs are long and the pasterns have good slope. A good walk and trot and a rocking-chair canter are characterized by high action. In show horses, the feet are permitted to grow very long in order to accentuate the action. Most Saddle Horses stand 15.2 to 16.2 hands, with some slightly taller.

American Saddle Horses have been successful in dressage competitions. At the 1932 Los Angeles Olympic Games, Captain Isaac Kitts and the American Saddle Horse American Lady were members of the U. S. Silver Medal Team.

Grasshopper, a Connemara member of the U. S. Olympic Three-Day Team, ridden by Michael Page.

Connemara

Native pony breeds evolve in areas where the terrain is rugged and feed scarce, such as the Shetland Islands, the highlands of Scotland, the mountains of Wales, the depths of the New Forest, and the moors of Dartmoor and Exmoor. Ireland's breed of native ponies comes from the mountains of Connemara, on its west coast, in County Galway.

Four hundred years ago, virtually all horses were of pony size, except for those used by the cavalry in warfare and by the nobility for parade purposes. So, in that sense, the ponies of today are the horses of the sixteenth century, which have remained largely unchanged in the more remote districts.

Ponies run loose and in droves on the Connemara mountains the year round, being caught only when needed for working the tiny hill farms or for carrying their owners under saddle. The Stud Book was founded in 1923 by the Connemara Pony Society. No animal is accepted for registration until it is two years old and has been passed by the Society's inspection committee for soundness and type. All stallions must be licensed by the Irish Government. Animals over 14 hands are not eligible.

Connemara ponies resemble small hunters in conformation. Thirty years ago, two Thoroughbreds and an Arabian stallion were admitted to the Connemara Stud Book. As a result, some of today's Connemaras have heads that resemble the Arabian, while others resemble the Thoroughbred. Their bodies are much like a three-quarter-bred Thoroughbred, hunter in type, with sloping shoulders, long legs, and sloping pasterns, although they travel with action a little higher than the Thoroughbred's. Gray and dun are the most prevalent colors, the latter with black points and a list (stripe) down the middle of the back. There are also bays, blacks, and browns, with an occasional chestnut. Connemaras have particularly good temperaments.

Connemara breeding stock was brought to the United States in the early 1950s by the late George L. Ohrstrom, Sr., of The Plains, Virginia. Since then, the breed has become very popular, not only in this country but also in Canada, Australia, New Zealand, Sweden, Germany, France, Belgium, and the Netherlands. The only problem encountered by importers has been the tendency of Connemaras to grow over pony size when removed from their native mountains to more fertile soils.

Connemara ponies have distinguished themselves as mounts for youngsters and for smaller adults in Pony Club rallies, horse shows, Combined Training events, Endurance rides, the hunting field, and many other spheres of equestrian sport. Part-Connemaras in international jumping competition include America's Little Squire and Great Britain's Dundrum, winner of the Grand Prix at Dublin and Brussels in 1963. Little Model represented Britain in the 1960 Rome Olympic Grand Prix de Dressage and placed third in the Grand Prix at Aachen in 1961. Copper Coin, later known as Grasshopper, competed in three Olympic Three-Day events.

Appaloosa

The Appaloosa takes its name from the valley of the Palouse River, which flows through the states of Idaho, Washington, and Oregon, where the Nez Percé Indians practiced horse breeding in the nineteenth century.

The Appaloosa is distinguished for its coat markings, which are classified into six pattern types: The leopard, most spectacularly marked of Appaloosas and also the most prepotent source of color in the breed, is white with large, well-defined dark spots all over its body. Leopards almost always pass "loud" color marking to their offspring, although not necessarily in their own image. Leopard Appaloosas often produce blanket-patterned offspring: A blanket of white hairs just covers the rump or sometimes extends all the way to the withers. Well-defined dark spots are present in the blanket. The remaining color patterns range downward to a mere sprinkling of white hairs over the croup, and in fact, some Appaloosas are totally with-

An Appaloosa.

out the characteristic coat markings. But all members of the breed, regardless of coat pattern, inherit a white sclera around the eyes, mottled skin at the muzzle and genital region, and vertically striped hooves.

Representatives of Appaloosa-type spotted horses are found throughout the entire history of art, and even in prehistoric cave paintings in France. Horses of these color patterns were probably brought to the New World by the Spanish conquistadores.

At the time the stud book was founded, the Appaloosa was a rather coarsely built horse, hardy but lacking refinement, distinguished chiefly by its coat color. Arabian outcrosses were admitted to the stud book to infuse quality, and later the book was opened to Thoroughbreds and Quarter Horses. Massive infusions of outside blood successfully upgraded the spotted horse but so influenced conformation that there is no uniform type. Some Appaloosas look like Quarter Horses, some like Thoroughbreds, and many more fall somewhere in the range between the two.

Thanks to this variety of type, the present-day Appaloosa has become a multipurpose horse used for everything from reining to Endurance riding. Appaloosas are frequently seen in the hunting field and in show jumping classes.

Quarter Horse

Since the first volume of its Stud Book was published in 1941, the American Quarter Horse Association has registered more than a million and a quarter horses, the largest equine breed registry in history. These tremendous numbers are due largely to the versatility of the Quarter Horse, which is unsurpassed today.

The foundation Quarter Horses in the early volumes of the Stud Book were "bulldog" types. Short legs with powerful gaskins and forearms; heavily muscled bodies and necks; straight shoulders; low, broad withers; short, straight pasterns—all contributed to a short but immensely powerful stride. The bulldog type had unmatched ability to make a fast start and to sustain speed for very short distances.

With the growth of Quarter Horse racing in recent years, distances have lengthened. Massive infusions of Thoroughbred blood have improved the staying qualities of the Quarter Horse while bringing about major changes in type. The old Quarter Horse seldom exceeded 15.2 hands. The modern Quarter Horse may pass the 16.0 mark. The new Quarter Horse is structurally sounder, with a more sloping shoulder, more pronounced withers, and greater length and slope of pasterns.

The feet tend to be disproportionately small, due to the esthetic preferences of halter-class judges, and are a source of unsoundness.

A Quarter Horse jumper, Texas, ridden by John Simpson, of the Canadian Olympic Team.

The head has quality, with large, powerful jaws and small ears. The neck, carried level, is short and deep, compared to the Thoroughbred and the Arabian. The stride is low but shorter than the Thoroughbred stride.

The origin of the Quarter Horse can be traced back to English, Scottish, and Irish settlers of the Atlantic seaboard. Sporting men, they created racecourses by hewing them out of the forest. For this exercise, a quarter of a mile was quite long enough, hence the term "quarter running horse," shortened to Quarter Horse.

During the eighteenth century, as quarter racing moved westward, there were added to these racing strains the bloodlines brought from Spain by the conquistadores, thus producing a very hardy, tough horse that could get along with small amounts of feed and not much care, ideal for working cattle on the range.

Because of his background, the modern Quarter Horse is not only superior for short-distance racing, but also excels in barrel racing and in rodeo sports, roping, and cutting. His quiet temperament and his ability to thrive with minimum feed and attention have made him particularly suitable for the hundreds of thousands of relatively inexperienced first-time owners and riders added to the ranks of horsemen annually.

Quarter Horses have invaded sports heretofore largely associated with Thoroughbreds: fox hunting, show jumping, Combined Training, even dressage, a development facilitated by the considerable percentage of Thoroughbred blood now found in the majority of pedigrees.

The popularity of Quarter Horses has spread to Canada, England, continental Europe, South Africa, Australia, and New Zealand, and it is still growing rapidly.

A Quarter Horse halter-class champion.

CONFORMATION IN ACTION

The horse's conformation is not merely a question of beauty. What the horseman sees (conformation) is related to what lies under the skin (structure), and structure is very closely related to athletic skills.

Horsemen consider a certain type of neck, withers, back, pastern, etc., as "good" not because it is the most pleasing to the eye, but because it denotes a structure that permits the horse to perform the work required of him with the greatest ease and efficiency. An experienced horseman can often predict the way a horse will move by examining him standing still. Movement simply confirms his observations.

What should you look for in a riding horse's conformation? And how should you evaluate your findings? To start with the one part of the horse that is an exception to the general rule, let's consider first:

The Head

A good head means a pretty head and nothing more. Of course, vital functions go on inside of it. Eating, drinking, breathing, seeing, hearing, and housing of the brain are life-and-death responsibilities. But structure, in this case, does not reflect usefulness.

A good head is small, and short from eye to muzzle. The ears are small and set alertly. The eyes are large, prominent, and set wide apart, forming "corners" at the sides of the face. The profile is flat or slightly concave. The nostrils are large and held open so that the soft tissue of the upper inside corners doesn't sag into the opening. The muzzle is small, with a tight lower lip and small chin. The skin over the head is thin, showing the bony framework and blood vessels clearly etched underneath. The hair is fine, with sparse growth in the ears and at the jaw.

Undesirable features of the head are as follows: any convexity of the profile; ears that are big or set too far forward, or that flop to the sides; small eyes; too much length from eye to muzzle; a large muzzle, especially with limp nostrils, so that the upper profile ends in an abrupt curve, while the chin juts out or the lower lip droops; indistinct bone formation, concealed by either thick skin or too much hair.

Prized features of the head are indicative of "quality," which generally means the presence of Thoroughbred blood. But heads vary immensely in every breed, including the Thoroughbred, with no obvious correlation to performing ability. The prettiest heads by no means always belong to the most talented athletes.

The most important information to be learned from the head comes not so much from studying conformation as from observing expression, which is a valuable clue to temperament. Drooping eyelids, flopping ears, hanging

 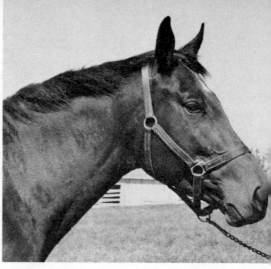

An attractive head: short, refined, with large, prominent eye, alert ears, and elegant throatlatch.

Not a badly shaped head, but spoiled by a small eye set too high and a closed angle between head and neck.

lower lip, and low head carriage (not due to conformation) are signs of a phlegmatic disposition. Head held high, eyes bulging to show the whites, and nostrils flaring are marks of an excitable nature. Ears repeatedly laid back are a sure sign of a spoiled or sullen disposition. Wrinkles above the nostrils indicate pain or discomfort.

Most imperfections of the head are of little practical importance. For example, if, by separating the lips, you discover a "parrot mouth" so severe that the upper incisors do not touch the lower ones at all, you can suppose that the horse has a hard time cropping grass. But, for the most part, one horse eats and drinks as well as another, jaw conformation notwithstanding —although abnormalities can cause bitting problems.

The angle at which the head is set on the neck might conceivably affect the horse's breathing. A good head set has an open angle, considerably greater than 90 degrees. The more open the angle, the less obstruction to air passing through the trachea. An oblique head set causes no problems when the horse is at liberty, but when he bends at the poll, the angle then becomes sharp enough to act as an obstruction.

The size of the head influences athletic performance to some extent, since the horse uses his head and neck as balancers. To lighten his forehand, he raises them. This occurs at every stride except the trot. Approaching a fence, he raises his head and neck to permit his forehand to leave the ground. In the air, the head and neck are lowered, enabling the hindquarters to clear the obstacle, then are raised again to lighten the forehand on landing. In general, the more a horse has "out front," the more he has to balance with. But the closer the mass to his body, the more easily he can maneuver it. The ideal combination for a jumper is therefore a small head on a long neck.

When his balance is in peril, a heavy head only makes matters worse, especially when it is carried on a slender neck. The horse's recovery depends in part on how easily he can lift his head and neck, shifting his weight to the rear. It takes a short, thick neck to support the weight of a heavy head and to supply the necessary bulk for balancing.

But these are all relatively minor points in the scheme of things. The most useful aspect of a good head is its resale value. If a horse is sound in other respects, you can forgive him for having a plain head.

The Neck

A good neck is a three-star quality. It's one of those features that immediately attract the horseman's eye. A horse may have a fine shoulder, good bone, all the soundness in the world, and considerable athletic talent to boot, but if he has a short neck he will never excel in conformation.

From the outside. A good neck is, first of all, long. Length of neck is measured along the topline from the ears to the point at which the neck meets the withers. Length is, of course, relative to other elements; for example, size. The lovely, long neck of a pony would look very short on a 16.1-hand horse. Moreover, while practically every riding-horse breed standard calls for length of neck, the interpretation varies from breed to breed. What is considered a long neck in a Quarter Horse would look absurdly short on a Saddlebred. And within the standard for any breed, length of neck is relative to other parts of the individual, in particular to length of back. Generally speaking, long necks tend to accompany long backs, and short necks short backs. A short-coupled horse is considered to have a long neck with considerably less out in front than a rangy individual. To evaluate length of neck, you don't look only at the neck. You stand back and judge the horse as a whole.

Shape is the next consideration. Again, the ideal varies from breed to breed, with the Thoroughbred occupying middle ground between the extremes of the thicker stock-horse types (Quarter Horse, Paint, Appaloosa) and the tapering saddle-seat types (Saddlebred, Arabian, Morgan). The ideal Thoroughbred neck creates the impression of a continuous gentle curve from poll to withers on top, and from jaw to point of shoulder below.

Undesirable features of the topline are as follows: crestiness (a bulk of muscle and fat creating an exaggerated upward curve), straightness, or a dip at the poll. Undesirable features of the underline of the neck: thickness at the throatlatch; a pronounced angle (instead of a curve) and/or a closed angle (90 degrees or less) of neck to head; bulges of muscle or fat producing a downward curve in the lower third.

The same principles are relatively valid for the necks of all riding breeds, although the best Quarter Horse neck will have less curve and more thickness of muscle and fat than the best Thoroughbred neck; and the best Saddlebred neck will have a much more pronounced curve.

Under the skin. The arrangement of muscle and bone under the skin determines the conformation that meets the eye. In the horse's neck, the length

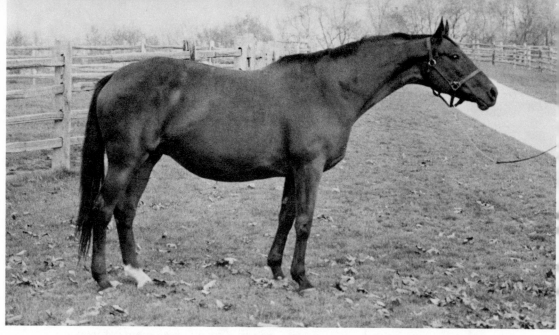

The ideal neck: Note the length and gentle curve of the topline from ears to withers, the perfectly straight underline, and the open angle at the throat-latch.

and shape of the cervical (neck portion) of the spine forms a framework for the muscles. The length of the cervical spine determines the length of the neck. Since every horse has seven vertebrae in its neck, it is not the number but the size of the vertebrae that causes the difference between one horse and another.

Each vertebra has four *articular processes*. ("Articular" refers to joint, and "process" is a projection of bone.) A pair of *anterior* articular processes project forward toward the vertebra in front. A pair of *posterior* articular processes project backward toward the vertebra behind. The posterior processes of one vertebra meet the anterior processes of the succeeding vertebra to form the joint between vertebrae.

The articular processes in the horse's back are short and blunt, fitting

A short neck, straight topline, and sharply angled throatlatch. Contrast downward bulge of brachiocephalic muscle here with graceful arch in horse in preceding photograph.

snugly together to form a tight joint. The articular processes of the neck are longer and loosely meshed. So the neck has considerable lateral and vertical flexibility, while the vertebrae of the back, packed together like Life Savers in their wrapper, can hardly flex at all. All else being equal, the longer the articular processes, the longer and more flexible the neck.

Length of neck is almost always a mechanical advantage. The neck, along with the head, is the horse's balancer. By moving it up and down, he can distribute weight backward or forward along the length of his body. With strong, agile movements of the neck, he can quickly shift weight both as a saving gesture when his balance is in peril and as a supplement to muscular strength when great athletic effort is required.

The flexibility that tends to accompany length is a boon to the horse. The more flexible his neck, the wider the range of adjustments he can make. This flexibility is useful to the rider, too. But at the same time, a horse can utilize a long, flexible neck to evade the demands of an unskilled horseman. At worst, the horse's head flies up at a pull on the reins; or, conversely, his chin drops to his chest. Even horses that have received very sophisticated training manage to produce such evasions if their conformation so disposes them.

The cervical spine is the blueprint for the shape of the neck. While it may not be apparent from the outside, the fact is that the horse's spine curves not once, but twice, following the form of a gentle S curve tipped slightly forward (when the horse is facing toward your right). Where the cervical spine emerges from the backbone, it curves downward and then gradually reverses to an upward curve in the upper third of the neck. The result is that in the lower third of the neck, the spine lies nearest the underline; but as it reverses its curve, it slopes upward and, in the upper third of the neck, the spine lies nearest the topline.

The shape of these curves has an important influence on the shape of the neck. If the spine curves sharply upward on emerging from the back, the complementary curve at the poll will in all likelihood turn sharply downward, and the section of spine between the curves will be nearly straight. The extreme result is for the neck to tend toward the vertical and meet the head at a hairpin angle. This is the peacocky look associated with the Saddlebred horse. When the downward curve at the base of the neck is abrupt, its covering of muscle may bulge forward, spoiling the straight underline of the neck.

At the other end of the scale, the Quarter Horse neck often emerges from the back at a nearly flat angle, and the head meets the neck at a very open angle. The result is a nearly horizontal head and neck carriage, with nose poked forward, the typical western pleasure-horse posture.

The Thoroughbred occupies middle ground, with individuals ranging from one extreme to the other. The ideal Thoroughbred spine curves gently but evenly throughout the neck. The neck emerges from the body at a me-

The American Saddlebred My My ⅃58720, six-time winner of the World's Grand Championship 5-Gaited Division at the Kentucky State Fair, illustrates the peacocky appearance associated with the spine that curves sharply at base of neck and poll.

By contrast, the Quarter Horse neck scarcely inclines at all from the body, and the head juts almost straight forward from the neck, suggesting that the spine curves very little. This conformation makes it natural for the Quarter Horse to carry its head low, while the Saddle Horse, above, is naturally predisposed to the high head carriage its training accentuates.

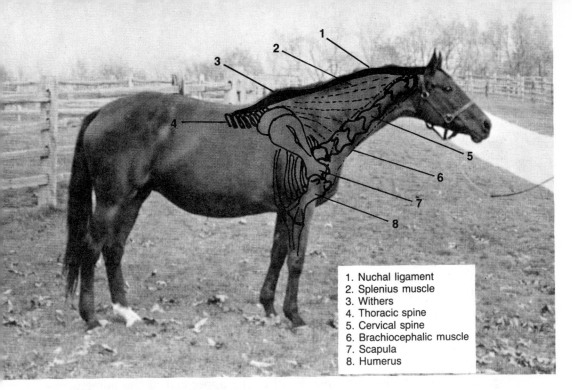

1. Nuchal ligament
2. Splenius muscle
3. Withers
4. Thoracic spine
5. Cervical spine
6. Brachiocephalic muscle
7. Scapula
8. Humerus

Inside the horse's neck and shoulder.

dium angle and curves smoothly upward to an arch at the poll and an open throatlatch. The impression is that the head does not just hang at the end of the neck, nor jut forward stiffly, but that the horse holds it a little away from the neck.

This is the most efficient head carriage for most of the purposes to which the Thoroughbred is put.

In motion. As a rule, this ideal Thoroughbred neck carriage is capable of a greater range of athletic movements than either the western pleasure neck or the peacock neck. The arrangement of the vertebrae not only dictates the shape of the neck, but also to some extent the way in which the muscles are able to move it. The *splenius* muscles, which are responsible for raising the neck (and, by their relaxation, allowing gravity to lower it), run from front to back in horizontal layers. Up front, they attach to the cervical spine. At the rear, the muscles in the upper part of the neck attach to the *nuchal ligament,* which runs from poll to withers. The muscles in the lower part of the neck attach directly to the withers.

Muscles have only one ability: to reduce their length by contracting. The various kinds of movement they produce are the result of the various arrangements of bones and ligaments to which they are attached. A muscle connects two bones, or sometimes a bone and a ligament. When it contracts, it pulls the bones closer together or, if one of them is immovable, it pulls one toward the other. For obvious mechanical reasons, the muscle is more effective when it meets both bones at right angles than if it lies along the bones in a parallel plane.

The relationship of splenius muscle to bone is determined largely by the arrangement of the vertebrae. If the neck curves sharply upward, the hori-

zontal layers of muscle lie more or less perpendicular to the spine, and raising the neck even higher comes naturally to the horse. If the neck juts forward in an almost horizontal plane, the same muscles lie almost parallel to
the spine and must labor to raise the neck. A trainer is obviously much better off if he starts with a horse whose conformation is suited to his purpose,
than if he tries to combat the natural tendencies of the horse's muscle and
bone.

The way in which the horse carries his head is a product of the length and
shape of his spine. To go a step farther, the way a horse moves his front legs
is largely dependent on the way he carries his head. The *humerus* (the bone
forming the lower half of the shoulder, which runs between the point of the
shoulder and the elbow) is more or less suspended from the head by the
brachiocephalic muscle, which meets the cervical spine at the poll, runs
down both sides of the neck, and connects to the upper end of the humerus
at the point of the shoulder. When the horse stands still, contraction of one
brachiocephalic muscle turns the head to that side. When the horse is moving, contraction of the same muscle raises the upper end of the humerus toward the head. Since the humerus is strung from the head like a puppet,
wherever the head moves, the humerus and the leg must follow.

It is easy to visualize how a difference in length and carriage of neck
affects the movement of the humerus. On a long-necked horse with a low
head carriage, the tug of the brachiocephalic, when it contracts, is only
slightly upward and very much forward, producing a long and relatively flat
stride. A short-necked horse with a low head carriage, for example a Quarter Horse type, will characteristically have the same low stride with little
bend in the knee, but a shorter stride because of the shortness of neck. The
higher the head, the more of an upward pull and less of a forward pull the
brachiocephalic exerts on the humerus. A long-necked horse that carries his
head in a moderately elevated position will show some bend to his knee, but
his stride may still be quite long if his head, although high, is held out in
front of him. The Saddle Horse type, with a very high head carriage, moves
very high off the ground, and the extra bend of knee naturally detracts from
length of stride.

Within the limits of his natural capabilities, the way a horse is ridden will
affect his movement in the same way. If ridden forward, with head and neck
extended on a loose rein, any horse will move with a relatively long, flat
stride. As increased contact causes the horse to raise his head, his stride becomes higher and somewhat shorter. A horse attempting to evade the bit by
holding his head high in the air or tucked against his chest, moves with exaggerated knee action and appears to go nowhere.

Draw an imaginary line from the poll to the point of the shoulder. The
knee tends to move in a plane parallel to this imaginary line. Training and
riding can alter head and neck position within a certain range. Conformation sets the limits of that range.

The Shoulder

The horse's shoulder is vital in discerning athletic ability. The efficiency of a good shoulder (as well as the limitations of a poor one) are reflected in every galloping stride and in every jumping effort.

The shoulder joint is the junction of two bones: the upper one, the *scapula* (shoulder blade); and the lower one, the *humerus* (upper arm). The scapula lies at an angle roughly parallel to the base of the neck, extending from just below the withers, downward and forward to about the middle of the chest. Here the humerus meets the scapula. A prominence on the upper end of the humerus juts forward, just ahead of the junction with the scapula, to form the *point of the shoulder*. From there, the humerus slopes downward and rearward to meet the combined *radius* and *ulna* (the forearm). This junction, the point where the leg joins the body, is the elbow joint. A projection from the ulna juts rearward from the joint to form the *point of the elbow*.

The traditional virtues of the shoulder are length and slope. Most horsemen, when they speak admiringly of a long, sloping shoulder, refer to the scapula and ignore the humerus, which forms the other half of the shoulder joint. But the two work as partners, so we will consider them both.

The points that indicate the slope and length of the shoulder are only

Appearances are deceiving. This horse's prominent withers make it seem that his shoulder slopes, when actually it is quite straight, as indicated by the outlined scapula. Short, straight pasterns such as these often indicate that the shoulder is also straight.

partly visible. Some may be located by sight, others only by feel. The path of the scapula does not necessarily coincide precisely with the clearly muscled band extending from withers to point of shoulder.

The withers consist of a row of *dorsal spines,* long, bony projections rising from the foremost vertebrae of the back. Except in a very low-withered horse, the upper edge of the scapula ends below the height of the withers. (In mutton-withered, or round-shouldered, horses, the withers project no higher than the scapula. The result is a wide, thick-shouldered effect that holds a saddle poorly.)

The upper edge of the shoulder, under its cover of muscle, should blend imperceptibly with the withers. In order to locate it, you usually have to feel for it.

Once you have found the upper edge of the scapula, you can determine its slope by feeling for the bony spine that bisects its length. Called the *scapular spine,* this ridge of bone, which provides attachment for important muscles, begins about one quarter of the way from the top of the scapula and runs all the way to the juncture of the humerus.

You can judge the exact length of the scapula by palpating the shoulder joint, or you can make an approximate visual judgment by sighting the point of the shoulder.

The point of the shoulder, seen from the side as a slight bony prominence about midway down the chest, is formed by a projection of the humerus called the *"lateral tuberosity."* Although the lateral tuberosity juts forward from the joint, forming a lopsided T juncture with the scapula, its uppermost surface is at about the same height as the lowest point of the scapula. So although the two don't actually meet, one is an indication of the boundary of the other.

The point of the shoulder is a landmark in the location of the upper end of the humerus too, although the major shaft of the bone is set somewhat to the rear of the visible prominence. The bone slopes downward and rearward to the elbow joint, which you can palpate or locate roughly by spotting the point of the elbow.

The point of the elbow is formed by a projection of the forearm (ulna) behind and slightly above the joint itself, just as the point of the shoulder is slightly ahead of and below the shoulder joint. So for the purpose of evaluating conformation, the point of the shoulder and the point of the elbow are useful visual landmarks. In order to determine scapular length and slope, palpation is usually required.

The angles of humerus and scapula are measured when the horse is standing still, because movement alters not only the planes in which the bones lie, but also the angle at which they meet. At rest, the scapula forms an angle with the horizontal of about 55 to 60 degrees or less. The humerus meets an imaginary horizon at an angle of 50 degrees or more. The angle they form with each other is about 110 degrees.

The forward and rearward phases of the galloping stride exhibit the pendulum action of scapula and humerus that prescribes length of stride.

The scapula and humerus can move in different planes. Not only can they pivot from the joint, but the pivot point itself has a significant range of movement. Because the scapula is only loosely joined to the body by long muscle fibers, the shoulder joint floats, within limits, of course, in relation to the ribs.

At the gallop. As the horse extends the front leg forward in the galloping stride, the scapula tips back and the humerus straightens up. This enables the foot to land as far ahead of the body as the horse's conformation permits. From the time the foot touches the ground, the horse's body commences to swing forward over the foot. As it advances, the scapula straightens and the lower end of the humerus tilts back. In both phases of the galloping stride, the angle of the shoulder opens to its maximum. The length of stride is directly related to the combined length of the two bones and to the range of movement of the lower end of the humerus (forward and back).

The horse can stride only as far in front as his hindquarters are capable of carrying him. But a powerful thrust behind is naturally limited by a short reach in front. The long, galloping stride covers most ground with least effort. The horse spends maximum time in the air while he decelerates, to some extent, but also rests. The long stride is best suited to galloping over a distance.

The sprinter is a shorter-striding horse. He spends less time in the air and more time pushing against the ground. Each stride has greater acceleration content but less resting time. He works harder and faster and tires sooner.

The leg swings like the pendulum of a clock. The longer the pendulum, the less effort is required up top to move the bottom in a longer arc. The longer the shoulder bones and the greater the ability of the joint to straighten, thus increasing their combined length, the longer the horse's stride. According to the pendulum principle, a small increase up top is multiplied many times in the increased distance the toe travels over the ground.

All else being equal, the longer the scapula, the more it will have to slope to fill the space available. The greater the slope of the scapula, the higher the shoulder joint and the more the humerus will tend toward the vertical. This combination—a long, sloping shoulder and upright humerus— produces the longest forward swing of the pendulum. Shortening or straightening of the shoulder or the approach of the humerus to the horizontal, contributes to a shorter stride. The longer the humerus, the longer the stride. But, all else being equal, the longer the humerus, the more it must slope toward the horizontal to fit the available space. Length of humerus is thus desirable, provided that uprightness is not sacrificed.

During a jump. While all horses gallop in much the same way, varying only in speed and length of stride, horses have varying jumping styles. When jumping at his best, the horse bends all the joints of his front legs: ankles, knees, elbows, shoulders. The shoulder angle closes as much as it is ever likely to do. The horse's intention is (or should be) to keep his feet and legs out of the way of the fence. The more successfully he accomplishes this feat up front, the less effort he is forced to exert behind. Over a low fence, he may find it easier to push a little higher from behind than to fold tightly in front. But every horse has a natural height limitation, at which, unless he can keep his front legs out of the way, he cannot produce enough power behind to clear the fence. At this point, he must raise the front of his shoulder blade so that the scapula approaches as nearly as possible the horizontal. This raises the point of the shoulder, which now moves up in the chest, nearing the base of the neck. As the joint moves up, the humerus

Inside the horse's shoulder during a jump. (Wilkinson photo)

1. Withers
2. Scapula
3. Lat. Tuberosity
4. Humerus
5. Radius
6. Ulna
7. Point of Elbow

This horse uses his shoulder well to fold his legs up in front of his body. The point of the shoulder has risen, the scapula flattens nearly to horizontal, and the humerus is almost upright.

approaches the vertical; the elbow joint closes, pointing the knee upward; the knee closes, directing the feet down and back; the ankles bend, holding the toes clear of the fence. This chain of events is somewhat muscular, but also mechanical to the extent that, as knee and elbow flex, they tend to push the humerus and the scapula into position, providing that the two are correctly conformed and positioned in the horse's structure.

Another jumping style, at its best, also signifies supreme athletic effort but is not as effective in reducing the requirement for push from behind. Ankles, knees, elbows, and shoulders close well, but the shoulder joint does not rise. The scapula remains nearer the vertical, and the folding of the elbow therefore nudges the humerus closer to the horizontal. The result is that the tightly folded legs, instead of being held out in front of the chest,

This highly successful jumper makes less use of his shoulder than the horse in the preceding photo, folding his front legs under his body. His scapula is relatively upright and the humerus horizontal.

are pressed up underneath it. Now the horse must jump high enough to allow room for his legs to clear the fence.

The worst front-leg jumping fault, variously referred to as "hanging," "hanging back," or "dropping the shoulder," occurs when the horse thinks that he hasn't the time or space to clear with his front legs in the conventional way. So he tries to trail them behind. The scapula approaches the vertical, the shoulder joint drops, and the humerus nears the horizontal. At worst, the elbow straightens and the knee points down. This is a bad mistake. It produces an unattractive picture, transmits an unpleasant sensation to the rider, who feels that he has somehow shot ahead of his horse, and it requires an even greater jumping effort in order to clear the dangling forearm, which threatens to hook the fence. Meanwhile, the landing gear trails.

The success of a jumping effort depends on the horse's ability to slide his shoulder blade up in front, raising the joint and the humerus to nearly vertical. This ability is partly due to effort, enhanced by training; but it is also due to conformation. The greater the natural slope of the shoulder, the higher the shoulder joint, and the closer to vertical the humerus, the easier it will be for the horse to lift his legs up in front of himself and well clear of the fence.

The Hindquarters and Hind Legs

All else being equal (which it never is), you can estimate the relative performance ability of two horses by comparing their hind legs. If it were possible to have two horses identical in every respect except for the hind leg, the shape of the hind leg would determine which horse would make the better jumper and which the better racehorse.

Of course, in selecting a horse for a particular job, there are many other variables too. In some cases, you have to fall back on guesswork and even on luck. But if you can identify the type of hind leg that is best suited to the job, you can at least narrow the odds in your favor. You will still have to guess right in regard to temperament, soundness, and dozens of other factors, but at least you will have one vital aspect working for you.

Landmarks of the hind leg. The hind leg originates well up in the hindquarter, where heavy muscling conceals its structure from the eye. The shape of the hindquarter itself is an important clue to athletic ability, but not in the way many people interpret it.

1) *The point of the croup:* The highest point of the hindquarters, actually two points padded with muscle, formed by prominences of one of the pelvic bones, the *ilium,* just above where it anchors on either side of the spine.

2) *The point of the hip:* Another projection of the foremost end of the ilium, in front of and below the point of the croup. Not to be confused with the hip joint.

3) *The croup:* The topline of the hindquarters between the point of the croup and the tail. Its length and slope are determined primarily by the height of the point of the croup, by the length and slope of the underlying vertebrae, and to a lesser extent by the muscles around the vertebrae.

4) *The point of the buttock:* The rearmost point of the hindquarters, about a third of the way down below the attachment of the tail, consisting of another projecting pelvic bone, the *ischium,* well padded with muscle.

5) *The stifle:* At the bottom front of the hindquarter, the joint that connects the femur (the uppermost bone of the hind leg, well concealed under the muscle of the hindquarter) to the tibia, the bone that bridges the stifle and the hock.

6) *The hock:* Juncture of the tibia above and the cannon below.

What lies under the skin. It is easy to visualize the bony structure of the hind leg, as it is thinly veiled by skin and a minimum of muscle. But the arrangement of bones in the hindquarters is buried under the heaviest muscling of the horse's body and can be only partially visualized. The rest must be surmised from a distance or determined by palpation.

From top to bottom, the bones of the hindquarters are as follows: *the spine,* a scaffolding that supports the muscular roof of the quarters; *the pelvis,* hung from the spine; and *the femur,* hung from the pelvis. The spine is easy enough to visualize, since it more or less coincides with the croup. The ilium (front branch of the pelvis) flattens and fans out at its forward

Inside the horse's hindquarters.

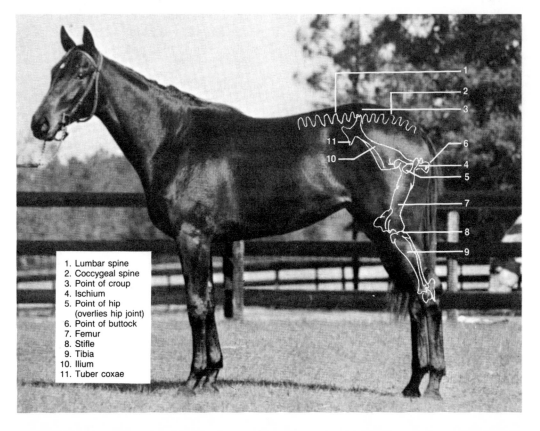

1. Lumbar spine
2. Coccygeal spine
3. Point of croup
4. Ischium
5. Point of hip
   (overlies hip joint)
6. Point of buttock
7. Femur
8. Stifle
9. Tibia
10. Ilium
11. Tuber coxae

end to form the easily located point of the croup and point of the hip. The ischium (rear branch of the pelvis) is easy to locate at its rearmost end as the point of the buttock. The bottom of the femur emerges from the hindquarters at the stifle.

But what about the rear end of the ilium, the front end of the ischium, and the top of the femur? The "missing link," obscured by muscle, is the *hip joint*. All three join at the hip joint to form a lopsided Y. The ilium and ischium fuse to form the top part of the Y, the pelvis. The ilium, longer than the ischium, slopes more sharply toward the juncture. The femur, the tail of the Y, fits into a socket at the lower surface of the juncture. From the hip joint, the femur slopes downward and somewhat forward to the stifle. The hip joint, deeply buried beneath heavy muscles, is neither visible nor palpable. But a bony projection from the top of the femur protrudes outward several inches from the joint itself, and this can be felt beneath the muscle. It provides the best clue to the location of the hip joint. Once you know the location of the hip joint, you know the lengths and slopes of ilium and ischium, as well as the length and slope of the femur. If you can't palpate the hip joint, you can at least draw an imaginary line from the point of the hip to the point of the buttock. This will give you a rough idea of the sum length of ilium and ischium (although you still don't know their relative length or the angle at which they meet), as well as an idea of the plane in which the pelvis lies, whether it tends toward or away from the horizontal. You still have to sketch the upper end of the femur in your imagination.

Many people make the mistake of judging the slope of the pelvis by the slope of the croup. The only meeting of the two is just below the point of the croup, where the ilium joins the spine. From that point rearward, the pelvis slopes away from the croup. It is the length and slope of the pelvis, much more than the length and slope of the croup, that determine athletic ability in a horse.

How length and slope affect ability. Generally speaking, one can say that:

1) Bone length tends to be consistent with the individual. A horse with a long neck tends to have long legs, a long back, and high withers; a horse with a short neck tends to be short all over. Of course, you can find individuals with long necks and short backs, or long backs and short legs, but these are exceptions to the rule. Quarter Horses, as a breed, are short-boned horses when compared to Thoroughbreds, for example. And each breed, within its own ranks, has its short-boned, chunky types and its long-boned, rangy types.

2) In a horse of a given size, with a given girth, the longer the bones, the more they will have to slope to fit the given space. This means that vertical spines and shoulder and leg bones approach the horizontal, while the pelvic bones (ilium and ischium) approach the vertical. The longer the sum of the ilium and the ischium, the more toward the vertical the whole pelvis must be oriented.

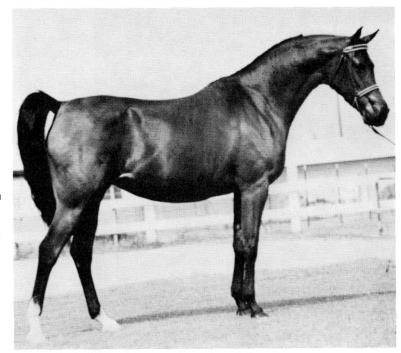

The Arabian horse, with its characteristically straight hind legs, is a superb Endurance horse but not typically distinguished for jumping ability.

3) The more the vertical bones approach the horizontal, the more the angles between them tend to close and the more angle you find in shoulder, elbow, stifle, and hock. As the pelvis tilts toward the vertical, the smaller the angle between the ischium and the femur becomes.

4) The closing or opening of the angles tends to be uniform throughout the horse. If a given horse has an open angle at the hock, he will probably have an open angle at the stifle and hip joint, and even the shoulder, as well.

These tendencies produce individuals of two major types, each with its own athletic predisposition. The closed-angle type makes the better jumper and sprinter. The open-angle horse is the better long-distance galloper and stayer. The types are splendidly illustrated by the Arabian horse and, to

At the other end of the spectrum, the white-tailed deer can produce a sharp burst of speed for short distances but is most remarkable for its ability to clear obstacles higher than its head.

The more angular the hind leg, the more readily it folds to store energy for the takeoff, in the same way that a tightly coiled spring packs a powerful rebound.

borrow from another hoofed species, the white-tailed deer. The deer is a superb jumper and fast runner over short distances. His hind legs are immensely long and folded in tight angles to accommodate his relatively small stature. The tibia meets the femur in a sharply angled stifle and approaches the horizontal as it slopes rearward to hocks that are far behind the point of the buttock. In the Arabian, the low point of the croup in relation to the point of the buttock hints at a nearly horizontal pelvic angle from which the hind leg hangs almost straight down, with little bend at stifle or at hock.

Long-distance galloping requires a long, ground-covering stride. The longer the stride, the more time the horse spends in the air in proportion to the time he spends pushing against the ground. In the air, the horse rests, but he also decelerates, which is why the long stride is not conducive to extreme speed but is indispensable to extended effort. Given two hind legs,

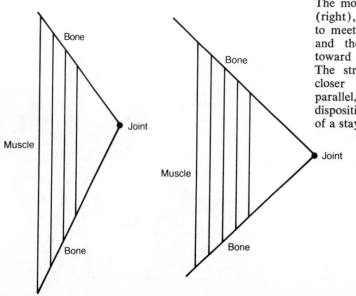

The more natural the bend in a joint (right), the closer the muscle comes to meeting the bone at a right angle and the greater the predisposition toward a sprinting or jumping effort. The straighter the joint (left), the closer the muscle approaches the parallel, and the greater the predisposition to the long, swinging stride of a stayer.

composed of bones of equal length, the straighter of the two will have the longer reach. The open-angle leg need only flex at the hip and slightly at the stifle to clear the ground and swing forward to its fullest extent, while the angular leg is expending energy in folding and unfolding, but never opening to its full extent.

On the other hand, for a short, powerful effort as in jumping, the closed-angle hind leg has a mechanical advantage. When the jumper shifts his weight onto his hind legs preparatory to takeoff, the legs fold up like a spring, storing energy, awaiting the rebound. The more tightly you press a spring, the farther it bounds back when you let go. The same is true of the hind leg. The more tightly the angles are capable of closing, the more spring they produce when they open. A sprinter, overcoming the inertia of a standing start, benefits from the same coiled-spring effect, although he bounds forward, rather than upward.

How the muscles work to close the joints. The galloping stride and the jumping effort both start with the closing of the joints of the hind leg. The muscles that bring about the closing are longitudinal fibers that bridge the inside of the joint, attaching to the bone above and the bone below. When these muscles contract, they draw the bones closer together, and the joint between them flexes.

It is easy to see why the angle at which muscle meets bone is important to the efficiency with which it exerts its pull. If the muscle lies along the bone, in a more or less parallel plane, its contraction cannot exert nearly as much force as when it is attached to the bone at right angles. The more natural bend there is in the joint, the closer the muscle comes to meeting the bone at right angles. The straighter the joint, the closer the muscle approaches the parallel.

The sprinter battles against inertia in his need for a flying start. The jumper battles gravity. Both efforts rely on immense muscular effort, which is provided by the built-in power boost of closed-angle-type conformation.

When the pelvis tends toward the vertical (right), the attachment of muscle to bone tends toward the perpendicular, making the effort of propelling a jumper into the air and a sprinter away from the gate easier. A nearly horizontal pelvis and vertical leg bones (left) compensate for lack of power by length of muscle. Long muscle means more ground covered with each stride.

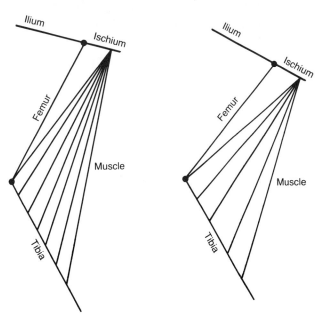

Of course, such intense muscular effort cannot be sustained over an extended period of time.

The open-angle conformation of the natural long-distance galloper predisposes him to an easy, swinging stride that requires little effort to maintain but takes a little time to work up to. The closing of the joints required to initiate each stride is powered slowly because of the relatively disadvantageous position of muscle in relation to bone; but once he has built up speed, momentum helps to maintain the free swing of his stride with a minimum of muscular effort.

How the muscles work to open the joints. The major joint-opening muscles of the hind legs run from the ischium to the lower end of the femur and the upper end of the tibia. The shortening of these muscles causes the straightening of the hip and stifle and, through the reciprocal action of the superficial digital flexor muscle, of the hock and fetlock.

When the pelvis tends toward the vertical, closing the angle between the ischium and the femur, the attachment of muscle to bone tends toward the perpendicular. At this angle they function in a direct and powerful effort to open the joints and straighten the leg, creating the mighty effort that propels the jumper into the air and the sprinter away from the gate.

In the typical stayer, with the pelvis approaching the horizontal and the bones of the leg itself approaching the vertical, the angle between ischium and femur opens, and muscular power diminishes.

Muscle power versus amplitude. Not all of the advantages lie on the side of the closed angle, however. When muscle meets bone at right angles, what it gains in power it loses in amplitude. The tendency is toward stronger but shorter moves.

As the angles between bones close, enabling the connecting muscle to approach the perpendicular, the distance between the bones naturally shortens. And so angular conformation goes hand in hand with shorter muscles. The contracting power of any muscle is the sum of the contraction of its cells. The more cells, the greater the total contraction. Consequently, the longer the muscle, the more it is capable of shortening its length and the farther it is capable of moving the bones to which it is attached.

In the typical *sprinter,* the forward slope of the femur closes the hip joint. The downward slope of the pelvis shortens the distance between ischium and femur and ischium and tibia. This is the conformation that generates powerful right-angle attachment of muscles, but it is not the ideal condition for muscle length. The result is a tendency toward the typical short but powerful stride of the sprinter.

The *stayer,* on the other hand, with his nearly horizontal pelvis and vertical leg bones, compensates for lack of power by length of muscle. Long muscles mean more ground covered at each contraction. The hip swings far forward, propelling the toe well under the body. The body moves forward over the leg, and the stride is prolonged, as opposing muscles, whose job it is to prevent over-opening of the joints, permit added extension of the hind leg behind the body, due to their length.

Horses that have relatively long bones for their size and height tend to have closed angles at the joints. Closed angles work mechanically in favor of spring and against swing. They favor intense, brief muscular effort over sustained performance. They favor power and push over length of stride. The sloping pelvis with angular stifle and hock works to the advantage of the sprinter and the jumper. The nearly horizontal pelvis with straight hock and stifle favors the long-distance galloper.

HOW THE EXPERTS JUDGE A HORSE'S WAY OF MOVING

Hunters and Jumpers

KAREN HEALEY, having worked with George Morris at Hunterdon, Inc., and coached junior riders in New Jersey, runs her own boarding and teaching establishment, in Scarsdale, New York, preparing horses and riders for competition in equitation, hunter, and jumper classes.

A good show hunter has a long, low stride, close to the ground. He doesn't show appreciable break in the knee or action in the hocks. Unfortunately, a classic mover on the flat sometimes moves poorly over fences. Many of the horses that don't bend their knees don't use their shoulders, either, and they're not much over a fence. I'll forgive a little break in the knee to get a long, reaching stride from the shoulder. But I consider good engagement behind essential. If my prospect doesn't bring his hocks well under himself on the flat, he'll probably trail them behind over a fence.

I begin my inspection routine with the horse standing before me in a bridle. I stand about ten feet away, opposite his midpoint, and look first at his hocks. Does he stand with his hocks well under him? If not, he probably won't bring them far enough under at the canter or in front of a fence. Second, the shoulders: Do they have a good slope? If his shoulders are straight, he's probably straight all the way down and he'll move short. No short movers for me.

Next I ask to move to a sand ring or some other soft area where the horse will leave prints as he walks. It's easy to be fooled as you watch the horse in motion, but the prints give you something to study later. As he walks past, I concentrate on his feet. Does he wing or paddle? A clever trimming job can make a paddler straight, but he'll still go a little short. Paddlers are out.

Does he stand squarely on his feet? A toe–heel or heel–toe landing, besides being unattractive, distributes the horse's weight improperly and produces strain. Does he overtrack at the walk? I'd like six to eight inches. A good overtrack tells me that the horse engages behind and has a long stride.

To measure his overtrack and evaluate straightness of movement, I study his prints. They should be clear, absolutely straight, and of equal depth all around. If he rolls his foot, the prints will be blurry, with one side deeper than the other.

Next, I move around behind the horse and have him walked away from me. I look at his hips first. Are they the same height, and do they move easily and evenly on both sides? If one hip rises higher than the other at the walk, the leg it belongs to is moving shorter than its fellow.

Are the hocks moving straight? Each hind leg should follow exactly in the plane of the one in front.

Back around to the side, I want to see the horse jogged past me on a loose shank. Does he show me a long, reaching stride? Does he land evenly or does he flip his toe? Toe-flipping, indicative of corrective shoeing, shows up pretty clearly at the trot. It's ugly and strains the shoulder area. I won't touch a toe flipper.

Does he have much break in the knee? If he breaks a great deal, he'll also break in the ankle. The more he breaks, the shorter he'll move and the harder he'll land. He will not be a good show hunter if he pounds, or if the arc of his stride is rounder than it is long.

How much action is there in the hocks? They should be active, but the legs should come forward and overtrack, not just come up.

For my final check on straightness of movement, I'll have the horse jog toward me and then away. Any slight tendency to wing, not noticeable at the walk, will show up here.

Tack on and rider up if the horse looks promising. From ring center, I watch the horse ridden in small circles around me at all three gaits. I'm interested in his natural cadence, so I ask for a loose rein. If he dives on his nose when the rein contact is released, he's not for me. I want to see him bring his hocks underneath himself and lighten in front with no coaching from his rider. I expect to see the same thing now that I saw in hand, except perhaps a longer stride.

My major interest is the canter. The hunter jumps from the canter, so it is his most important gait. Does he bring his hocks well under? Does he maintain a crisp three-beat gait? Lazy hind legs four-beating the canter eliminate him. Can he maintain his stride in small circles without shortening to rebalance himself?

His fence test comes next: two little verticals, three feet to three feet three inches high, set sixty-six feet apart. I want to see him do it in five strides and then in six. If he's the kind of athletic mover I thought he was on the flat, he should have no trouble shortening for the six strides and lengthening for the five. If he can't make the distances easily, he's out.

For his final exam, I get on, myself, for a sort of quick quality-control check. Are the rhythm, balance, and adjustability I thought I saw really there? A brief run-through of the same things I just asked to see tells me whether the horse will do.

Combined Training Horses

JIM WOFFORD, a member of the U.S.E.T. Three-Day Team since 1965, has amassed an impressive collection of gold, silver, and bronze medals, individual as well as team, in Olympic Games, Pan American Games, and National and World championships, and in 1980 was awarded the coveted Whitney Stone Cup. In addition to running his hundred-acre Fox Covert Farm, in Upperville, Virginia, he is a director of the U. S. Equestrian Team, the U. S. Combined Training Association, and the American Horse Show Association, of which he is also first vice-president and member of the F.E.I. (Fédération Équestre Internationale) Committee.

Straight, even, precise. If his hind feet don't follow the track of his front, if he wings, if he ambles instead of walks, he's not going to be my Event horse.

Before I see him move, I want to look at the physical material. I usually start on the near side and work my way around.

First, his withers and shoulders: High withers and a long, sloping shoulder are promising signs. A good gallop and a clean jump require complete shoulder freedom. My horse must reach out with his front legs. Reach out, grab the ground, and swallow it. The more prominent the withers, the more the horse can rotate his shoulders. In fact, if his withers are very prominent, I can forgive a little straightness in the shoulder.

A tight topline, with a high head and neck, is acceptable. A low-necked horse is naturally more on his forehand and can be very difficult to bring on the bit. It's harder to hold him together galloping, and much harder to get a good dressage score. Deep chest; large forearms; long, flat knees; short cannon bones; moderate slope to pasterns; large feet. I check the straightness of his forelegs from the side and move to the front.

I want symmetry in the front and rear views. I should be able to draw a straight line down the leg from forearm to hoof. Both knees should be attached the same way to the forearms, cannons should come straight out of knees, and hooves should sit directly in front of forearms and cannons. Often I can tell that a horse paddles by studying his frontal symmetry.

Looking between the front legs to the hind legs, I should see a wide triangle in the hock area, wider at the top and equilateral. Both hind toes should be pointing straight at me.

I move back to study the motor area. I want to see good length to hip. A straight hock may be fashionable in conformation circles, but it's not good performance material. The horse gallops from his hip, rather than using his entire rear end. An efficient, powerful galloper really bends his hocks. A suggestion of cow hocks or sickle hocks is acceptable; at least it means the hocks are under the body, where they belong.

Now around to the rear. The good prospect is shaped like a wishbone. His hips are wide and the seat of his pants is slightly wider still. These features give him power to propel himself forward and jump big spreads.

Hocks underneath the body concentrate power. I'd rather his hocks be a little close than too far apart. I can always protect him with boots if he brushes. But if he travels wide, he'll dissipate power to the side and waste energy, particularly as he jumps. He should not, however, rope-walk (swing one hind leg in front of the other). Like winging and traveling wide, rope-walking means turbulence in the horse's motion. Any turbulence or loss of gait purity is wasted energy.

If he has the physical material, does he use it properly? The next part of the exam takes place on hard ground, preferably pavement. It's easier to see whether the horse moves straight and evenly on an unyielding surface. Moreover, I want to hear him move.

I like to start with him walking away from me. I'm concentrating on the lower legs from hocks and backs of knees on down. Does he move straight? Hind feet should follow front. He may travel a little close. He may not travel wide. He should have a straight four-beat walk, each foot striking flat.

Does he wing? If he does, I look to see whether his foot is trimmed correctly. I flex the ankle and study the leg. Can I draw a straight line from the point at which the tendon comes out of the knee down through the cleft of the frog? If the ankle flexes straight, with no discomfort or tendency to curl sideways, he probably travels straight normally but needs a new farrier.

Next, I want to see him trot toward me. How do his feet hit the ground? I should hear a good two-beat trot: one-two, one-two, his feet making hollow, cupped sounds. If I hear a double beat, I know he's rolling a foot. A little turbulence at the walk or the trot will be much worse at the canter or the gallop.

Finally, I'll move to the side while the horse is walked and trotted past me, so I can measure the mechanics and quality of his paces. Do his shoulders and hips move freely? Does he reach out with his front legs and over-track behind? I don't mind a horse that moves a little high in front. Many half-breds are round movers. Horses that are tense or high-necked are apt to be a little high. Sometimes the rounder-moving horse jumps better.

Time for the saddle. Usually I'm the rider. I give the horse no help, very little rein contact. Painful as it is to the ego to look inept on a horse, it's much more useful to find out what the horse can do on his own.

He should show me the same things at walk and trot that he showed me in hand: regular cadence, striding out in front and bringing his hocks under behind. At the canter, I want a definite three-beat gait. Whatever his stage of training, he should feel level, go forward and straight, and bring his hindquarters under. He can pull, he can be hard to get on the bit. But as long as he feels level and engaged behind, he's a definite prospect.

Dressage Horses

GUNNAR OSTERGAARD, 1976 Professional Dressage Champion of his native Denmark, trained with Karl Diehl in Germany and Gunnar Andersen in Denmark before moving to the United States, where he has achieved great success as a dressage rider, trainer, coach, and judge.

A dressage prospect should cover as much ground as possible. He must travel straight, with a great deal of shoulder freedom, swinging his front legs well forward but not with the flat arc of the show hunter.

He should pick up his hind hooves, bring them forward, and overstep the track of his front feet. I want a definite bend in the hocks, too. He'll need that energy and activity later for collected work.

If I'm looking at a young horse, I like to see him first at liberty in a ring or an indoor school. I stand in the center and ask someone to urge the horse forward.

Are his gaits regular and precise? I'm looking for an active walk with a one-two-three-four cadence. An overstep of one and one half hoof lengths is just about right.

The trot should be a two-beat cadence: one-two, one-two. I'm looking for straightness, activity, and regularity. If he's a Thoroughbred, he may not have enough shoulder freedom for a really good trot. Many don't. But, providing he has a really good walk and canter, I may be able to improve his trot.

I look for balance and cleanness at the canter. He should bring his hocks forward as far as possible under the center of gravity, with a clear three-beat rhythm. A four-beat canter is a serious fault, indicating lack of activity and engagement behind.

Once I've seen him in his natural state, I want to see him under saddle. I stand beside the track while the horse is ridden toward me at the walk and trot. Does he travel straight? The hooves should land in the direction they are pointed, with no toe-flipping. If he has a minor paddle and he's otherwise perfect, I won't discard him out of hand.

Next, I'll have him ridden away from me. I want straight hind legs, no cow hocks. He should neither cross over behind nor track to the outside of his front feet. Both are major faults. Dressage judges particularly dislike the latter.

Now I move to the middle of the ring and ask to see all three gaits in both directions. Does he maintain the correct rhythm of the gaits when ridden? Is he one-sided or does he bend equally well in both directions? Is his stride even in both directions and at all three gaits?

If the horse is young, I ask for some lengthening; if he's an older animal, I ask to see shortening, too.

If the horse seems suitable, I get on, myself. I ride each gait on a loose rein. Can he maintain his balance and stride around corners with a rider's weight but without his help? Does he feel even, level, and straight? If he is a young horse, I finish by picking up rein contact, riding all three gaits, and asking the same questions.

Suppose the horse is older, say five or six. I ask for a little collection at the trot and canter. I might also try some small circles. If he bends well and places his inside leg well underneath his body, he should be able to do pirouettes later.

A prospective Fourth Level horse must pass more difficult tests. Flying changes are an important factor. If the horse changes late behind, or if he swings sideways, front or back, I might be able to correct him; but if not, he'll be faulted in competition.

I ask for a little bit more than the horse has been taught. If he performs nice changes every three strides, I'll ask for changes with every two.

A Fourth Level horse must have extensions. How much, depends on the state of his training. He must lengthen his frame, stretch his neck, and give me a longer period of suspension without hurrying.

He should shorten at the canter. I'll also try a few collected trot steps to see if the potential for piaffe dressage is there.

I ask for a collected walk. If he loses the one-two-three-four beat and starts to amble or pace, I discard him. At the higher levels of dressage competition, the walk is heavily weighed in the judging. A Fourth Level prospect that paces has a dark future.

LOOK BEFORE YOU RIDE!

Illustrated by Custer Cassidy

Professional horsemen don't have to fall in love with every horse they buy. They don't even have to get along with them well. All they require is that the animal possess enough attributes to make him attractive to a large number of potential buyers. On the other hand, a nonprofessional, who does not usually expect to make the quick-turnover sale that is the livelihood of the pro, has no reason to please anyone but himself.

When you are evaluating a horse with the idea of making a purchase, there is a lot to be learned from watching him ridden before trying him out for yourself.

If you have a chance to see his behavior as he is caught in the stall or pasture, you can discover quite a lot about his temperament. If the horse is easily caught and handled, it is a distinct plus. When you reach for his head with halter or bridle, does he pull away, make himself tall, or give evidence of being head-shy or otherwise uncooperative? Does he stand quietly while the saddle is placed on his back and positioned? Does he fidget or resist or snap his jaws as the girth is drawn up? Does he seem to resent the entire act of being bridled, or does he accept the bit willingly? When given a choice, the latter attitude is obviously preferable. If the prospect of being ridden seems to excite or frighten the horse, if he becomes nervous and tense, he is obviously no horse for a novice rider or a timid one. Even when the behavior is all in fun, he can develop into a genuine bully in the hands of an inexperienced rider.

These may seem to be trivial considerations, but they can be pertinent, even decisive, factors when the horse under consideration is destined for a novice rider or a child. Of course, a horse that dozes calmly through the above preparations may not be ideal either, but at least he will pose no threat of bodily harm.

It is always a good idea to let the seller "show" his horse. The circumstances are all in the horse's favor and you will see him at his best. He is in familiar territory, being shown by a person you can assume to be his regular rider, and he is being asked to do only what he does well. You therefore have every right to expect him to perform in a relaxed and cheerful manner, with an evident desire to please. Signs of resistance under such favorable circumstances should make you wary. Why acquire a horse that is basically

SAY "PLEASE" —

"If the horse is easily caught and handled, it is a distinct plus."

unhappy about being ridden? There are too many others who enjoy their work. Of course, a green or unfinished horse may be a bit confused by some of the demands placed upon him, but if he cannot maintain a kindly disposition, a cool demeanor, and a willing attitude in the hands of his present owner, you shouldn't expect him to do any better for you.

By insisting that the owner make the initial demonstration of the horse's talents, you also absolve yourself of responsibility for any possible missteps or misbehavior. You don't want to unwittingly ask somebody else's horse to accomplish a feat beyond his present means. And you certainly don't want to cause the horse to react badly, resist forcefully, and perhaps damage himself and/or you in the process. So start by letting the seller demonstrate the movements and exercises that interest you. You cannot then be blamed for "ruining" the horse.

The shrewd horse dealer may exaggerate when he points an accusing finger at an innocent novice and shrieks, "My horse! My horse! You've ruined my beautiful horse! It will take me a [month, year, forever] to [restore his confidence, re-school him, get him out of that bad habit, make him do it correctly, etc., ad infinitum]." While the probability of a horse so suddenly acquiring an enduring bad habit or losing confidence completely is not very likely, a clever dealer can nevertheless make a buyer feel guiltily responsible and thus lead to a horse sale that was not all that much decided in the buyer's mind before.

If a horse is supposed to be a jumper, ask to see him jump a fence or a series of fences. If he is a reining horse, ask to see a reining pattern. If he is of a breed characterized by a specialty gait (a Tennessee Walking Horse, for example, or an American Saddlebred), ask to see the gaits performed in both directions. In other words, under no circumstances should you consider riding, much less purchasing, any horse just because someone said it could do something.

Much of what you see in a demonstration ride is contingent on the type of schooling the horse has had and the level to which he has been trained. But, in all cases, the horse should stand quietly and patiently for mounting. Those which are nervous about being mounted may be fine for agile types, fearless children, professionals who will educate them, and persons with an endless supply of ground help, but they are poor choices for less-coordinated, more-timid individuals, passive children, and generally insecure riders, who may find their enthusiasm vanish at the prospect of a daily hassle to secure a seat in the saddle. Moreover, horses know when they have the advantage, and a horse that puts his rider on the defensive before he is even in the saddle is apt to maintain the upper hand, and furthermore is unlikely to make much progress.

At the *walk,* you should like to see a long, rhythmic four-beat gait, moving freely from the shoulder and ending with the hoof planted squarely on the ground. It should be a flat-footed gait, minus prancing, sidestepping, and jigging. If a horse is so nervous that he cannot relax and walk correctly, he is a poor candidate for pleasure horse.

You hope to see a *trot* and a *canter* also characterized by long, fluid strides, with a definite cadence and a minimum of excess movement. These qualities represent the ideal, rather than the average, but the closer a horse comes to meeting these standards, the greater are his chances of remaining sound and performing well over an extended period.

Since a horse's action is a direct result of his physical structure, it is generally true that the better his conformation, the better his movement. The better he moves, the smaller the risk of interference while he is in motion and the lighter the concussion and structural stress. Also, the better he moves, the more comfortable he is to ride.

On the other hand, no matter how well a horse is constructed or how beautifully he moves, if his mental outlook places him in the dunce percentile or, worse, in that of the calculating rogue, he is practically useless. In fact, you may be well advised to forgive certain minor structural defects in a horse that may fall short of the mark physically but is blessed with the temperament, good nature, alert mind, innate intelligence, athletic ability, and common horse sense that make him an apt pupil or a reliable graduate. Bombproof ponies and unflappable horses are worth their weight in gold despite obvious physical imperfections if only because of the confidence they inspire and the assurance they provide their tiny and/or timid passengers.

A horse that responds willingly and promptly to the cues of his rider is giving proof of a good education. Absence of head-throwing, restlessness, and other petty annoyances attest to his good manners. Smoothness of gait, ease of steering, lack of stumbling, and general pedal dexterity will tell you almost everything you need to know about his balance and coordination.

Another quality that should not be overlooked is the horse's willingness to stop. While it may seem to be more a matter of training than a natural asset, it is a subtlety that can greatly affect a horse's usefulness and performance. Horses rarely hurt themselves or their riders when they are standing still or moving slowly. They get into trouble going fast, and especially when the speed exceeds what is suitable for the terrain and footing. Most horses will stop on command. Avoid the one that doesn't. There are too many instances during riding when it is important to stop, for you to risk a ride on a horse with faulty brakes. If you have any doubts after seeing the horse go, ask the rider to gallop a short distance and then halt. If the horse performs well, so much the better. If it takes a hundred feet of rider persuasion plus a tug-of-war, you probably don't need that horse.

Remember, a pleasure horse is meant to be just that: a pleasure.

PRECAUTIONS THE PROS TAKE

DAVID HOPPER, with his partner, Ira Schulman, has bought and sold countless famous show-ring stars, some of them for fabulous prices. Nevertheless, the majority of his purchases are for under $15,000—his "breadbasket," as he puts it, being the $5,000 horse. The most modest horse buyer can therefore profit from his experience and advice.

In order to get horses to sell, I have to buy them from other people. Whenever possible, I buy from people I know. When I go to a stranger, I'm scared to death of being taken in.

I buy most of our horses at the racetrack. That's where I can resell a mistake, either in a sale or directly back to the track. Before I buy a horse at a racetrack, I do a little research into the horse's pedigree and performance record, so that I have a rough idea of its value as a racehorse in case I have to sell it back.

Whenever I buy from somebody I don't know, I save myself a lot of driving by checking him out in advance. If I see an ad that interests me, I call up the dealer and find out where he's located. Then I call other horse people in the area and ask them whether they know the seller, or even the horse. Every once in a while, someone goes and buys a horse out from under me. But, overall, I save a lot of gas.

Even if I didn't know anyone in the area, I'd find a way to check out an unknown dealer. I'd call him and ask him for the names of three or four people to whom he's sold horses, and I'd call them. If the dealer is straight, he won't mind giving out the information. One bad report wouldn't bother me; every now and then a buyer bears a grudge that may not even be justified. But if everybody I talked to expressed the same reservations, I'd worry.

I look at hundreds of horses in a year, but if I weren't experienced, I'd take along someone who could interpret the horse's way of going and assess the whole package in terms of both my wants and my needs. An experienced horseman can save a novice from buying a horse with a potentially serious problem; he can also keep a novice from passing up a horse because of some insignificant fault.

If I were an amateur buying a horse for my own use, I wouldn't just watch it being ridden. I'd ride it myself to be sure I *could* ride it. Sometimes a very good rider can make a horse look a lot farther along than it really is. If I were buying a horse that was going to be ridden cross-country, I'd take it for a hack. If the seller told me the horse was fine with traffic, I'd ride it beside a road.

When I first arrive at the seller's, I ask about the horse's turn-out and riding schedule and about what has been done with him already that day. Quite often a seller will give his horse a little work in the morning to settle him down for a buyer in the afternoon. If the seller has nothing to hide, he'll probably say something like, "We had the horse out for half an hour this morning." But if the answer I get doesn't quite ring true, I ask the question again sometime later in my visit to see whether the stories match.

I also ask about the horse's idiosyncrasies, his quirks, what makes him tick. He may be the kind that goes sour if he is schooled three days in a row but is fine if he is hacked or let alone every third day. The seller is bound to make the horse appear simpler than he really is, if I don't press for information. I keep an eye on the horse throughout my visit. Once, I bought a horse and then discovered that he had a phobia about concrete. He would come into the barn and lean against the wall like a drunk. It took me twenty minutes every day to get him from barn to paddock. Now I observe every horse I inspect in his stall, in the aisle, on the driveway, wherever he goes.

If the horse were on a large dose of tranquilizers, I could probably spot some of the signs myself: dull eyes, sheath dropping down. But the best way to tell whether a horse is drugged is to have a veterinarian do a blood test. If I don't know the dealer and if his references seem shady, but if I like the horse anyway, I'll take my vet out and have him take a sample of his blood. I encourage buyers to do the same thing with my horses.

I usually trust my own judgment as to soundness, but if I were an amateur buyer, I would have the horse vetted and ask the vet to X-ray the horse's feet, at least. The three basic X-ray angles will show any sign of navicular disease, coffin-bone rotation from founder, ringbone, or sidebone. A hock flexion test will usually show up trouble in the hocks; but if I were very cautious, I might have the vet X-ray the hocks too, even if the flexion tests were negative.

What I like about this business is that it's like the "last frontier." There's an element of risk in it, like shooting craps. You shouldn't spend more for a horse than you can afford to lose. On the other hand, if you're patient and very lucky, $1,500 might get you a $3,500 horse.

DR. JOSEPH HEISSAN and Dr. William Bradley, his partner in the New England Equine Practice, in Ridgefield, Connecticut, perform more than 250 pre-purchase vet exams a year, specializing in show hunters, Event horses, and jumpers.

Before you even go to see a prospective new horse, you should have firmly in your mind the kind of horse you want, what you plan to do with him, and how much you are prepared to pay. There is no point in bringing out a vet if the horse doesn't meet one of your basic requirements.

You may also be able to save yourself the price of a wasted vet call by looking over your prospective purchase for obvious physical flaws. A serious conformation fault, such as severe calf knees, sickle hocks, or a misshapen foot, will probably give your vet reservations about the suitability of your prospect.

Look for eyesight problems. Does the horse shy in inappropriate situations? Or when going one way of the ring but not the other? Take note of his breathing. Does he wheeze? make a noise when he's ridden? Is he coughing?

If the horse is lame, try to determine why. If you can see a bump (swelling) or if the owner says that the horse rapped himself over a jump the day before, the lameness may be temporary. Ask whether you can try the horse again when he is sound. Don't waste a vet call on a lame horse unless the horse is a superstar and you feel that you can live with a chronic lameness.

When you send your vet out, make sure he knows what you plan to do with the horse. Is he a show prospect? a dressage performer? a field hunter? An old bowed tendon might be insignificant in a prospective pleasure horse; but if your vet knows that you are buying this horse in hopes of taking him to the top in Combined Training competition, he will give the bow an especially thorough going-over.

You will have spent several hours with the horse and his owners. Your vet may have only an hour and a half. Give him the benefit of your observations. If you know, for example, that the horse seldom gets out of his stall, tell him so; it will help to explain poor muscle tone. Tell your vet about any lumps and bumps, peculiar behavior, signs of cribbing in the stall. Mention anything that worries you, so that he will take special notice and be prepared to comment on it afterward.

Your vet has a standard examination routine that he will follow in lieu of instructions from you, so if you want him to perform any special procedures such as X rays or drug tests, be sure to request them specifically.

X rays are often a wise precaution when you're buying a young horse. They can provide an early warning of trouble to come. In an older horse, X rays usually show only bony changes the horse has already lived with for a while; if the horse is sound when you X-ray him, he is probably never going to be affected by the changes you find on the film.

A drug test is simply too expensive to do on a routine basis nowadays.

But there are certain situations in which the expense is justified. A horse that is lame the first time you try him, and miraculously sound a day and a half later; a horse that is nervous and jumpy the first day, dead quiet when you come back to ride him again—these might merit the expense of drug testing. If the seller has a questionable reputation or is unknown to you, you will have to weigh the expense of testing against the penalty of making a mistake. In our practice, we run a spot check for drugs in about every tenth horse we vet, at our own expense. The sellers in the area know we do it, and it helps to keep everybody honest.

RICHARD ABBOTT is a horseman's lawyer with a private practice in West Chester, Pennsylvania. He is also a partner in Charlton, Inc., a Thoroughbred bloodstock agency and public stable that trains and conditions young horses for shows and sales. He is an A.H.S.A. judge and steward and a director of the Pennsylvania Horse Breeders Association.

If you buy at public auction, you are probably already pretty well protected, although you may not know it. An established sales company will take a horse back for a wide range of defects you may discover within seven days of the date of the sale; but if you are familiar only with the very limited warranties included in the conditions of sale printed in the front of the sales catalogue, you won't benefit from the recourse open to you.

Before you go to the sale, do not only read the conditions of sale in the catalogue, but also obtain from the sales company a copy of the contract all sellers must sign when they consign their horses. You will discover that there are a number of circumstances, not mentioned in the conditions of sale, under which the seller agrees to take back his horse. If a racing prospect, for example, is found to have a defect of bone structure that adversely affects its suitability for race training, the consignor must take it back. You, the buyer, in effect have the opportunity to vet the horse after you get it home. If the horse is defective for the purpose for which it was sold, you can return it within seven days for a full refund.

Private transactions are more hazardous, because so seldom is anything set down in writing. People spend tremendous amounts of money in a casual manner that they would never dream of applying to any other form of business transaction.

My advice is very simple: *Get it in writing.* If the seller tells you the horse is suitable for a five-year-old child to ride, get it in writing. If he tells you the horse is capable of winning at the "A" shows, get it in writing. Anything the seller tells you about the horse's performing ability, suitability, or soundness that influences your decision to buy should be in writing. Any seller who is not willing to enter into a reasonable written agreement is not the type of person with whom you should be dealing.

If you are buying an expensive horse, you should handle the purchase just like a real estate transaction, beginning with a written agreement of sale expressing all warranties and designating a date for settlement.

At the time of the signing of the agreement, you give the seller a down payment.

If the horse doesn't pass the vet, you get your down payment back. But if you simply decide not to go through with the purchase, you forfeit the down payment to the seller.

At settlement, you pay for the balance of the horse with certified funds and the seller transfers the papers to you. Agents' commissions, the vet bill, and any other charges related to the transaction are also paid at settlement.

The advantage of this system is that it leaves no room for misunderstanding. You and the seller know exactly what to expect from each other at every stage of the transaction and later, should a problem arise.

HOW TO TEST A HORSE FOR SOUNDNESS

You've been out horse shopping, you have found a horse you like, and now you're about to get him vetted. Pre-purchase vet checks are cheap insurance with today's horse prices what they are, but there's a catch. This horse may not pass the vet, nor may the next one you find, nor the next. You can spend several hundred dollars riffling through faulty prospects (many buyers do), or you can do the preliminary weeding out yourself. If a prospect passes your own inspection, you can then call in the vet to check for shortcomings you may have missed.

Your examination should consist of two parts: a ridden test and a closeup inspection from the ground.

The Ridden Test

When the horse is led up for you to mount, note his general condition. He should have a bright, alert expression and a healthy-looking coat. A dull coat or a dropped penis may indicate a hefty dose of tranquilizer. You can also ask his owner for a brief medical history. Has the horse ever been lame? had laminitis? colic? pneumonia? Frequent colics could mean an intestinal obstruction or a destructive parasite load. A long, severe bout with pneumonia might have left his lungs riddled with scar tissue. Although most owners are not eager to volunteer information about their horses' health problems, few of them will lie outright. If the answer seems vague, make a mental note to explore that area in detail later on. Finally, find out how much work the horse has done recently. You don't want to mistake an unfit horse for one that is unsound in the wind.

When you mount the horse, does he hump his back, buck, or drop his hindquarters as soon as he feels your weight in the saddle? He may merely be sensitive, but these reactions could also be the warning signs of a back problem. Note also if he coughs when he starts to work, for this is often a symptom of heaves. And as you ride, keep a sharp eye out for obvious signs of pain: a nodding head at the trot, uneven strides at any gait, a hind leg that stabs the ground abruptly, or hindquarters that seem to fall away beneath your seat.

The walk. You can't tell much about soundness at the walk, so you might as well use the time you spend walking to familiarize yourself with the horse's way of going and to plan your maneuvers at the trot and the canter. To begin with, you'll need a level area with good footing and room to ride large and small circles, from sixty down to ten feet in diameter. If the area is too cluttered with jumps for this, request that some of them be removed.

Change rein at the walk and continue to plan your test. Lay out a second circle sixty feet in diameter, so that you will be able to ride a large figure of eight. If there's room for only one large circle, plan instead to change rein through the center of it, using an *S* pattern. Also, pick a spot where you can ride a smaller figure of eight, one with two circles of ten-foot diameter.

The trot. The trot is the best gait for spotting lameness. Begin on a sixty-foot circle and keep an eye on the horse's head carriage. A sound horse holds his head steady at the trot. If he is severely lame in a front leg, he'll probably raise his head as the lame leg strikes the ground. If he's very lame behind, he may drop his head as the lame leg lands. Any head movement at the trot is an ominous sign.

The trot is a two-beat gait, and there should be equal emphasis on the beats. Your circle is big enough for the horse to use both sides of his body equally. Listen to the sound of his hoofbeats. If he's only slightly off, his head may remain still, but you'll hear and feel the unevenness. One beat will seem slightly longer and a little more emphatic than the other.

Change directions, using the *S* pattern (or, if space permits, a figure of eight), and continue to circle on the other rein. Pay close attention to the horse's strides during the change. He may be stiffer in one direction, and in order to avoid stretching those stiff muscles, he may throw his quarters to the outside and hurry around the turn; but if he's sound, his strides should hurry equally, so that the right and left forelegs cover the same distance with each step. If he moves symmetrically but seems jerky, short-strided, or otherwise awkward, it might be his natural way of moving; on the other hand, it might be indicative of a problem. Make a mental note.

Once you have the feeling of his normal trot, gradually decrease the circumference of your arc until you are riding a circle ten feet in diameter. Small circles require the joints of the legs on the inside of the arc to bend more than those on the outside, and to support more than half the horse's weight. They require the legs on the outside of the arc to make a longer reach. If this extra effort causes the horse discomfort, you'll see his head bob or hear an alteration in the rhythm of his stride.

(Since you won't detect unsoundness at the walk, use that time to lay out a course for the tests you'll perform at the trot.) Begin the trot on generous, 60-foot circles in both directions, monitoring the rhythm of the gait and position of the head for signs of lameness.

Tight circles at the trot, first left, then right, put extra stress on the legs, making it easier to spot subtle problems. As you change your posting from one diagonal to the other, there should be no change in the thrust you feel from the horse.

Take your time. But be sure to keep the trot active. You will find it easier to judge the soundness of the horse's hind legs if you oblige him to keep his hindquarters well under him.

Make three or four small circles and then spiral back to the larger circle. Change direction and repeat the exercise on the other rein. By asking the horse to perform large circles and small ones in rapid succession, you will discover whether he is able to change the degree of flexion of his joints easily.

Once you've ridden small circles in both directions, try a figure of eight using two circles of ten-foot diameter. The figure of eight gives you a basis for rapid comparison: Does the horse move the same to the right as he does to the left? And it puts even more stress on the joints. The legs that are on the inside of the first circle will be on the outside of the second, and must quickly adapt to the different degrees of flexion and stretching that the figure of eight requires of them.

If you notice any irregularity in the horse's stride through the change of direction, repeat the figure several times to confirm your impression. A horse that is green or uncertain of your aids may hurry around the turns; but his stride should remain even, with both front legs hurrying at the same rate. If one leg seems to hop or to catch the other when you change direction, something in that leg is probably hurting.

You have been trotting the horse for about fifteen minutes, and he has covered roughly two miles. Any leg problem should be making its presence felt by now. Urge him forward on a big circle and monitor his reaction carefully. Does his head remain steady? Is his stride even? Does he place each foot firmly? An uneven stride, reluctance to move forward, and a loss of rhythm are all signs that he may have a problem.

If you can find some sloping ground, you can perform a test that is particularly useful for exposing weak stifles. Although a severe stifle problem will probably have shown up as you circled the horse, minor difficulties are easier to spot when the horse works on a hill. Jog up and down a short slope, and notice whether the horse's hind legs push him steadily up the hill and support him firmly as he descends. A loose, jolting downhill or a feeling of unsteady support on the way up is a bad sign.

If the riding area is flat, you can use a different test to check the horse's stifles. Lengthen his trot down the long side of the ring, ask him to shorten before he reaches the turn, and bring him to a halt in the middle of the short side. Although he may be too green to halt immediately, his hindquarters should feel secure throughout the exercise. You should feel each leg give a firm, definite stride through the turn and the downward transition to halt. If his legs drag behind him before and during the turn, or if he rocks to and fro on his hindquarters before coming to a full halt, you should suspect weakness in the stifles.

The canter. The canter will show you whether the horse has breathing problems; it can sometimes show up heart deficiencies as well. The canter will also give you another chance to check for joint pain in the hind legs.

Begin, as you did at the trot, with a circle sixty feet in diameter. Canter two or three circuits and then change direction with a simple change of lead through the trot. Make several changes to compare the horse's performance in one direction with that in the other. If the trotting test led you to suspect a problem in a hind leg, pay particular attention to that leg when you canter. You'll probably find that the horse is reluctant to pick up the canter lead on that side or, when he does, that he switches leads behind. Although a horse that's one-sided isn't necessarily lame, you should add this piece of evidence to your mental list.

If your prospect has been in light work—for example, an hour and a half a day of easy walk-trot-canter—the five minutes of cantering you'll need for your circles will probably also provide an adequate test of heart and lungs. If he's a fit Event horse or just off the racetrack, you'll need up to ten minutes more of a medium canter in order to stress him.

As you canter, listen to the horse's breathing. Unless he's supremely fit, it will become progressively noisier, just as yours does when you jog for more than a few minutes. But it should always be regular and relaxed, with no strange sounds, other than the normal "blowing." If it isn't, take note. After you have cantered long enough to test his level of fitness, change to a walk and monitor the time it takes his breathing to return to normal. It should be no longer than the canter period.

If the horse makes a rasping noise as he inhales, as though his air passage is restricted in some way, he may be a "roarer." This condition is caused by the partial paralysis of a nerve, which permits a portion of the larynx to flap in the airway. It's possible to confuse the huffing and puffing of an unfit horse with roaring. If you decide to have the horse vetted, mention the noise to your veterinarian and ask whether the horse should be "scoped" (the air passages visually examined with an endoscope).

If the horse's owner claims that he has been galloping five miles every day, and yet the horse seems reluctant to canter for the fifteen minutes of your test, beware. Shortness of breath in a supposedly fit horse or, worse, unsteadiness after moderate exercise, may be the warning signs of a cardiovascular problem.

Jumping. You have placed more strain on your horse's joints with your tests at the trot and canter than you will by jumping a course of small fences. However, jumping is useful, because it gives you another means of checking suspicious areas. Remembering that even perfectly sound horses often do strange things over fences, be on the lookout for styles of jumping that suggest the horse is attempting to avoid pain. He may not perform faultlessly, but if he's sound, he should trot and canter down to his fences without shuffling his stride for the takeoff. He should maintain a smooth, even gait and perform like an athlete. If he chips in or switches leads before each fence, you should suspect that he feels discomfort when shifting his weight to the hind legs; if he throws his hind legs to one side in the air, rather than tucking them up, this is another sign that they are hurting him; and if he unfolds his front legs too quickly or dives on landing, he may be trying to reduce the length of time during which his knees are bent.

Ground Check

If your prospect hasn't disqualified himself by this time, on the basis of either soundness or performance, it's the moment to take a closer look at his physical conformation. In this part of your examination, you'll probe for abnormalities, using some such techniques as joint flexion tests, with which you may be unfamiliar. So before applying these procedures to someone else's horse, practice them at home on a sound and healthy one. You should know, for example, what a normal eye looks like, and how a sound horse jogs away from a flexion test. You should be able to run through your examination briskly and efficiently. Nothing brings a supercilious smile to the lips of an owner more quickly than the prospective buyer who fumblingly raises a foot, stares at it vaguely for a moment, then sets it down, having concluded nothing.

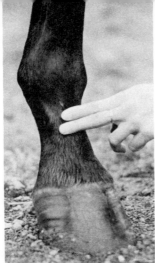
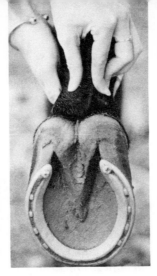

1. Squeezing just above the heels, you should feel flexible cartilage. If nothing gives when you press, the cartilage may have calcified into sidebones.

2. Run your fingers down the front of the pastern from fetlock to hoof. Lumpiness at the pastern joint or coronary band could signify ringbone.

3. Two small scars or a few white hairs at the back of the pastern may be evidence that the horse has been nerved.

4. Working your way up each front leg, carefully palpate the tendons for signs of heat, swelling, or soreness.

Begin by standing a few feet away from the horse and slowly walk around him. Pay particular attention to the legs. They may not be textbook perfect, but they should match. If they don't, if one knee points north while the other faces east, or if one hoof is large and round while the other is small and narrow, trouble may be brewing. Viewed from behind, the muscle masses over both sides of the croup, hips, and gaskins should match. If they don't, the horse may be using one side less vigorously than the other. Note any differences, and pay special attention to these areas when you move in for a closer look.

The hoof. Begin by examining the outside of the hoof. A flared wall on one side tells you that the horse puts more pressure on that side, perhaps in order to avoid using sore tissues on the other side of his leg. You should also be on the lookout for parallel rings in the hoof wall, which are a telltale sign of *founder*. Feel the hoof, checking for heat and swelling at the coronary band.

Next, pick up the foot to check for *contracted heels* and *dropped soles*. The latter, another sign of founder, are caused by the downward rotation of the coffin bone. If the horse has foundered, you'll probably need X rays to determine the extent of damage.

The leg. Most horses have stray lumps and bumps on their legs, and the horse you are examining is probably no exception. You might miss out on a perfectly good horse by making too much of an old injury that has healed. In many cases, you'll have to ask a vet to evaluate its importance. But don't hesitate to ask the owner about it too. When did the injury occur? How was it treated? You might also request permission to consult the horse's regular veterinarian.

Work your way up each leg, feeling for heat, swelling, and sore spots. Test for soreness by pressing on the spot you suspect and observing the horse's reactions, remembering that some horses are more sensitive than others. You can check your findings by applying pressure to the same spot on the other leg and comparing the reactions.

Keep in mind the unsoundnesses commonly found in each area. The first trouble site is located just above the hoof. Press down at the coronary on either side of the foot; you should feel two pliable cartilages beneath your fingers. If, instead, you feel bony lumps, the cartilage has calcified and the horse has *sidebones*. Once they have set, sidebones may or may not bother the horse again.

Ringbone, bony growths in the neighborhood of the pastern or coffin joints, may cause the horse pain, which would have shown up during your ridden test; but ringbone is usually quite severe before you can see or feel it. You will probably have to have X rays made in order to confirm your suspicions.

The examination of the pastern may also turn up a small scar on either side, just below the sesamoid bones, evidence of *"nerving."* This is a last-resort treatment for navicular and some other chronic lamenesses. Al-

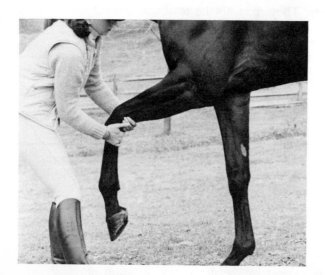

Stretch each front leg forward in turn. The horse may try to pull his leg away, but he shouldn't react by sinking toward the ground.

Pull the leg back and then . . .

. . . pull it out to the side. Repeat with the other front leg and compare the response.

Hold each ankle in a tightly flexed position for sixty seconds and have the horse jogged away. If he takes more than one or two bad steps, you may have irritated a sore spot.

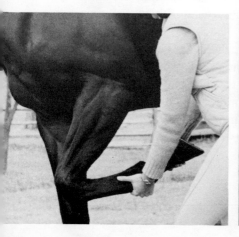
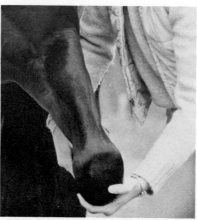

though the scars are often difficult to spot without clipping the coat, you may see a few telltale white hairs.

Wind-puffs (little soft swellings just above the ankle) do no harm as long as they are not accompanied by heat or soreness.

Osselets, another problem you might find in this area, are bony lumps on the ankle. Whether or not they will affect the horse's usefulness depends on their location. If they interfere with the tendons or ligaments, or are so positioned that the horse is likely to strike them with his other foot, they can cause problems.

Continue up the horse's leg, palpating the major tendons and ligaments in search of heat, swelling, or soreness. A puffy knee or tendon, even an old *bowed tendon,* is not necessarily grounds for rejecting the horse on the spot; but it is a warning signal.

You may discover that the horse has *splints,* little lumps of bone along the sides of the legs between the cannon and splint bones. Splints, like osselets, vary in seriousness according to their location. Many are merely unsightly, but some cause lameness by interfering with the nearby tendons and ligaments. Splints situated near the suspensory ligament or close to the knee are more often a problem than those farther forward or lower.

Some horses that have been raced will have parallel rows of small, circular scars on their shins or ankles, the marks left by *pinfiring.* They may be unsightly, but they do not bother the horse. The important question is, What prompted the pinfiring? Was it merely preventative, or was it an attempt to cope with some specific problem?

Conclude your examination of the horse's front leg by briefly flexing the knee and ankle and pulling the whole leg forward and back. The horse should stand quietly while you flex his joints; if he flinches and tugs his leg away, you can assume that one of the joints hurts. When you stretch his leg forward and back, it is normal for him to try to pull it away; but if he sinks toward the ground, he may be telling you that his shoulder is sore.

Return to the ankle and hold it in the flexed position for sixty seconds. Have a helper ready to jog the horse forward as soon as you release the leg. Flexing the joint for a minute will aggravate any soreness and make lameness more apparent. Even a sound horse may take a bad step or two as he starts off; but if all is well, he will recover quickly.

Begin your examination of the hind leg with the hoof, as you did with the front legs, and work your way up. When you reach the hock, remember that it has a set of ailments all its own. Soft swellings such as *thoroughpin* and *capped hock* are usually harmless; they merely indicate that the joint capsule was strained at one time. *Bog spavin,* a soft swelling at the front of the hock, is also not serious in itself, as long as it is not accompanied by pain. Some vets, however, consider it a sign of weakness in the hock that can lead to further problems.

If you find a firm but pliable lump on the back of the leg below the point of the hock, the horse has a *curb,* an injury to the plantar ligament, which anchors the point of the hock to the head of the cannon bone. Once the curb is healed, it will cause no trouble. *Bone spavin,* a hard, bony growth at the front of the hock, is more serious. It often indicates a degenerative joint condition that will leave the horse permanently lame.

Conclude your examination of the hind leg with another flexion test. Stand beside the horse's stifle, facing his tail, and raise the near hind leg. Clasp the fingers of both hands together and slide them under the fetlock so that your arms form a sling for the horse's leg. If you position yourself close to the horse, standing erect with your arms hanging straight down, it will not take much strength to hold up the leg. Maintain the flexion for sixty seconds. Stand behind the horse as he jogs away; if he is favoring one leg, his hip on that side will rise higher as he trots. Since the test flexes both hock and stifle, you may not be able to pinpoint the problem, but you'll be alerted to the likelihood that there is one.

Back and hindquarters. When you have finished your examination of the horse's legs, you are ready to check the muscles of his back for weakness or soreness. Starting at the withers and working toward the tail, press your fingertips along his spine with short, firm movements. If all is well, the horse will dip his back as you cover the area between the withers and the point of croup. He'll tense his quarters upward as you pass down over the croup to his tail. If he tenses upward against your fingers as you work in the saddle area, or sinks down as you pass over the croup, you'll know he's hurting.

Before leaving the horse's hindquarters, take a quick look at his flanks. If his muscles seem to contract twice every time he exhales, beware: this "double breathing" is a sign of *heaves.*

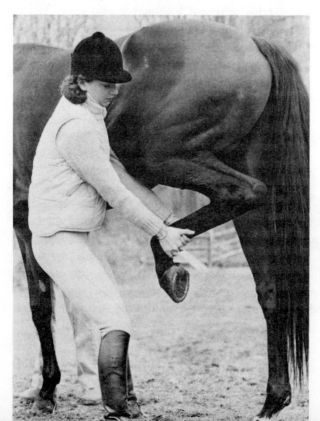

Hold each hind leg in a stifle flexion test for sixty seconds and watch for signs of soreness as the horse jogs off. Since you've cramped hock and hip, too, trouble in any one of these joints could show up now.

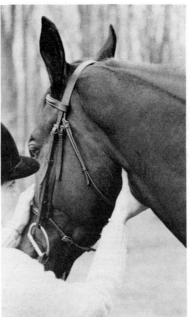

1. Probe between the jaws. The glands should be of equal size.
2. If you feel lumps when you palpate the larynx, or if the horse goes into a coughing fit, he may have a throat problem.
3. Run your fingers down the front of the neck, feeling for the cartilage rings of the trachea. An empty space may mean that a sunken cartilage is obstructing the horse's air passage.

Head and neck. Open the horse's mouth and check to make sure that the incisors meet squarely. Also, bad breath is a danger sign: An abscess gives off a foul odor.

Palpate the underside of the head, probing between the jaws to check that the glands are of the same size; they should feel like little bunches of grapes. If you cause the horse pain, something is amiss. Now move your hand over the larynx, palpating the tissues gently. If you feel lumps here, or if the horse goes into a coughing fit, he has a throat problem. Run your hand down the trachea to ensure that the rings of cartilage are of regular shape. If your fingers hit an empty space, the horse may have a sunken cartilage, which is apt to obstruct his breathing.

You have to take the horse into a dark place in order to check his eyes. Shine a penlight into the eye. If it is normal, you'll see reflections from three structures: the cornea, the front of the lens, and the back of the lens. If any one of these structures is abnormal, the light will not pass through it and you won't see its reflection.

Now you've kicked the tires, peeked under the hood, and taken a test drive. If your examination turns up nothing to stop you cold, it's time to call in the professional. Your vet can perform a detailed examination, take X rays, give various tests, and evaluate the problems that may have turned up during your own exam.

PRE-PURCHASE VET CHECKS

There is no imaginable set of circumstances under which anybody should buy a horse without a veterinary opinion. Every horse that is expected to perform in or out of competition should be vetted for soundness. So should any horse purchased for breeding, or any young horse purchased as a performance prospect. Yet, when the broodmare has a foal at her side or the yearling jogs sound, the buyer is sometimes tempted to spare the expense. We have, and we've learned. There's a lot more to soundness than clean legs.

Any horse that deserves to be bought deserves to be vetted. Even the horse acquired cheaply at an auction should be vetted when you get him home. The purchase price may not seem to warrant the additional expense, but consider your time, your hopes, plus future maintenance, which can make the initial outlay look like a drop in the bucket. So vet now, before you lavish loving care.

A veterinary certificate flaunted by the seller is no substitute for a vet check subsidized by you. Who knows how current the certificate is, or by what means it was obtained? Certainly the veterinarian who issued it knew nothing of your intended use of the horse. Any seller who seems to be using a veterinary certificate to divert you from a vetting of your own may know something that you had better find out.

The vet who does the job must be your man. This means that he must be paid by you and his loyalty must be to you. Don't assume that the latter ensures the former. If possible, use your regular veterinarian. In any case, never use the seller's vet, or even ask the seller to recommend one. Dealers frequently take pains to patronize most of the vets in their area, leaving few or none with uncommitted loyalty.

If your prospective purchase is so far from home that your own vet cannot go to the horse, make every effort to take the horse to your vet, or at least to some neutral territory, such as a university veterinary school clinic. Do not use a vet local to the seller, even if your own vet recommends him.

The seller probably won't let you take his horse home unless he has agreed to a trial. But he shouldn't object to sending his horse to an established veterinary clinic or hospital, at no risk or expense to himself, unless he has pretty good reason to believe that he'll be getting his horse back. You will have to pay transportation costs, back home again too, perhaps, and you should offer to assume responsibility for the horse. If anything happens to him en route, he's yours at the agreed price.

You, not the seller, should call the vet. Tell him how you plan to use the horse. Leave to him the decision of whether or not to X-ray, and to what extent, and authorize him to follow the course he thinks best. Tell him you will want his report in writing. If the horse fails, the seller is entitled to a copy of the report too.

But do not expect any veterinarian to advise you beyond the areas of health and soundness. It's not the vet's job to comment on performing ability or temperament, or to express an opinion as to whether the horse is fairly priced.

WHAT UNSOUNDNESSES ARE ACCEPTABLE?

DOROTHY MORKIS started out as a self-taught rider who was just "crazy about horses." After studying with Ernst Bachinger, of the Spanish Riding School, in Vienna, and acquiring a big gray Hanoverian called Monaco, she won the Individual Bronze Medal for Dressage in the 1975 Pan American Games, then placed seventh in the Grand Prix and fifth in the Grand Prix Special at the 1976 Montreal Olympics, helping the U. S. Dressage Team to win the Team Bronze Medal there.

A good dressage performance depends upon the horse's evenness of pace, willing attitude, and ability to extend and collect. Anything, physical or mental, interfering with these requirements eliminates the horse as a dressage prospect. Obviously, if you campaign at the lower levels your expectations for soundness can be lower. However, if you dream of Grand Prix dressage, your horse should be practically indestructible.

Remember, various jobs impose differing soundness standards. The show hunter, once he's made, is rarely worked hard between shows. Any infirmities can be nursed along. The dressage horse is in constant training and must be sturdy enough to withstand it. I'm not sure which is more frustrating: campaigning a sound horse with insufficient talent, or campaigning a talented horse with insufficient soundness.

Differing standards apply for dressage initiates. If you are just beginning or if your goal falls short of Fourth Level, the veteran animal that has developed infirmities or the less-expensive green horse with physical limitations may suit quite well. The lower levels do not require the brilliant extensions and collections demanded in Fourth Level and beyond. The emphasis is on obedience and basic maneuvers, rather than brilliance.

A dressage horse's hindquarters are his most important feature. Hock, stifle, hip, and back are major stress points. Their strength should approach that of structural steel. Moreover, his "motor" is there. While you may be able to patch problems in front, you cannot glue a motor back together.

The hindquarters must support weight as well as supply impulsion. If the horse cannot bring his hind legs forward under his body, using the hindquarters freely, then he lacks impulsion. Proper collection and extension are beyond his abilities. Any unsoundness preventing free use of the hindquarters eliminates a horse for advanced dressage.

Arthritic conditions or evidence of weakness in those areas such as spavins, curbs, thoroughpins, or spinal defects disqualify the candidate. Spinal problems produce unevenness of pace and prevent proper rounding of the back. Arthritis limits joint movement and usually gets worse. Flying changes and piaffes, difficult anyway, become impossible. The horse protects his arthritic side and refuses to change leads behind. Should you persuade the horse to sit down for the piaffe, arthritic hocks produce uneven steps as he shields his damaged area. Uneven steps knock you right out of the dressage ring.

There are no acceptable problems behind if you are thinking of advanced dressage. Spavins other than bogs are disasters and cause problems even with the use of bute. Resorting to surgery is not always successful. The horse still goes unevenly. Even bog spavins are iffy unless they occur in a seasoned horse. Should your boggy-hocked prospect be campaigning at Fourth Level or Prix St. George, then he'll probably hang together the rest of the way. I wouldn't accept bogs in a young horse.

Unsoundness in front, with the exception of the shoulder, is not quite so desperate. If I know what I'm treating, I might take a gamble here. The odd lump, bump, spur, splint, or wind-puff is certainly not alarming. Very few horses with any work experience at all escape such marks. Even an old fracture of the sesamoid, if properly healed, does not disqualify the candidate. As long as the questionable area is not at or near a joint, the horse may be suitable.

Any shoulder limitations are unacceptable. Extension comes right from the shoulder. Reduced flexion will inhibit full extension. A horse that can't extend properly has a dim future in advanced dressage.

Remember: Extension produces tremendous concussion in front. A really sore horse, whether in shoulder, knee, tendon, ankle, or foot, will not be able to extend. He'll back off the bit and refuse to stay round. Any foot problem such as sidebone, ringbone, or navicular can seriously compromise training. Intermittent lameness can throw your carefully planned work schedule into chaos. Full use of the knee joint is essential. You will not be able to keep the horse level and even when circling without full knee flexion. An afflicted animal, as he comes around a corner, may strain any of these problem areas. His discomfort may produce loss of rhythm. A dressage horse must cover the ground evenly. Loss of rhythm, particularly in extension, is severely penalized.

Osselets are acceptable provided they do not involve a joint. I don't like them in a young horse. In an older, high-level horse, calcium deposits accompany experience.

General stiffness often accompanies age and experience. If history shows that an older animal usually works out of his stiffness, I would not reject him. However, the four-year-old who crawls crablike from his box every morning is a poor choice.

Mental unsoundness is a catastrophe. A rogue, an unwilling or sour horse, is simply not worth the trouble. He's no fun to ride, eventually he'll embarrass you, and there are too many other horses with nice attitudes. There is also the occasional individual whose extreme nervousness produces rein lameness. For whatever reason, under stress he will refuse to take one side of the bit or use one side of his body. As a result, he's lame on one side. It's a difficult problem to correct, particularly in an older horse. Living outdoors does wonders for the nervous or flighty horse. However, when you have the choice, pick a more placid animal. If his temperament interferes with his performance, pass him by.

Dressage demands a high degree of soundness. Unfortunately, by the time a horse reaches Grand Prix level, he is no longer young. Bute can ease the pains that accompany experience, but under F.E.I. rules it is not permissible. And if a horse is truly unsound, bute is of little help anyway.

RONNIE MUTCH, former Equitation Medal winner and U.S.E.T. member, now a professional rider, trainer, instructor, and judge, has found, made, and ridden literally scores of top show hunters and jumpers during his lifetime career with horses—including Count Tuscan, Peace and Quiet, and the 1976 Amateur Horse of the Year, 20th Century Ltd.

There are few perfect horses. Those there are command breathtaking prices. Showing on the "A" circuit demands a quality animal, and providing a customer with affordable quality usually means coping with some unsoundness. By quality I mean not only looks, manners, and talent over fences, but a horse that moves well.

I frequently buy horses others won't touch, if they have the quality. Horses not up to the rigors of the track can often cope with the easier routine of the show circuit. The intended use of the horse influences the soundness standards I apply. Jumpers, because they are under the most stress, require the closest scrutiny. Show hunters have a more comfortable life, jumping fewer and lower fences. They can afford more physical problems. Equitation horses bear the least scrutiny of all. As long as an equitation horse can do his job, I'll nurse along almost any infirmity.

Buying a horse is a two-stage operation. First, I consult with my veterinarian and my blacksmith. We must decide if we can all live with the problem. If we can't decide what the problem is or the proper remedy, we reject the horse. Second, we bring in the prospective owner and describe soundness problems, proposed remedies, and any anticipated resale difficulties. Only after detailed discussion does the object of our collective speculation enter the barn.

Before us stands our prospective show hunter. He's attractive, willing, moves well, has eight good fences and an acceptable price tag. What little problems does he have? What is acceptable and what is not?

Let's begin with the feet. No horse goes far without them.

The most common cause for soundness rejection is navicular changes.

Realistically, there are very few active horses over five who don't have some arthritic changes of the navicular bone. I like to have comparative X rays. If the horse showed the same changes at four as he does now at eight, I'll take him. If current X rays show the changes are not remarkable, he's acceptable. I am leery, however, of gross changes, or of changes in a three-year-old.

Slight indications of founder do not alarm me, as long as there is no significant coffin-bone rotation. I do not reject a horse if my blacksmith decides that proper shoeing and good management can deal successfully with the problem.

Sidebones are iffy. I may reject the horse if they are quite large, or if the horse is young.

I will take a horse that has been heel-nerved, under two conditions: First, I must know why he was nerved. Runners are often "nicked" just to squeeze more races out of them. No problem. Some navicular changes are cause for a neurectomy. Each case must be judged individually. Second, the owner must find the situation acceptable. A heel-nerved horse is not a threat to himself or to his rider. He doesn't need sensibility in this area in order to remain a safe, reliable jumper. But I will never take a horse that has been nerved high. He has no feeling in his entire foot, and ultimately, since nerving inhibits circulation, the ligaments and tendons supporting the foot give way, leaving you with a cripple.

Coffin-bone chips at the front coronary band are often present in jumping horses simply because they've hit fences. I do not find this a significant problem. Bear in mind that a severe blow can cause further injury.

Now, what about the area from ankle to knee? If calcification results in greatly reduced ankle flexion, I might reject the horse. Bone chips, common in racetrack refugees, are not a particular cause for alarm unless they impinge on the joint.

Bows are acceptable as long as they are not unsightly. If my prospect is bowed, I prefer the bow to be low. A leg with a high bow is weaker than one with a low bow. I'll take the horse as long as the bow is old, set, and well healed. I don't like a bow behind. In a jumper, there is more strain on the hind legs and I want them to be as trouble-free as possible.

Full knee flexion is essential. Horses that cannot bend their knees may go through rather than over fences. Any chip or fragment that interferes with the free use of the knee is cause for rejection.

Now look at our prospect's hind legs.

I avoid horses with spavins. Once the spavin has calcified, it does not usually cause lameness, but horses that must jump for a living place heavy demands on the hock. A spavined hock is a weak hock.

Thoroughpins and curbs are acceptable if they are not recent. Rarely do they bother the horse.

I will take a horse that periodically catches his stifle (upward fixation of the patella), since the remedy is a simple surgical procedure.

Stringhalt is out of the question. While not a lameness, the upward jerking of the hind leg is ugly as well as incurable. A show hunter should cover the ground with long, reaching strides. A stringhalted horse has no future as a show hunter.

I don't take horses with nonspecific hind-end lameness or back problems. The longer you study such horses, the worse they look. If you cannot find the problem, how can you treat it?

Moving upward, how are our prospect's eyes, wind, and heart?

A horse with poor vision is an unreliable jumper. However, a spot on the eye does not necessarily disqualify him. Eye abnormalities require an examination by an equine ophthalmologist. I won't reject the horse if he has a history of injury or virus to account for the abnormality and if the ophthalmologist decides that his vision is not impaired.

I reject an obvious roarer. However, should the horse make a little noise when working, I have him scoped to determine the cause. A little flap or tear is not necessarily cause for rejection. The judicious use of glycerine and honey or Azium to combat laryngitis may be sufficient.

A horse with a heart murmur is not a suitable candidate. On the other hand, an irregular heartbeat is common in man and horse and is not automatic cause for rejection.

THE QUESTION OF
THOROUGHBRED UNSOUNDNESS

It seems that most of the Thoroughbred hunter prospects I find to buy are moving sound, but flunk their veterinary exams! All sorts of elusive bone chips, minor tendon inflammations, and calcium deposits turn up in just about any horse that has ever been in race training. Are there actually any "sound" Thoroughbreds around?

An answer from RODNEY JENKINS, one of the most successful riders of hunters and jumpers in show-ring history:

Since so many racetracks are racing all year round, it has become more difficult to find a hunter prospect from the track. The trainers have more places to race their horses, which means there is a better chance of making money with a "cheap" horse. But sound horses can be found. Indeed, it does take lots of looking. And then it is usually best to have it X-rayed. If you have a vet you know well, he should be able to explain any of the problems he might find, and how and whether you will be able to cope with them. If you intend to resell the horse after you train it for jumping, it's a good idea to explain this to the vet also. Reselling a horse with a "minor" problem might be difficult. It usually depends on the buyer and how educated he is on minor problems that you can live with. When a novice is buying a first horse, he usually shies away from such problems.

THE QUESTION OF WEIGHT-CARRYING ABILITY

What is the maximum weight a horse can safely carry?

An answer from DR. WILLIAM MOYER, of the University of Pennsylvania:

You can't point to a weight figure and say: "That's the limit." It depends on the individual horse. The size of the horse is not the most important criterion; his conformation and inherent strength have more to do with his weight-carrying ability. For example, an 18-hand, long-backed Thoroughbred can't carry as much weight as a smaller, shorter-coupled stablemate can. I've seen a 14.3-hand, 1,100-pound Quarter Horse carry 250 pounds efficiently through a hard day's work.

A horse intended to carry a great deal of weight should be short-coupled. His limbs should not be excessively long, nor should his joints be greatly angled. A pack donkey, for example, is a good weight carrier. He is quite small, but he has short pasterns, short legs, and a short back. He's capable of carrying a 500-pound elk for six or seven hours.

If a horse has any significant back or leg problem, extra weight will increase its susceptibility to damage. Any chronic problem—a bowed tendon, navicular disease, or a tendency to back-soreness, for example—may be aggravated. The horse with chronic ailments has trouble enough carrying his own weight, let alone anyone else's.

No one has scientifically determined the effect of the rider's ability on his mount's weight-carrying potential. I've always considered it important. A 95-pound bad rider probably creates more problems than a much heavier good rider on a well-built horse.

Chapter 2

OUTFITTING THE HORSE

WHAT YOUR HORSE NEEDS
AND HOW TO SELECT IT

BLANKETS

Lined. Standard cotton duck lined with wool. Variety of colors with contrasting binding, available with monogram. Washable, but stand up better to dry cleaning.

Weatherproof. Water-repellent canvas, wool-lined. Good for turn-out but not waterproof indefinitely in a heavy rain. Hose to clean. Dry cleaning destroys water-repellency.

Unlined. Sturdy, triple-woven synthetic blanket, durable and washable. Comes in characteristic plaid design.

Measure from center of chest to dock of tail, size corresponds to inches. Allow for two inches shrinkage. Should fit loosely across chest to prevent rubbed shoulders, and extend over top of tail.

STABLE SHEETS

Duck sheet. Lightweight indoor night and vanning sheet. Keeps coat clean for showing; keeps stable drafts off horse when woolen blanket is too warm. Assorted colors and bindings. May be monogrammed and stable colors specially ordered.

Measure as for blankets.

Fly sheet. Large square net for keeping flies off stabled horse during summer.

One size fits all.

Sweat sheet. Synthetic net sheet in square or contour shape used to absorb sweat and cool horse out quickly.

One size fits all.

Wool cooler. Plaid or solid-color rectangular wool cover. Absorbs sweat and keeps horse from chilling after exercise or bathing.

Two sizes, for medium and large horses.

HALTERS

Leather. Favored for looks and safety. Will break in an emergency. At the top of the line: English triple-stitched with brass nameplate. Domestic and other imports not as attractive or durable, but serviceable. One with adjustable noseband handy for growing horse.

Noseband should rest about 1½" below cheekbone, tightly enough to keep front feet out. Available in pony, average, and overlarge sizes.

Rope or nylon. Inexpensive, useful halter for leading and tying. Virtually unbreakable. Not safe for turn-out.

REINS

Round and half-round. Used with round and half-round bridles, although flat reins may be used with these bridles as well. Available in laced, plaited, and plain styles, with or without fancy stitching.

Prefer wrinkle-free, smooth-edged leather; small, close stitches; solid brass or stainless-steel hardware.

Plaited reins. Afford good grip for hunting and showing for all types of bridles.

Rubber-covered. For extra grip in wet weather.

Flat reins. Used on all types of bridles. May be either utility quality or dress stitched.

SADDLES

Forward seat. Standard saddle for hunting, with prominent knee rolls, forward flaps, and deep seat. Rider security sacrifices contact with horse.

Sized in inches from stud of pommel to center of cantle. Correct size varies with style. Rider's knee should meet but not overlap the knee roll while sitting in the deepest part of the seat.

Show jumping saddle. Lightweight with little or no knee roll, flat seat, forward flaps. For maximum contact with horse.

Dressage. Deep seat, places rider to rear; vertical flaps; and thick padding around leg.

Balanced seat. Combination jumping/ dressage saddle with moderately deep seat. Some with long billets and short girth, eliminating interference of buckles with leg contact.

GIRTHS

Leather. Sturdy girth with good appearance for hunt and show. Available in straight, folded, or shaped style (which contours around horse's front legs). Requires care to keep flexible or may chafe horse.

String. Inexpensive, non-chafe girth. Suitable for informal riding.

42–52″, measured from center of billets. Stretch with use.

SADDLE PADS

Felt. Inexpensive, school-quality pad for informal riding. Non-washable.

Quilted. Washable light cotton pad for informal riding. Serves more to keep saddle clean than protect horse's back.

Synthetic fleece. Popular replacement for traditional sheepskin. Fully washable and good appearance for showing.

Most pads available in forward-seat, dressage, and western versions.

LEAD STRAPS

Leather. For dress and usually with chain end, which aids control.

Rope. Good for stable use. Cotton-rope variety easy on hands, ties more easily than leather, but stock snaps are lightweight, break easily, and are not suitable for teaching horse to tie.

BANDAGES

Three-yard knit leg wraps for medicating and protection while shipping.

GROOMING TOOLS

Currycomb. Metal or hard rubber tool for loosening dirt and mud.

Dandy brush. Stiff bristles for removing bulk of dirt.

Body brush. Soft bristles for remaining dust.

Rub rag. Linen or terry cloth for final polish.

Sponge.
Mane comb.
Sweat scraper.

BRIDLES

Round. Popular show bridle of rolled, stitched leather. Flatters good head.

Half-round. Rounded straps with flat side toward horse. Crownpieces and browbands may be either plain or fancy-stitched.

Flat. Traditional English style, all-purpose. Available in top-of-the-line and schooling qualities. All bridles available in snaffle, Pelham, and double bridle varieties.

WHAT THE WELL-DRESSED HORSE SHOULD WEAR . . . AND WHY

The horse's clothing, as opposed to tack, consists mostly of blankets and sheets. They come in all sizes, most colors, various weights, and even a couple of shapes. They have a variety of uses, from keeping a horse warm to cooling him out, from fly protection to rain protection to just plain good looks.

You don't have to spend hundreds of dollars on blankets for every imaginable use. If your horse is clipped in the winter, he will certainly need some kind of protection from the cold. A horse in hard work will need a cooler of some sort so that he doesn't catch cold while drying out. Whether he needs additional blankets and sheets beyond these essentials depends on where you take your horse, the draftiness of your stable, the type of fly control you furnish, and when and where you turn him out.

Winter Blankets

If your horse is clipped or if you want to keep his coat down, there is a variety of winter blankets to consider. You should bear two things in mind: First, the biggest problem when you blanket a horse throughout the winter is keeping the blanket clean. Second, "heavier" does not necessarily mean "warmer." Just as with human clothing, the more layers you wear, the more body heat is retained. For winter stable use, you will probably do better with a lightweight blanket or blanket liner under a duck sheet than with a heavy wool blanket. This two-layer method involves less expense and easier cleaning, since the top sheet can be removed and cleaned faster than can a heavy wool blanket.

There are two general types of winter blankets: those claimed to be water-repellent, which can be worn outdoors; and those meant to be worn principally indoors.

There is a common misconception that water-repellent means waterproof. The only completely waterproof material is rubber. But if you put a rubber sheet on a horse, he would soon sweat off the weight you have been trying to put on him. Water-repellent fabrics are cotton or duck that have been treated in the same way as army tents. They lose their waterproofing if medication is spilled on them or if they are dry-cleaned. As with raincoats, they protect a horse for a limited time, but if worn all day long in a downpour, they will become soggy and eventually start to seep at the seams, through the stitching holes. No manufacturer has yet devised a way to prevent this.

If your horse is clipped and you turn him out during the day, he should wear a water-repellent blanket, especially if he is unsupervised. A clipped horse can be brought in during the day when the weather turns bad, but if you are often absent and there is nobody else to look after your horse, some kind of water-repellent covering is a must. Leg straps are also advisable if you plan to leave him blanketed in the field alone. The straps keep the blanket from twisting, a potentially dangerous situation if the blanket turns to such a point that his legs get caught in it.

A fully wool-lined blanket should not rub the hairs off your horse unless it becomes stiff with soil or mud. An inner hem of coarse outer material can cause rubbing, but you can prevent damage to the hair by sewing patches of sheepskin or soft flannel at the trouble spots. A horse that wears a blanket in the stable still needs daily grooming. Taking the blanket off once a day and properly grooming the coat underneath will do a lot to prevent the blanket from rubbing.

The best-known water-repellent variety is probably the *New Zealand rug*. Originally an English import, it is now made by American manufacturers as well. Consisting of a water-repellent duck outer covering, lined halfway down with 16-ounce wool, with leg straps to keep it in place, the rug comes

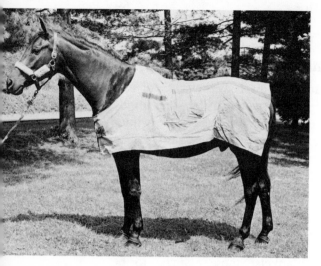

New Zealand rug.

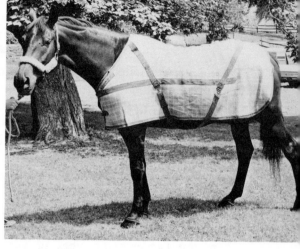

Baker blanket.

in all sizes. The only problem is cleaning, since dry cleaning will affect the water repellency and it is too bulky to be placed in a washer. It must be hung over two clotheslines, scrubbed by hand with a stiff brush and a detergent solution, and air dried.

A lighter version is the *Lavenham rug,* of Irish origin. It consists of a nylon quilted exterior and a brushed tricot lining (the material used for ladies' nightwear). Lightweight and washable, it is, however, criticized by users who say that the lining picks up stall bedding more readily than the New Zealand rug. It is also reported to be less durable, the nylon splitting after several washings.

A newer blanket which is gaining popularity in the East is the *Congress blanket.* Originally developed for use at the Quarter Horse Congress a few years ago, it consists of a nylon exterior with a fiber-fill interlining and a synthetic fleece lining, similar to the pile lining used in rainwear and winter coats. It is extremely warm and is popular among Quarter Horse trainers who wish to maintain a show coat all year round. Washable and tough, some varieties are water-repellent as well. Others are primarily intended for use as stable blankets. They are sold under a variety of trade names.

The *Baker blanket,* which comes in both blanket and sheet weights, is probably the best known winter blanket of all, due to its familiar black-and-tan plaid patterns and its proven durability. The plaid fabric is triple-woven, the three layers accounting for its ability to retain heat. Another characteristic is its crossed surcingles, which give the blanket a close fit and keep it in place.

Improvements have recently been made in the Baker blanket, which was first designed in 1885. It is now washable and unshrinkable; an acrylic plaid material replaces the cotton fabric; leather chest straps have been replaced by washable, nylon ones; and the former cotton surcingles are also now of nylon. But beware: There are authentic Baker blankets bearing the trademark of Ayres-Philadelphia, and there are imitations, generally of inferior quality.

Duck blankets, lined with wool or a mixture of wool and nylon, are a common type of winter horse covering. Some are water-repellent, and most of the nylon mixtures are said to be washable. This blanket serves the same purpose as a duck sheet over a woolen liner, but it is harder to wash, since the duck cannot be removed for cleaning. Many horse owners consider them "one-season" blankets, because the inferior grades can end up torn or worn out after a winter's hard use.

Summer Blankets

Summer clothing for a horse consists mainly of fly sheets, duck sheets, and rain covers.

Fly sheets, made of a cotton or nylon mesh, are becoming obsolete for home stable use. They shift and rip easily and are generally not as effective as other forms of insect control. But a fly sheet is still handy during horse shows for protecting a horse while he is standing around between classes.

A lightweight *duck sheet* is another useful item in the show horse's summer wardrobe. If you turn him out during the day, the sheet will protect his coat from sun bleaching and will keep it clean. On the show grounds, if you toss a clean sheet over your horse once he's had his final polish and is waiting to go into the ring, you'll keep the dust off his coat and prevent it from bristling under the effect of the hot sun.

Rain sheets are a show item seldom seen in the home stable. They are made of a very thin nylon material, covered with urethane, and are meant to protect your tack as well as your horse. Many horsemen find it convenient to tuck one into the tack trunk when they take off for a show. But they are unsuitable for home use, as they are loose-fitting, like a cooler, and they offer no warmth.

Cooling out. The traditional *cooler* is a loosely woven lightweight wool rectangle that is draped over the horse from ears to tail. At a horse show, it

Fly sheet.

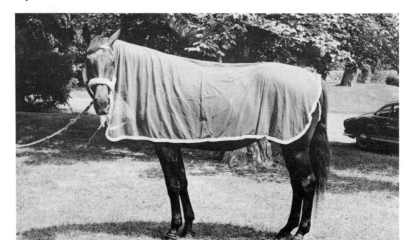

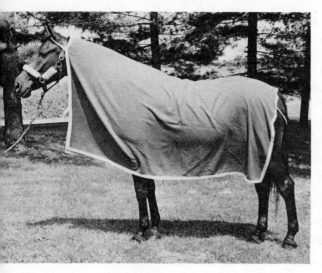

Wool cooler.

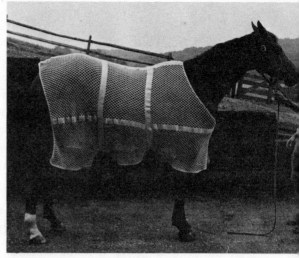

Anti-sweat sheet.

serves many of the same purposes as a light sheet, by keeping off the dust and holding the coat down, in addition to protecting the neck and supplying a little extra warmth. But its primary purpose is to prevent the horse from catching a chill while cooling out after exercise.

The loose-fitting cooler traps body heat while permitting air to circulate and dry the coat. A blanket would absorb the horse's sweat but would also cling damply and increase rather than decrease the risk of a chill. The cooler, on the other hand, stays dry. Wool coolers come in a variety of solid and plaid colors, either bound all around or unbound.

A relatively recent development with a similar function is the *anti-sweat sheet,* a washable synthetic garment of a special mesh weave like that used in thermal underwear. The ingenious weave traps body heat while permitting sweat to evaporate. Anti-sweat-sheet users claim that a horse could even go straight to his stall after exercise, without any walking. (But remember that a period of walking, aside from its effect on body temperature and evaporation of sweat, provides a valuable "unwinding" after strenuous exercise.) In winter, the anti-sweat sheet should be supplemented by a light sheet or wool cooler. Thermal underwear was not designed as outer wear. The anti-sweat sheet is available in a loose, "cooler" style, and also fitted like a standard stable sheet.

Cleaning your blankets. Consider washability when weighing blanket economics and convenience. That pale wool plaid cooler may be beautiful, but it will require careful home care or professional dry cleaning to maintain its good looks. You might want to choose instead one of the new washable anti-sweat sheets. New Zealand rugs, although initially rather expensive, are popular winter protection for a horse. But they must be cleaned by hand and require lots of scrubbing. A fleece-lined nylon blanket of the Lavenham type is just as warm, completely washable, but not as durable.

Most horse owners have their wool blankets dry-cleaned. If you intend to wash your sheets and blankets yourself, bear in mind that unless you own a heavy-duty washer, you will put great strain on your automatic washing machine. Wool blankets can be washed by hand or machine, but both ways are hard work. Blankets are very heavy when wet, and you must brush off the hairs by hand, since they are seldom removed during the washing cycle. You can wash three cotton duck sheets or two lightweight wool blankets in a heavy-duty washer at one time. If the blankets are badly stained, put them through a rinse cycle with slightly warm water and a weak solution of ammonia. Then wash them in tepid water and detergent and rinse in cold water to keep the colors from fading. The ammonia will also help preserve the color. Never place a blanket or sheet in an electric clothes dryer, since the heat will shrink them for sure. Air-dry them, by hanging them over two clotheslines so that the air circulates between the thicknesses and hastens drying. When they are dry, brush off any remaining hairs with a stiff brush before removing them from the line. Since coolers are made of a looser weave of wool than blankets, if you hang them on a line to dry they will stretch out of shape. Treat them just like your fine wool sweaters. Wash with cool water, then block them on a flat surface to their original dimensions.

Options. Like cars, horse blankets are sold with a variety of options . . . which bear a variety of price tags. For example, for horses whose manes are braided for hunting or showing, there is a blanket with a *cut-back* V shape at the withers, which will not disturb the braids. Depending on the tack shop, this "extra feature" will add from 5 percent to 15 percent to the price of the blanket. *Tail pieces,* flaps that come down over the tail in back, are good protection in drafty vans and are used mostly by the Quarter Horse set, whose vans are frequently made with open slats. The disadvantage of tail pieces is that they soil easily, and if they are not perfectly fitted, the blanket will pull and tear when the horse lifts his tail. The tail can also be damaged if the blanket binds the horse. *Leg straps,* which keep the blanket from turning, are another frequent option, especially useful with active, young horses. A *closed front* is popular. It makes the blanket a little warmer and helps prevent it from shifting. But it is more difficult to put on, especially since some horses dislike having a blanket pulled over the head.

The right size. Most people buy blankets that are too short, to start with. When the blanket is washed and has shrunk 1 percent or 2 percent, they end up with a really badly fitting garment. You should determine the size of your blanket in view of its utilization. A blanket or cooler to be worn between classes at a horse show should be two sizes larger than your horse, in order to fit comfortably over the saddle. A blanket for use around the stable should be one size too large, to allow for shrinkage and to increase its adaptability to other horses. A blanket with flaps overlapping a couple of inches or more in front will fit more horses than one with flaps that barely meet.

When measuring your horse for a blanket, run a tape measure from the center of his chest along his side, back to the farthest point of his rump. Some blankets come in size gradations of two inches, some three. Whatever your horse's measurement, get one size larger.

Surcingles on blankets should be adjusted just tightly enough to keep the blanket from shifting. The front surcingle should be comfortably snug, and the back surcingle loose enough to slip the palm of your hand underneath it. If it is too tight, a horse that bloats in its stall overnight may react to the rear surcingle as to a bucking strap. Leg straps should be loose enough to allow the horse freedom of movement, but not so loose that a horse getting up can put a foot through it or catch his stifle. Rubbing can be prevented by looping one through the other. Make sure that the spring on the clip is on the inside, so that it cannot catch on anything.

The latest development in blankets is *"contour cut."* Form-fitting sheets and blankets offer better fit than non-form-fitting and are adaptable to a wider range of horses. Cut in four or more pieces, they overlap generously in front, with another overlap and snap under the tail. A contour-cut blanket seventy-two inches long can be adjusted to fit horses from sixty-eight inches to seventy-six inches.

Repairs. Where you buy your blanket makes a difference when it needs to be repaired. A tack shop with its own repair service is a lifesaver if your horse turns up one morning with a broken buckle or a dangling surcingle. If you purchase from a mail-order catalogue, don't forget to add the shipping charges. These may outweigh a higher price at your local tack shop, especially if you have to send the blanket back for repairs.

HOW TO PUT ON YOUR HORSE'S BLANKET

Stand at your horse's left shoulder and toss the blanket over his back so that it lands forward of its final resting place. If the blanket is heavy or your horse is spooky, fold it in half before you toss it. It will be easier to manage and the surcingles won't flap as much.

Slip your left hand under the front edge of the blanket and smooth the mane flat.

Close the front fastening. If the closing is a buckle-type on a leather strap, use the next-to-last hole. Should the leather break at the buckle hole, you'll still have one hole left on the stub of the strap. If there are two fastenings, leave the bottom one undone, so that the blanket won't pull tight and rub the hair on your horse's shoulder.

Unfold the blanket and pull it back gently so that it rests loosely and comfortably across the front of the chest. As you do this, you'll smooth the hair. Never pull a blanket forward, or you'll end up with a rough, dull coat.

THE ART OF BLANKETING

or How the Experts Keep Their Horses' Coats
at Their Best Throughout the Winter

SANDY VAUGHAN, who trains Quarter Horses for Jon Riker's Westenhook Farm, in Southbury, Connecticut, in eastern as well as western styles, has developed a blanketing program particularly adapted to the Quarter Horse breed.

Halter horses must be slick the year round. We blanket and hood the horses from the middle of September to April. The rest of the time, they wear sheets. In addition, our barn is heated to about 50 degrees, and we use stall lights to lengthen the daylight hours, beginning in August. The idea is to convince the horses that it's summer all year round, so they don't grow winter coats.

I've tried all kinds of blankets and settled on the heavyweight quilted type that slips over the horse's head, and contours to his body. These blankets have foam insulation, which makes them extremely warm. The outer covering, of heavy woven nylon, is resistant to rips and tears. They're available with either fleece or flannel linings. Both of them keep a nice polish on the horses' coats. We remove the blankets when we turn the horses out. The best blanket in the world will rub shoulders and hips if the horse runs around in it.

I've tried the Baker blanket, the New Zealand rug, and the lightweight quilted type. They're all warm, but they slip. Contoured blankets stay put. And if you order the optional leg straps, even the most accomplished escape artist can't slither out.

To keep the neck sleek, we use a silk-lined hood, with no seams that might rub. The hood is attached by three connectors to the blanket and a strap around the jowl. It cannot slide around. Nevertheless, you must take it off every day or so or the horse will start to lose his mane.

I don't bother with undersheets or oversheets. One blanket is warm enough. And it's washable, although it takes a big machine.

1. With the blanket adjusted properly in front, it should cover the top of your horse's tail.
2. This blanket is too short. It should reach the spot indicated by the handler.
3. This sheet is too long.

The surcingles must be adjusted tightly enough that your horse can't put a foot through one when he's lying down, but not so tightly that they make him uncomfortable. This is about right for the front surcingle, leaving just enough room for a hand's breadth. The rear surcingle should be looser, leaving room for another hand's breadth. Diagonal surcingles that cross in the middle can both be adjusted to the snugness of the front surcingles.

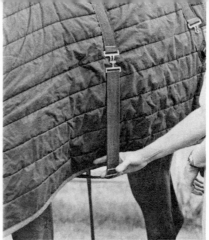

If your blanket has a single, wide surcingle, like this one, adjust it so that you can just fit a hand's breadth into both sides.

A tail cord helps hold a blanket in place on a young horse. It belongs here, below the prominence of the hindquarter, not up under the tail.

Once the horse is accustomed to the feel of the blanket, leg straps are a surer method of holding it in place; they are necessary if the blanket is to be worn outdoors. This shows the proper adjustment of the leg straps: not so tight as to restrict movement or to rub the hair, but not loose enough to snare a foot. Make sure the snaps face inward, so they don't catch on a stall screen or the handle of a water bucket.

Some horses manage to shift any blanket, no matter how it is equipped. The answer is a separate body roller, adjusted snugly just behind the withers. Place a folded towel underneath to protect the withers.

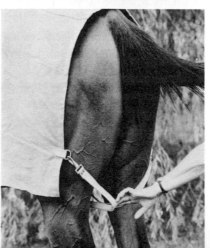

BONNIE BYRNES, who trains gaited and fine harness horses for Mrs. Donald Ferguson's Royal Scot Stables, in Richmond, Illinois, is careful to maintain the coats of the numerous World Champion show horses in the stable in top form. This is how she does it:

We have tough winters in Illinois. We blanket the show horses early, starting in October, to prevent hair growth, and keep them blanketed until May. If they're going to work much during the winter, we often clip them. For turn-out, we use the indoor ring and remove the blankets.

I like to put one sheet under the blanket and another on top. A closely clipped horse needs these layers for warmth. The undersheet keeps a soft material next to the horse's skin and protects the hair from rubbing. The top sheet keeps the blanket clean. Instead of dry-cleaning the blanket, I just wash the sheet.

Often, I'm short of sheets, and then I use just the oversheet to protect the blanket. I've had very little trouble with horses rubbing spots bare. If I notice one developing on a shoulder or hip, I rub baby oil on it to eliminate friction. If the horse is showing, I line the chafed areas with cotton. You have to keep a sharp eye out for the first signs of rubbing. Once a spot is established, it's usually there until the horse sheds out.

For convenience, I like lightweight nylon quilted blankets. They're warm and washable, but I have trouble keeping them on the horses, and the nylon rips. So I've resorted to the Baker blanket, although it requires dry cleaning. The cross straps hold it in place. It's warm, durable, and easy on the horse's coat. The part that is blanketed is always smoother and shinier than the rest.

RAY DUNPHY, manager of Mrs. Miles Valentine's stable, in Unionville, Pennsylvania, handles its numerous hunters, broodmares, young racing stock, and pensioners with painstaking care and respect for tradition acquired during a lifelong career with horses.

We clip our Thoroughbred hunters three times during the hunting season. We keep sheets under the blankets, because I think the softer material keeps their coats nicer. If the weather is very cold, I might add a top sheet, too.

When the horses are in their stalls, they wear Baker blankets. Fleece-lined blankets are fine if you bed on straw, but on shavings or sawdust the bedding clings to the inside of the blanket and you have a dirty horse. The Baker's cut-back neck accommodates high withers and doesn't rub the mane. It doesn't shrink, it doesn't show dirt as badly as some other blankets, and it's quite durable.

When we turn the horses out, we take off the Baker and replace it with a New Zealand rug. The New Zealand, with its heavy canvas, keeps the horses warm and dry in the field.

Both styles shift around a little. The only solution is careful supervision. I keep the straps pretty snug and check the blankets each time I pass by the stalls. For a horse that rolls a lot in his stall, I anchor the blanket with a surcingle, putting a pommel pad underneath to protect the withers.

The only real problem is rubbing. Thoroughbreds tend to have thin skin and, if I'm not careful, I end up with bare patches at the shoulders. This usually happens when the blanket doesn't fit correctly. As soon as I see signs of roughened hair, I switch blankets until I find the proper size.

We wash the sheets and dry-clean the Bakers. New Zealands are a little more work. They're too big to put in a washing machine, and if you dry-clean them they lose their water-repellency. So we spread them on the pavement and sweep them inside and out with a stiff broom. Then we hose the mud off the outside and hang them over a fence to dry.

LEG BANDAGES

by DONNA SMITH

The Exercise Bandage

Purpose. To support the leg during exercise.

Use. When riding or longeing a horse with strained or weak tendons or ligaments; or a horse just returning to work after a layoff due to a tendon injury. Care must be taken not to use this type of bandage for more than four or five consecutive days, as the horse's tendons may become dependent on them.

Equipment. A track bandage, known as a stockinette or knit wrap; or a four-inch Ace elastic bandage. The Ace bandage has more stretch and gives greater support than the track bandage. When using a new Ace bandage for the first time, wash it, and while it is still damp, secure the ends so that it remains stretched not quite to its maximum overnight. This will help prepare the bandage. Caution should still be used when applying a new Ace because of its extreme elasticity. You also need a single layer of sheet cotton cut to exact size.

Procedure. Apply a single, smooth-fitting layer of cotton just wide enough to expose one half inch above and below the finished wrap. After cutting the cotton to size, stitch around the edges with white coat or mane thread in order to reinforce and preserve its shape for longer use.

With the cotton in place, begin the wrap by applying the edge of the bandage at the center face of the cannon just below the knee, with the rolled remainder of the bandage facing outward, toward your hand.

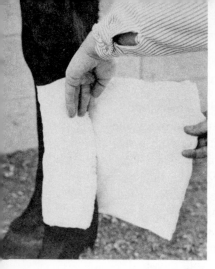

Draw the wrap toward the outside of the leg, to the rear around the tendon, inside forward, and again around the face of the cannon bone. Hold the roll of wrap close to the leg as you go, to produce an even pressure all around the leg.

For a great deal of support, make each succeeding turn very close to the first when descending the leg. At no time should angles be very great, and each turn across the face of the cannon should be as horizontal as possible. It is very important to maintain equal pressure all around the leg throughout the entire wrap. Wrap down the leg in this manner to just above the fetlock joint, then reverse and wrap up the leg, ending the wrap just below the knee. On the way back up the leg, the turns may be spaced a little farther apart.

When bandaging to support a check ligament, keep the bandage as high behind the knee as possible.

After wrapping up the leg to just below the knee, end the wrap on the outside of the leg. If the end of the wrap should coincide with the face of the cannon or on the tendon (and if the wrap is an Ace), just fold it back under itself to shorten it, and pin it in place. When pins are used to secure a wrap, always use two, with one pinned through the other to form an X, and cover the pins with masking tape. The tape should completely encircle the leg and overlap a couple of inches. For competition or cross-country, the end of the bandage should be sewn down, rather than pinned or taped, for greater safety.

When the bandage is finished, check for equal distribution of pressure. Insert one finger between the bandage and the leg in the depression between the cannon bone and the superficial flexor tendon at both top and bottom of the bandage. The pressure should feel equal, not tight around the top and loose around the bottom or the reverse. It should not be necessary to strain and pull at the bandage in order to insert a finger, and the bandage should not pinch the inserted finger. Pressure should increase slightly when the finger is moved toward the rear of the leg and over the tendon.

If the pressure is uneven or too great, the bandage must be removed immediately and reapplied from scratch. It should be removed at once after work, even when return to the stable is delayed.

If you are inexperienced with this type of bandage, either have someone observe your first few efforts, or apply this bandage to your own leg and wear it around for a while. You will soon appreciate its restricting capacity, especially if applied too tightly.

So remember:

—Never draw any part of the bandage tighter than any other part.

—Never draw tape or strings tighter than the rest of the bandage.

—Never bandage so tightly that circulation is restricted.

—When applying an Ace bandage, always roll it on.

A special application: supporting the fetlock. When applying an exercise bandage to a leg that has an injury to the lower tendon area (such as a low bow), suspensory ligament, fetlock joint, or bursal sack, begin the wrap just outside the fetlock joint. Starting with the edge of the wrap on the outside of the leg just above the fetlock, come forward around the cannon to the inside and rear around the tendon (this first turn is made without the wrap being snug). In coming to the cannon again, catch the overlapping edge of the first turn and angle down and across the face of the fetlock joint, around underneath the fetlock in the rear, and up and around the top of the fetlock joint a second time. Moving up just slightly, repeat the crisscross wrap and then continue to wrap up the leg to below the knee in normal fashion. When you reach the knee, simply wrap down again until the remainder of the wrap is used. This will usually be about halfway down the leg. A wrap applied in this manner has a sort of lifting support, but care must be taken that extreme angles are not used to increase the lift. Each successive turn across the cannon should remain as horizontal as possible, with the exception, of course, of the crisscross turns over and around the fetlock joint, which form an inverted V at the front of the leg. Only elastic wrap should be applied in this fashion. Wool or flannel wraps must always start just below the knee, because they are not elastic enough to conform to the contours of the joint.

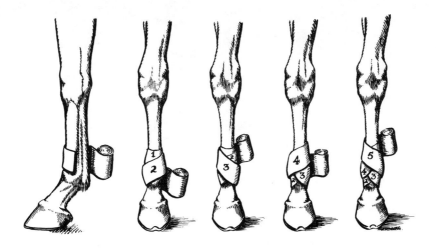

The Support Bandage

Purpose. To rest and give light support to tendons and legs after hard work; to prevent legs from filling.

Use. In the stable.

Equipment. Track wrap seven to eight feet in length. Track wraps have limited elasticity and are approximately four inches wide. When using a track wrap, it should be rolled in such a way that the tie strings sewn at one end will be on the outside of the leg when the wrap is finished. To do this, unroll the wrap and, gathering the strings in a small roll or figure of eight, lay them on the triangular end of the wrap, which has a sewn edge showing; then roll the point of the wrap forward over the strings toward the remaining wrap until it is completely rolled.

A double thickness of cotton or quilted pads.

Procedure. The stable bandage is applied in the same way as the exercise bandage which covers the fetlock joint. The only difference is the addition of more cotton (double sheets) or specially quilted leg pads. Keep each turn very smooth as you wrap, and keep the turns close together, using only very slight angles to descend and ascend the leg. When the wrapping is completed, divide the strings, run them once around the leg in opposite directions, and tie them on the outside of the leg. Fold the top edge of the last turn of the wrap down over them. This will prevent them from being loosened by rubbing or banging.

To test the bandage, insert two fingers at top and bottom. Pressure should be equal. As you run your fingers around the leg, you should feel an even pressure with no pinching anywhere.

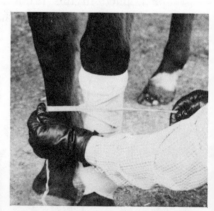
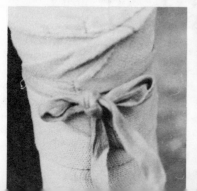
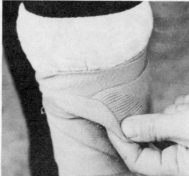
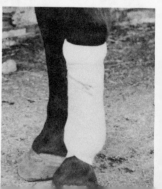

The Warmth Bandage

Purpose. To provide warmth for the leg; for a sick horse.

Use. In the stable.

Equipment. Wool or flannel wrap. Wool and flannel bandages are six inches wide and have no elasticity. A wool or flannel wrap is used when warmth is the only requirement. They are relatively safe for a novice to apply, as it is difficult to wind them tightly enough to harm the leg.

A double thickness of cotton or quilted pads.

Two safety pins.

Tape.

Procedure. The procedure is the same as for the exercise bandage. Wool or flannel wraps must always start just below the knee, because they lack the elasticity to conform to the joint. When applying wool or flannel wraps, use lots of cotton underneath. Keep each turn smooth as you wrap, and keep the turns close together, using slight angles. Since flannel has no stretch, this procedure will give a well-fitting wrap that will stay in place. Flannel and wool bandages must be secured with pins and tape. Use two pins, with one pinned through the other to form an X, and place masking tape over them, completely encircling the leg and overlapping a couple of inches. Test the bandage with your fingers in the same manner as with the support bandage.

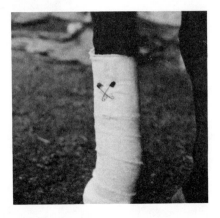

The Shipping Bandage

Purpose. To provide protection to knees, legs, coronet band, and heels.

Use. During transportation.

Equipment. Four double-length track wraps; four layers of sheet cotton.

Procedure. Place the cotton to cover the leg from the lower half of the knee to below the coronet and heels. Using the double-length track wrap for each leg, start at the lower quarter of the knee and wrap down the leg in the same manner as for the stable bandage. When wrapping the fetlock joint, use crisscross turns to allow the joint freedom of movement and comfort. Continue down the pastern and over the coronet and heels. At this point, it is easiest to pick up the leg and, supporting it on your knee, make the turns that cover and secure the upper hoof area. They must be snug or the wrap will work up, exposing these vulnerable areas during transit. When the coronet and heels have been covered, wrap back up the leg and secure the bandage by the same method described for stable and exercise bandages. You can make a double-length wrap by sewing two regular track wraps together at the straight edge and eliminating the tie strings from one end. Or just tie the strings of two regular wraps. This method is not advisable, however, for other than emergency use, as it causes the tie strings to be situated in the first layer of wrap, closest to the leg, and if great care is not taken, pressure in this area will be uneven.

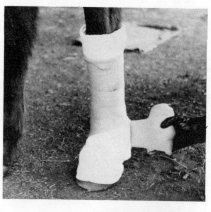

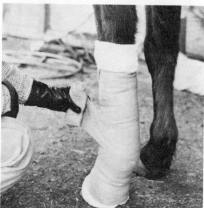
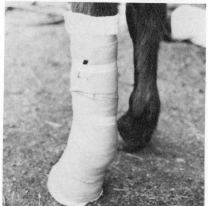

The Tail Wrap

Purpose. To protect the tail during shipping; to prevent braiding from being rubbed out overnight or during transportation; to make the upper tail hairs lie smooth in order to give a neat appearance in halter showing and the illusion of broader hindquarters.

Use. During transportation and in the stable.

Equipment. Track wrap, sponge, water.

Procedure. Stand at the horse's rear and, with a damp sponge, wet the hair of the tail (unless the tail is braided). Place the tail over your shoulder (facing the horse) so that the end of the tail bone rests on your shoulder. You will now have both hands free to apply the wrap. Most horses will permit the tail to be handled this way when they know no harm will come of it and if the procedure is done slowly and gently.

Begin the wrap at the top of the tail as close to the body as possible. Hold the starting edge of the wrap on the hair side (the underside of the tail is hairless and can be damaged very easily). Wrap around the tail. Returning over the starting edge, fold down a corner of the starting edge over the top of the second turn. Wrap one more turn, staying in the same place to catch and secure the folded edge. Then proceed to wrap down the tail to the end of the bone and upward again, securing the wrap at the top of the tail with the strings. Turns should be kept close together while wrapping, and care must be taken to maintain an even pressure. Under no circumstances should the wrap be pulled snug as it passes under the tail. The tension should come as it is passed over the top (hair side) of the tail, and the wrap should be merely "rolled" as it crosses the tender underskin of the tail. The wrap is applied in this manner because the hair acts as a sort of cushion on the top

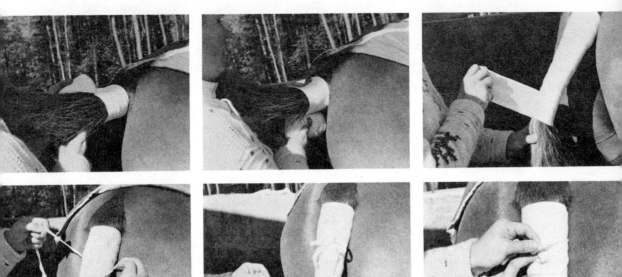

side, whereas a wrap wound too tightly on the hairless underside can cut off the blood circulation and even cause the hair of the tail to fall out. When securing the strings after the wrap has been completed, care must be taken not to pull them any tighter than the wrap itself.

A QUESTION ABOUT TAIL WRAPS

The Question: How do you keep a tail wrap from sliding off a shiny, clean, unbraided tail?

An answer from JOE FERGUSON, well-known hunter/jumper trainer and conditioner, of Norristown, Pennsylvania:

Using either a string bandage or elastic bandage (which requires great care to avoid cutting off the circulation in the tail), I would start wrapping the tail from the top. On about the third wrap, I would take a good-sized clump of hair from the center of the tail at the bottom edge of the bandage, turn it up so that it lies against the part of the tail already wrapped, and continue wrapping down from there. This may be done once or twice, depending on how secure you want the bandage to be.

LEG BANDAGES: A QUESTION, AN ANSWER, AND AN IDEA

The Question: Concerned about leg protection for my horse during the cross-country phase of Three-Day Events, I wonder if wrapping the front legs in a sheet of cotton and Vetrap from just below the knee to over the fetlock and then putting on bell boots would offer protection as well as support. How would this combination compare to galloping boots and bell boots, and how should the hind legs be protected, if at all?

The Answer from DR. MATTHEW MACKAY-SMITH, an active Endurance rider and eminent equine veterinary surgeon: There is no way currently available to wrap a leg so that you increase any supportive functions of bones, tendons, or ligaments. The mechanical basis of that statement would take too long to go into, but just accept it as a fact that you cannot support a leg by wrapping it. You can prevent swelling, protect wounds, keep a horse from injuring himself, but mechanically it is impossible to increase the lifting force of the leg in any way by wrapping it.

I prefer boots to bandages in every instance, because the danger of putting them on too tight is less, the danger of their becoming disarrayed by some accident on the course and thereby strangulating the leg is less, and they afford much more protection from the edge of the horse's hoof, which is what is really likely to damage him. I wouldn't bother to protect the hind legs except on a horse that interferes, in which case I would use ankle boots.

The Idea: For bandaging your horse, you don't have to buy expensive knit track bandages, and you don't have to throw away piles of cottons every time they become soiled. You can make inexpensive, washable bandages for shipping and standing by doing as Julie Steele, of Norwalk, Connecticut, does, and buy a yard and a half of gray or white flannel, a package of shipping cotton (from any tack shop), a package of fine-mesh cheesecloth, and a spool of masking tape. Take the cotton, which usually comes in packages of twelve sheets, unfold it, and divide it into four piles of three sheets each. For the front legs, fold the cotton once lengthwise; for the hind legs, fold it in half the other way. Cover the cottons, front and back, with the cheesecloth. Either by hand or machine, stitch all around the edges and then diagonally through the center. Now you have bandaging cottons that can be washed and reused. Cut the flannel into strips a yard and a half long by six inches wide, or slightly smaller for ponies. Any extra can be used for tail wraps or spares. Secure the bandages with masking tape.

WHEN, HOW, AND WHY SHOULD A HORSE WEAR LEG BANDAGES?

There is a wide difference of opinion among horsemen, as you can see from the answers to this question by outstanding experts in various equestrian fields.

> FRANK WRIGHT, a successful racehorse trainer based at the New York tracks, and an award-winning CBS and WOR television racing analyst and commentator:

I'm a great believer in preventive bandaging. The minor stall or training injury that knocks a carefully prepared horse out of a race is one of the big headaches of this business. I keep my charges well wrapped. I work them in bandages, ship them in bandages, run some in bandages, and they all wear bandages in their stalls.

When a horse comes in from racing or work, if he's hot, I do him up in cold-water bandages first, to take the heat out of his legs. I soak cotton quilts in a solution of cold water and Epsom salts and wrap them around every one of his legs from just below the knees and hocks down to cover the ankles. I wind flannel bandages over the quilts to keep them in place and secure the flannels with pins. Every five or ten minutes, while the horse is cooling out, I pour more ice into the quilts. They take heat out of the legs fast, they soothe stinging shins, and they reduce the swelling in minor sprains. Before I put my horses away, I always do up all four legs in standing bandages. I rub the leg with liniment, wrap it in three to five sheets of cotton, and secure the cotton with a flannel bandage. For standing, I cover the horse's leg from just below the knee or hock to below the ankle. For shipping, I wrap all the way down over the coronet band.

The standing bandages over liniment promote circulation and reduce filling. They protect the horses against not only stall injuries, but flies in summer and cold in winter.

In theory at least, a racehorse might spend twenty-four hours of his day in bandages of one kind or another. These horses are fit and on the muscle. I have to protect them from themselves as well as from the normal strain of racing.

MELANIE SMITH, Horsewoman of the Year in 1978, member of the U.S.E.T., star of the Grand Prix circuit, and World Cup Champion in 1982 with Calypso:

My horses do not live in bandages. I don't want them to become dependent on them. I wrap only when the activity demands it: when a horse has worked hard, when he's traveling, or when he's at a show.

The bandages I use are simple and inexpensive. I sew six or seven sheets of cotton into a gauze "slipcover." I rub alcohol or liniment on the horse's leg, wrap the cottons around, wind flannels on top, and secure them with bandage pins. Pins stay in better than tape; they're neater, and cheaper in the long run.

I always keep horses' hind legs in thick protective bandages at shows. Horse-show stalls are usually built of slats, like large packing crates. If a horse gets caught, he usually catches a hind leg. I wrap them so thickly that he can't fit them in between the boards.

I wrap front legs if the horse has a hard school or does quite a bit of jumping. Which means that at home I don't do much wrapping. Our horses don't school much at home until it's time to leave for Florida.

At a show, any horse that jumps goes into front wraps right after its class. The alcohol or liniment tightens the leg. The wrap provides a thick protective cover, prevents swelling from coming up after a hard work, and keeps the area warm and the blood circulating.

In the summer, I sometimes do up my jumpers in a poultice overnight. When the ground is like concrete, all that pounding makes a horse's feet sting and tires his legs. At night, after the last class, I mix some white rock granules in water, pack the paste into his feet, and stick a piece of plain brown paper over his sole to keep it in place. I mix up a thick paste of Antiphlogistine and liniment or vinegar and tack it around his legs from below the ankles to below the knees. Saran Wrap or brown paper goes around that, with the regular cotton or flannel bandages on top. Vinegar or liniment makes the poultice draw a little bit better, while moist heat takes the sting out of the feet and shins.

WINKY MACKAY-SMITH, like her husband, the famous veterinary surgeon Dr. Matthew Mackay-Smith, is a consistent winner of Endurance riding competitions, an expert trainer and conditioner, and an active promoter of the sport. She has won the Old Dominion 100-Mile Ride twice, finished in the top ten of the Tevis Cup twice, and won the Ontario 100-Mile Ride, generally being awarded the trophy for Best Condition as well:

I don't wrap my horses at all.

An Endurance horse doesn't have to be beautiful, but it does have to be sound. Training is pretty rigorous, seventy to eighty miles a week, including a once-a-week ride of twenty to thirty miles, trotting and cantering uphill and down.

A horse that needs help from standing or support bandages is not a good candidate for Endurance competition. There is a weakness somewhere that bandaging won't correct. I can't take a horse on a hundred-mile ride if he gets touchy after twenty.

Horses wear standing bandages to protect their legs from stall injuries and to prevent stocking up. But our horses live outside twenty-four hours a day. They come in to eat and go right back out. Horses at liberty don't stock up, and stocking doesn't worry me anyway. Every once in a while I do keep a horse in overnight for some reason, and his legs fill; but after ten minutes of movement the next morning, they're fine.

I don't use shipping bandages, although our horses travel all over the country. Horses scramble and hurt themselves when they can't spread their legs and brace, but because the center partition of our trailer doesn't go all the way to the floor, our horses can spread their legs as they please.

I don't even use shin and ankle boots in competition, although they are permitted. Their only purpose is to prevent horses from interfering and overreaching. But horses with such gait defects waste energy and tire easily. I concentrate my efforts on finding horses with pure gaits. Then I make sure they're shod properly.

If I have chosen the right horse, sensible, sound, with true gaits, there is nothing bandages do that he can't do for himself.

ALL ABOUT SADDLES

Expert advice on selecting and caring for saddles and tack from CLINTON HANKS, former president of the Smith-Worthington firm of saddlemakers, and a horseman himself.

Good leather should have a tallow quality to it, so that it appears to be almost squeaky with grease it has absorbed. To get this in quality saddlery, mutton tallow is worked well into the leather after it has been tanned. The high grease content of the mutton lard keeps the leather from drying out, stops cracking, and makes it more pliable to work with. Many times, people buying new saddlery will mistake the whitish-looking mutton tallow on it for wax and try to remove it. Removing it will dry out the leather.

Tanning. There are essentially two methods of tanning used in English saddles. Our firm uses bark tanning, with bark from oak or hemlock trees. We prefer this method because bark-tanned leather takes oiling and cleaning and absorbs grease to give it that tallow quality. You can recognize bark-tanned saddles by their color, which ranges from light tan to brown.

Chrome tanning is a more recent chemical process. It is recognizable by its gray-cream or greenish color. While it is very durable, it does not have a high grease content. Some manufacturers use chrome-tanned leather for certain parts of the saddle that take a lot of stress, such as the billet straps, and bark-tanned leather for the visible parts.

Saddles that have been completely chrome-tanned are difficult to clean and do not appear very pliable. Sometimes, if you look at the edge of the skirt of a cheaper saddle, you will notice that the leather is brown on the outside and gray or green on the edge. The leather has been chrome-tanned and then dyed to look as if it were bark-tanned.

The hide. Leather is made from five parts of the animal's hide. The butt is the section from tail to shoulder and is the most desirable for saddlery use. It is the most durable part of the hide and has the least stretch. The belly, which is good for other uses, should not be used in saddlery, because of its elasticity. When buying a stirrup leather, make sure that it comes from the butt and not the belly. Stretch it as much as you can. If it gives as much as a quarter inch, don't buy it.

The shoulder of the hide is as good as the butt section in quality and durability, but it is wrinkled where the animal's head joined the body. If this is noticeable in the finished saddle, you might not want it, for aesthetic reasons, but it is just as strong as butt leather. The back is the entire area from tail to neck, including both shoulder and butt. It's simply another way of sectioning the leather and is just as good in quality as the butt section—again, if you don't mind the wrinkles. The last and least desirable part of the hide is the shank, or leg, section, from the belly down. The shanks are hard, crack easily, and are unsuitable for saddlery. They are not used by any saddlemakers that I know of.

Grades of leather. Leather is further divided into five grades, which various manufacturers use in various parts of the world, so where the leather is bought is just as important as which part of the animal it comes from. Leather from India is rated at the bottom of the list in quality, mainly due to the tanning processes used in that country. Leather in Indian saddlery is tanned in clay vats and comes out too dry, so that the grease content is very poor and the leather won't absorb additional grease. We won't touch Indian leather or Indian-made saddlery for this reason.

Japanese leather also leaves a lot to be desired, but for a different reason. It has very poor tensile strength, meaning that the fibers don't hold together well. You'll find that it tears easily around the tongue holes and also stretches easily. Although the Japanese haven't started to make saddles yet, they make a line of bridles and halters. I'd consider their leather about grade D.

Leather from southern Europe and South America rates a grade C but is still inferior to English, German, and American leather. If we were to purchase Argentine leather, we'd have to watch it carefully because of grub holes, which appear when the leather is stretched. South American pigskins are especially susceptible to grub holes and must be used with discretion. In addition, South American leather is on the hard side. It takes more work to make it flexible.

A- and B-quality leather is tanned in Germany, England, and the United States. Manufacturers in these countries use it almost exclusively. It is the best unblemished leather and is usually bark-tanned to make it soft and pliable, but it is the most difficult leather to obtain and also the most expensive. The higher prices of German, English, and American saddles is largely due to the better quality of leather used in them.

Unfortunately, the consumer has no way of knowing what kind of leather he's getting in his saddles. No government regulations require specification of the grade and section of animal used. Such a regulation would be impossible to enforce anyway, since leather is cut up and sectioned so frequently.

Parts of the saddle. Our saddles have five kinds of skins in them from three kinds of animals. Other firms use different combinations, but this seems to work best for us.

Pigskin is used in the seat portion of most saddles. We find that it is more pliable than cowhide, takes abrasion better, and lasts longer. The actual seat portion takes more strain than any other part of the saddle, since it supports the weight of the rider. So this is where the strongest leather must be used. We use nearly an entire pig hide for every two seats. Because pigskin has a certain amount of give to it, we stretch it five times before we sew it over the frame.

There are upper and lower skirts or flaps on the saddle, which are the sections between the rider's leg and the horse. For the skirts, we use eighth-inch-thick butt cowhide that has been put through a roller to make impressions on the leather so that it resembles pigskin. We call this "hogprinting," and it is purely for aesthetic purposes, so that the saddle skirts match the seat. We make our skirts as thin as possible to give the rider the greatest contact with the horse. The more leather between the leg and the horse, the less feel for the horse the rider has. Pigskin skirts used to be popular with some manufacturers in place of cowhide, but the pigskin tends to curl up with use and nobody I know uses them any more. Because of the curl, pigskin skirts can be quite easily recognized on a used saddle, and many people avoid them, because it is an unattractive feature. In most saddles, there is a slight difference of color, because the skirt is cowhide and the seat pigskin, but this decreases as the saddle is oiled and used.

The stirrup leathers are taken from the butt of the cow, as is the skirt, but they are not hogprinted. Billets are also taken from this cut, but are made thicker and heavier than the stirrup leathers because they should not have to be replaced during the life of the saddle. Tallow is worked well into them so that the thicker piece of leather is as pliable and easy to work with as stirrup leather.

The panel of the saddle is the padded part sitting on the horse's back. The seat is attached to the top of the panel, so this is not a visible saddle part. Some makers use felt for the top of the panel. We use a very thin, four- to five-ounce shoulder hide, since it gives the most strength with the least weight. For the underside of the panel, which lies against the horse, we use glove-tanned horsehide, which is much more pliable than cowhide. Horsehide doesn't have as much grease content as cowhide, even though it is also bark-tanned, like all our leather. We use horsehide because we feel it wears longer than cowhide and the horse's sweat doesn't seem to crack it as much as it does calfskin. It's simply a tougher hide. If you ride without a pad, this part of the saddle should always be wiped off after each ride so that the salt from the horse's sweat doesn't eat into the leather.

The tree. The second-most-important part of the saddle, after the leather, is the frame, or tree. Saddlemakers will put fine leather on frames of all qualities.

Frames are made principally in England and Germany. The cheapest is a wood-laminated plywood, not reinforced with steel and therefore very soft. A lot of Argentine saddles have soft wood frames, and they often gradually open up with use. To compound the problem in Argentine saddles, barrel-hoop iron is used in the frame. This type of iron is very soft and can break when all of the rider's weight is on the stirrups—during jumping, for example. It is scary to think how much the rider's safety in jumping depends upon the saddle.

A good wooden saddletree should be reinforced with steel along both sides in order to give the saddle a springy quality. A saddle that is too rigid can crack and break from strain. We use a frame of hickory, birch, or beech wood, reinforced with flexible spring steel. This tree was developed and patented in 1936 and is guaranteed for the lifetime of the buyer. With normal use, it is absolutely unbreakable.

We also make a patented leather tree, the only one I know of. Riding in it is like sitting in a hammock, because it conforms to the horse's back as well as to the rider's leg and seat more than a wooden frame does, giving the rider greater feel for the horse. There is almost no break-in period. With most saddles, it takes several hours of riding for the leather to shape itself to fit the contour of the rider's leg, for the knee rolls to gradually shape up and

1. Smith-Worthington saddles start with a wooden frame of hickory, birch, or beech. The tree is then reinforced with spring steel for flexibility.

2. Irish-linen webbing is stretched directly over the frame and covered with canvas.

3. Underside shows billet straps sewn to the webbing. Notice that the stirrup bars are recessed between the wooden frame and the steel.

4. Foam rubber is cut and glued on the canvas directly under the seat portion of the saddle.

the skirts to shape in. But with a leather tree, the saddle is more flexible and the leather shapes to the rider's leg immediately. The pommel and cantle are still wooden, because you need a frame over which to shape the leather. Spring brass joins the cantle to the pommel, just as spring steel joins our wooden-frame saddles. The brass runs along both sides from front to back.

What goes between the frame and the outer leather is important to the rider's comfort. On some cheaper saddles the leather is stretched directly over the wood. You can feel the wood with your hand if you press down hard on the seat. After you've ridden for a while, the saddle becomes hard and uncomfortable. Better saddles have webbing stretched over the wood, which is what the rider actually sits on. We stretch pure Irish-linen webbing from front to back and from side to side over the frame. Canvas goes over the linen, and a foam pad is cut to fit over the canvas, directly under the seat. With three thin layers between the rider and the tree, there's no chance of his feeling a hard frame underneath him.

Buying used tack. Some leather has reached the point of no return, and you must be sure this is not the case with the used tack you buy. Check a saddle by bending back the skirts and observing whether they appear to be cracked or flaky. Look especially hard at the billets and stirrup leathers. Billets that have cracked must be replaced if you want a reliable saddle, and this can be quite expensive. If you have doubts about the stirrup leathers, put them in a vise and pull with all your might. If there is no cracking, they are safe to use.

If you find a piece of tack that is cracked and dry, remember that you can never restore deteriorated leather to its original condition; you can only prevent it from getting any worse. All the mutton tallow in the world won't remove the cracks from a saddle.

Saddle myths. There are a lot of myths about saddlery. One of them is the more stitches per inch, the better the quality. The truth is that there is a variety of lengths of stitching in quality saddles. Areas that undergo the most strain should be sewn with as long a stitch as safety will allow, because the more stitches per inch, the more you are weakening the leather by breaking the fibers. Billets are stitched to the saddle with no more than six stitches per inch for this reason. The seat, skirt, and breastplate rings underneath the saddle are stitched together before the saddle is assembled, with a very tight stitch of about twelve per inch, since there is little direct strain on them. Ornamental stitching around the flap has ten to fourteen stitches per inch.

Thick leather is not necessarily better than thin leather. You want the saddle skirts to allow for as much leg contact with the horse as possible. Skirts that are one eighth inch thick will last for years if they have a good tallow content and are kept soft and not permitted to crack. In all cases, the tallow content and the part of the animal from which the piece was cut are more important than the thickness of the leather.

Another myth involves the continual use of neatsfoot oil to care for saddlery. If you want to darken a new saddle, use neatsfoot oil or compound until the piece of tack is of the desired color. Then let it dry out and put the oil away. Continued use of any oil has no purpose and in time will rot the stitching. Cod liver oil is also used to darken tack and serves the same purpose as neatsfoot oil, but I recommend only animal oils for darkening. You can get a chemical reaction from vegetable oils, and for this reason I don't recommend caster oil or olive oil for saddlery. Stick with like to like and you won't be disappointed.

Tack care. Water damages leather more than anything. That is why I am just as happy to see people avoid saddle-soaping their tack. The fats contained in saddle soap are good for the leather, but people like to get things done in a hurry, and in soaping their saddles they often do more harm than good by using a lot of water. If you keep your sponge as dry as possible, just barely damp, then saddle soap is beneficial. Glycerine soap also keeps the leather soft, but it, too, should be used with as little water as possible.

It is a mistake to remove mud from a saddle with water. If your saddle is muddy, the best thing to do is to let it dry and then remove the mud by brushing with a dry brush. This will remove the mud without working the grit into the leather, which is the unfortunate result of using water.

For regular leather conditioning, I'd recommend a commercial product containing lanolin, such as Lexol or Leather Care, which keep the leather pliable and water-repellent. But you don't really have to use a commercial product. When I lived in the country, we used skunk grease occasionally as a leather conditioner. It did the same job and was a lot cheaper. Unsalted chicken fat can be used regularly for keeping leather in condition.

If you find that your saddle is losing its tallow content and becoming dry after continued use, you can add mutton tallow to it. Get the lard from your butcher. Just make sure that it has not been salted, which would cause leather corrosion. Heat the tallow gently until it is just melted, work it well into the saddle, and let it dry. The leather should be pliable and almost squeaky with the grease it has absorbed. Wipe off any excess tallow. The final result should be a hard finish. If you leave any sticky substance, the saddle will pick up dust from the horse's coat. You can also improve the durability of lesser-quality tack by treating it with mutton tallow. Whatever the conditioner you use, always wipe off any excess in order to prevent dust from adhering to the tack.

Storing leather properly helps to prolong its life as much as keeping it soft does. Storing it in the barn can shorten its life, since leather reacts chemically to the urine content in the air. I'd also keep tack out of the attic, where the dryness of the air will dry out the leather, and out of the basement, because the humidity there will cause the leather to mold. Storing tack in the house in a cool, dry place away from any heating element will help prolong its life.

FAVORITE SADDLES OF FAMOUS RIDERS

BETH PERKINS, of Monkton, Maryland, was a member of the Gold Medal-winning U.S.E.T. Three-Day Team and placed fifth individually in the 1975 Pan American Games at the age of nineteen; she is a successful Event rider and trainer:

I use various saddles for the various phases of Eventing. For dressage, I have two: a Passier and a Martin-Kinlet. I liked the Passier a lot, but heavy use spread it hopelessly out of shape and I needed a replacement. I wanted a saddle similar to the Passier, but my budget demanded something cheaper. The Martin-Kinlet, which costs about one-third less than the Passier, seemed to be the best compromise.

Dressage requires effective use of seat and legs. The deepest part of the saddle must be in exactly the right place. I need a fairly small saddle, sixteen to sixteen and one half inches, or my seat slides too far back. And I need a narrow seat so I can place my legs where I want them.

The Passier was narrow through the gullet and relatively unpadded. In contrast, a saddle like a Steuben Parzifal presents real problems for me. It has a wide seat, a lot of padding, and feels rather like sitting on a barrel. Try getting an extended trot out of a barrel!

The Martin-Kinlet is even narrower than the Passier and has a deeper seat. It fits a narrower horse. If I used the Passier on a horse with a high front and sloping topline, I always felt as if I were falling off the back.

For all my conditioning work at a gallop I use a Pimlico exercise saddle. It's light and well balanced and puts very little saddle between me and the horse. Its light weight reduces the strain on the horse's legs. A galloping saddle must be well balanced. You're up there riding with short stirrups, and balance is what keeps you there. I balance well with this saddle and therefore can keep the horse in balance well. It's an unobtrusive saddle. I can really feel what the horse is doing.

I use a thirteen-year-old Hermès for the cross-country and stadium phases. I used to ride in a real knee-roll saddle and felt locked in. I'm freer in the Hermès. I can get up in galloping position with less effort. So my energy is conserved and my horse gets the freedom he needs.

The Hermès is a close-contact saddle, which means that I can be tighter with my legs, more athletic, and therefore more adjustable. I fell off much more when I had a knee-roll saddle. I was inclined to pinch with my knees. When you ride in an Hermès, you learn to keep your leg tight.

It takes a lot of leg to ride cross-country. You have to keep your horse in gear. The Hermès lets me put my leg where I can use it best.

My model has a slightly higher cantle than the newer ones and so is a little deeper. It makes quite a decent seat to sink into when I drive with my seat the last few strides before a fence. And should the horse check, I'm not sliding around on a flat surface.

The Hermès is a competition saddle. It's not particularly comfortable over a long period. For hacking and flat work, I prefer the Martin-Kinlet.

MELANIE SMITH is world-famous for her jumping partnerships, first with Val de Loir, Grand Prix Horse of the Year in 1978 (when Melanie herself was Leading Lady Rider, Grand Prix Rider of the Year, and Horsewoman of the Year), and then with Calypso, a Dutch-bred gelding. Melanie and Calypso were the first horse-and-rider team to win the "Triple Crown of American Jumping," consisting of the American Gold Cup, the International Jumping Derby, and the American Invitation. In 1982 they won the World Cup Finals.

My horses range in size from 15 to 17 hands and come in all shapes. Radnor and Val de Loir, for example, are built quite differently. Radnor is narrow and Val is broad. The Hermès fits each horse very well. It does sit me fairly forward and close to the withers, so I use a pommel pad as a matter of course.

My Hermès has a regular, rather than a cut-back, pommel, which I find more comfortable. It rubs neither me nor the horse. But I do like to use girth guards. A close-contact saddle gives you a good feel for the horse, but it also gives you a good feel for the girth buckles. The guards keep the buckles from rubbing my legs and also protect the saddle.

I did some hunting at one time and used a Steuben Lorelei, an amply padded and knee-rolled saddle. It was very comfortable. When I first used an Hermès, I had a terrible time staying in the saddle. Now I'm so accustomed to being close to the horse that I can't ride with a full knee roll.

I like the position and the versatility the Hermès gives me. The deepest part of the saddle is right behind the pommel, which is close to the horse's center of balance. There is no padding to dictate leg position. I can put my legs wherever I want them.

The Gold Cup saddle and the Riem are similar to the Hermès and less expensive. Some riders may find them a good compromise. The Crosby Prix des Nations resembles the Hermès, but I don't think it's quite as well balanced. It rides you farther back. I've been spoiled by the Hermès. It molds to the horse better than the others.

I ride eight horses a day, so I need several saddles. I like to keep two Hermèses in use, and let two others rest. My favorite saddle is eight years old and is just like a pair of comfortable old shoes.

BERNIE TRAURIG, of Hartland, Wisconsin, one of America's leading professional riders, is a specialist in Grand Prix competitions. He has won more than fifteen of the most important ones and placed in more than one hundred others. A member of the North American squad at all of the F.E.I. World Cup Finals to date, he was winner of the Grand Prix at the World Cup Finals in Sweden in 1982. Among the famous jumpers he has ridden are Eaden Vale and The Cardinal, with which he won the U. S. Open Jumping Championship in 1979:

I use an Hermès and a Gold Cup saddle and like both. They are close-contact saddles and similar in design. Basically, the only difference between them is the price, the Hermès being considerably more expensive. Both saddles give the rider a good feel for the horse, because they put so little between rider and horse.

As a junior, I used a Steuben Siegfried. The Siegfried is a heavily padded saddle with ample knee rolls. It's a comfortable, secure saddle for a child. The Gold Cup and the Hermès are much flatter. The cantle and the pommel are low and the seat is shallower.

Both Hermès and Gold Cup break in well. They are soft and comfortable in a short period of time. Their best selling point is good balance. I'm right on top of the horse's center of balance and I can alter my weight distribution at will. Freedom to shift forward or back is extremely important in Grand Prix jumping. The courses demand precision riding and often force some drastic maneuvers over the fences.

DOROTHY MORKIS, who runs a boarding stable and teaches a few students in Raynham, Massachusetts, is one of America's leading dressage riders. Since the retirement of her Olympic horse Monaco, she has been training his successor: a Thoroughbred-Oldenburg ex-driving horse called Pandur:

I like both the Kieffer models: the Standard and the Bavaria II. They have lightweight trees, foam-padded fronts, and cut-back withers. The Bavaria II features an extra thickness of leather at the leg and better stitching and is covered with a remarkable chrome-tanned leather. The surface is softer, darker, and has a nap; not suede, but the effect is similar. The result is better grip.

The Kieffer is available in a regular as well as a deep seat. I have both. I use the regular seat on horses like Monaco, which present no particular conformation problems. I use the deep seat on horses whose backs drop a bit behind the withers.

I am rather difficult to fit with a saddle. I have a long leg, so some flaps (on the Steubens, for instance) are cut too short for me. I've also used a Passier, but I find it too hard.

There is an interesting new custom-made English saddle called the County Competitor. Ernst Bachinger, with whom I trained at the Spanish Riding School, helped with the design. It's like a Kieffer: has the same kind of tree and is available in the same kind of leather. If you provide your horse's measurements, an exact description of his withers, and his photograph, they make the saddle to fit him. I'm eager to try one.

CAROL HOFMANN THOMPSON was a member of the U.S.E.T. Jumping Team from 1962 to 1972. Now married to J. Willard Thompson, who trains and races Thoroughbreds, she shares her experience with junior riders as an equitation instructor at their quiet winter farm, in Colt's Neck, New Jersey, and also continues to train and show hunters and jumpers:

I use an Hermès. It's reasonably comfortable for show jumping, it puts me close to the horse, and it fits most horses quite well. While it is a good basic saddle for the show ring, it has a fairly hard seat and I would not recommend it for fox hunting or long hours of hacking.

Nor would I recommend it for juniors, and certainly not for children. Aside from the price, I like a junior saddle to have a bit of padding or a little deeper seat. A child's saddle should have a little knee roll. Most children and many juniors simply don't have the strength of leg to use an extremely close-contact saddle to good advantage. A child really needs the security of a knee roll. Not the over-stuffed German variety, but still more " 'twixt child and horse" than an Hermès.

One of the Hermès cousins, either a Devon Gladstone or a Riem is a nice choice. Both are close-contact saddles but not quite so flat. The Twentieth Century, with its little knee roll, is a suitable saddle for a child. It offers a good combination of security and sensitivity. Proper saddle fit is particularly important when dealing with children and junior riders, and proper balance, too.

> EDITH MASTER, who owns a farm in Chester, New Jersey, is a prominent dressage competitor, trainer, instructor, and judge. As a member of the U. S. Dressage Team, she competed in three Olympic Games (helping to win a Bronze Team Medal in 1976, riding Dahlwitz) and in two World Championships. In 1978 she won the U. S. National Grand Prix Dressage Championship, with Paloma, a Hanoverian mare she purchased as a three-year-old and trained herself.

I'm not a theorist and I'm not familiar with the intricacies of saddle design. However, I do prefer the comfort and balance of the Steuben Parzifal and the Steuben Tristan to other dressage saddles.

The Kieffer is too straight and slippery and I don't like the cut-back pommel on the Passier. Long hours working on the sitting trot bring appreciation for a really comfortable saddle.

The Tristan and the Parzifal both have good balance. Some dressage saddles are built too high in front and tip the rider back. This slight shift in proper position makes effective work difficult. I can sit properly straight in either of my saddles and use my seat and legs to good advantage.

All saddles settle with use and require periodic reupholstering, but one that is unbalanced to begin with will become worse as it settles.

The Parzifal is a fairly heavy saddle, possibly too heavy for a young horse. The Tristan is lighter and has the added advantage of lower cost. I use both saddles on all my horses and employ pads as necessary. My Thoroughbreds and Trakehners come in all shapes and sizes and tolerate either model well.

> TAD COFFIN won the Three-Day Event Individual Gold Medal in the 1975 Pan American Games, and again in the 1976 Olympics, with Bally Cor, along with many other Eventing awards. He owns and operates Flying Horse Stables, in Hamilton, Massachusetts, a stone's throw from the headquarters of the U.S.E.T. Three-Day Team, of which he is one of the brightest stars.

For top-level Eventing, you need at least two saddles, and I use three.

I like the Fontainebleau, a French saddle, for dressage. It's ideal for flat work. Mine looks very much like a forward-seat saddle with a higher cantle, which keeps me snug in the seat, right up against the pommel, where I want it to be for dressage. The newer models have a lower cantle.

The Fontainebleau doesn't have knee rolls, but it does have a little bit of a thigh roll. The flaps are like those on an all-purpose saddle. They are cut more forward than most dressage saddles. I do some slow gallops and jumping in the Fontainebleau, so the slight forward cut is quite useful.

This saddle bothers some horses if I am not careful. There is a lot of weight in back, which can produce a sore-backed horse. I have been using a flow-form saddle pad for the past six months, which solves the problem. It's filled with the same material as ski boots, and molds itself to the horse's back.

The Fontainebleau's standard-height pommel can bother a particularly high-withered horse. That problem, of course, is not unique to the Fontainebleau. You must fit every saddle carefully, and this one is no exception.

I use a British saddle for cross-country. There are many good cross-country saddles available, but most of them are pretty heavy. The Parker is designed for the better rider having trouble doing 165 pounds. It is lightweight but more substantial than the Hermès. It doesn't impede the horse, but there is more to hold you in than an Hermès offers. I wouldn't suggest the Parker for much flat work. It's pretty uncomfortable for long sitting but ideal for galloping and jumping at speed.

I have a Passier All Purpose for stadium jumping. The Passier is acceptable. I don't much like jumping in either a Crosby or an Hermès. There's not really enough to them. But truthfully, I'm not all that keen on my Passier, either. It's biggest point is that I already own it.

The Passier is cut back at the withers and therefore sits low on the horse's back. I always use a pommel pad in addition to the regular saddle pad. The flaps aren't as forward as a true forward-seat saddle. The seat is bigger and the saddle is heavier than a forward-seat saddle. I would call it a cross between a cross-country and a dressage saddle.

ALL ABOUT SADDLE PADS

If your horse has a chronically sore back, you may have researched the saddle-pad market already. But if you only use a pad to keep the bottom of your saddle clean, you may never have given much thought to the vast selection of products on the market today. Among the many styles, materials, and other variables, there may be features from which you and your horse have yet to benefit.

The first step is to put your priorities in order. If your horse has a sensitive back or if you're engaged in a sport that is likely to make his back sore, such as Endurance riding, *protection* for him should be your primary concern. Protection means cushioning, but it also means absorbency. A hot, sweaty back is subject to irritation.

Appearance may be important to you. If you compete in a subjectively judged sport such as show hunting or dressage, it should be. A neatly fitted pad of the style that's in fashion in your sport gives you an edge.

And there is the *convenience* factor. It's nice not to have to clean the bottom of your saddle every time you ride, and your saddle will last longer if it's not in direct contact with your horse's back, exposed to sweat, heat, and friction. But if this is your prime objective, any pad that fits your saddle will fill the bill. Your choice becomes a matter of merely eliminating undesirable characteristics:

—You don't want the pad to slip and bunch under the saddle.
—You don't want it bulky under your leg, so that you lose contact with your horse's sides.
—You don't want it to fall to pieces before you've had your money's worth of service from it.
—And you'd probably rather not have to take it to the dry cleaner's every time it gets dirty.

If there were a modestly priced pad embodying all the good features and none of the bad ones, it would be the best seller, and all the others nowhere. This is an impossible dream, unfortunately, because some of the desirable features are mutually exclusive. In other words, the presence of one by its very nature rules out the other. So, by establishing your priorities, you will know which features you can afford to do without, and where you must stand firm.

The single most important feature of a saddle pad is its material, since this is what determines most of its characteristics. Today most pads are made from synthetics: synthetic fleece, synthetic felt, or polyurethane foam rubber. Some of the materials that inspired the synthetics are still around too. There's no real foam rubber any more, but there are real sheepskin pads and 100-percent-wool felt pads. There are also a couple of types of cotton pads.

Despite this array, where protection for the horse is concerned there are only two operative characteristics: density and absorbency. Each material consists of fibers separated by air spaces. The more air relative to fiber, the less dense the material.

Density can easily be evaluated by feel. Felt is denser than fleece, wool is denser than cotton, while the density of foam varies according to the size of the air spaces or pores selected by the manufacturer.

All else being equal, the less dense the material, the less of a cushion it provides between horse and saddle, as the weight of saddle and rider compress the air spaces. (Of course, if all else is not equal, and if the less dense pad is the thicker of the two, this thickness will offset the compression of air spaces to some extent.)

You can evaluate *cushioning* by squeezing the material between your fingers. Press hard. This is what will separate your saddle from your horse. Remember that it is also what will separate your leg from the horse's side.

However, there is a very important point about cushioning, and it's not all pro density. There are two kinds of cushioning: support and padding. Density provides support. A dense pad, for example, helps hold a wide-throated saddle off a high-withered horse. But while it preserves clearance in some areas, it focuses pressure on others. It may save the withers from an ill-fitting saddle, but it could at the same time be concentrating weight under the cantle.

A less dense pad more readily conforms to the shape of the horse and saddle. If the material is thick without being dense, it fills all the little nooks and crannies and equalizes pressure. So more density is not always better. You must decide whether your horse needs padding, support, or something in between the two.

Absorbency, the ability to keep the horse's back relatively cool by absorbing sweat is the other critical protective feature. Like density, it is a function of the air spaces—not their size but their arrangement. If each pore is insular, isolated from the others, moisture will not permeate easily and the material will be comparatively unabsorbent. If the pores are connected, forming a network of tiny channels throughout the material, absorbency is good.

It is impossible to evaluate with the naked eye the air-space structure of a saddle pad. You can know the properties of a material, for example that the pores of real wool have more interrelationships than those of synthetics. Or if you're comparing two materials and can obtain samples of each, you can conduct your own test.

Take the sample and weigh it. Then soak it in water and weigh it again in order to measure the amount of water it has absorbed. To compare samples, divide wet weight by dry weight. The highest score is the absorbency winner.

But there's a complication. By the time you've girthed up and lowered your weight into the saddle, you will have mashed your pad down, compressing a good many of those air spaces that you were counting on to hold moisture. This brings us back to density. The denser the material, the less air space relative to fiber, the more compression it will withstand before its air spaces close down, and the more moisture it will hold under pressure. If absorbency is important to you, density gains in desirability.

Breathability is a characteristic that saddle-pad manufacturers like to claim for their products, suggesting that the pad promotes heat discharge by permitting air circulation. No question, some materials have better breathability than others, following the principles that apply to absorbency. Dense pads, resistent to compression, with interrelated air spaces, can receive more of the heated air rising from the horse's back. But, for a real cooling effect, warm air must be exchanged for cooler air from the atmosphere. With both its large surfaces pressed between horse and saddle, very little air exchange can take place in a saddle pad while it's in use. Breathability is thus a dubious selling point.

Of these qualities, you'll find some, but not all, in most of the pads on the market. So decide which features are most important to you as you take a closer look at each material.

Synthetic fleece is probably the biggest seller. There are three kinds: acrylic, polyester, and Kodel, a type of polyester fiber patented by Eastman Kodak. These pads have a neat look that's right for most competitions, and they're machine washable and dryable.

The most expensive of the three is Kodel. Its chief advantage is its heat resistance. If you put an acrylic or non-Kodel polyester pad in the dryer on high heat, the tips of the fibers will melt and mat together. Gradually the appearance of the pad and its absorbency will deteriorate. Kodel fibers, able to withstand temperatures up to 300 degrees, will retain their like-new aspect longer.

While Kodel fibers have a distinctive, silky look, you won't be able to distinguish acrylic from polyester by sight, and the cost is roughly the same. Polyester withstands slightly higher temperatures than acrylic, but the difference is academic, since neither can endure high dryer settings and should be removed from the dryer when still slightly damp. Polyester is a stronger fiber than acrylic. It takes more wear and tear, but it is also less absorbent.

Synthetic fleece pads come in single-ply, double-ply, and single-ply with rolled edges. *Single-ply,* consisting of one layer of material worn fleece side down, is least expensive and puts the least bulk under the rider's legs. It is most likely to shift and bunch under the saddle, and for most tastes it is the least attractive, since most of what shows around the edge of the saddle is backing. Single-ply pads are made of acrylic and polyester but not of Kodel.

Double-ply pads are manufactured in all three materials. They show fleece on both sides. They're naturally more expensive, since they use twice the material and require more workmanship. They tend to stay put under the saddle, and they provide twice as much protection for the horse's back as a single-ply and twice as much bulk under the rider's leg.

The *rolled-edge* pad is in some respects a compromise. It's usually a single thickness of fleece with the edges turned up, sometimes backed with sailcloth or some other reinforcing material. The backing or lining is hidden by the saddle; only the fleece edges show. The appearance is distinct from the double-ply, because the saddle flap sits in the depression formed by the rolled edge. It provides a single layer of fleece protection for the horse's back and, except at the edge, a single thickness under the rider's leg. The rolled-edge pad is generally as costly as the double-ply, sometimes more.

While *real sheepskin* pads (the English call them "numnahs") have been jostled out of the limelight by their synthetic imitators, they still possess qualities that no synthetic has been able to duplicate entirely. Real wool has the edge in absorbency. The horse's back stays cooler and drier. If these benefits make the difference between a sore back and a usable horse, you'll cheerfully pay the premium for real sheepskin and put up with the inconvenience of a pad that requires dry cleaning.

Wool felt shares the absorbency benefits of wool fleece, and it's denser. The fibers are closely matted and resist compression. Like wool fleece, it requires dry cleaning.

There are a couple of *synthetic feltlike materials* that are machine washable in warm (not hot) water; they air-dry quickly. The densely matted synthetic fibers provide more support and absorbency than synthetic fleece but less absorbency than real wool.

Quite an assortment of *foam rubber* pads have burst upon the market, some of them horsey adaptations of materials developed for other purposes, such as bed pads under hospital patients. All of them are forms of polyurethane and all possess the same chemical properties. They vary mainly in porosity and thickness. Thickness ranges from one to two inches; some feature very large pores and some smaller ones.

The *thickness* decision is a trade-off. The thicker the slab of foam you put under your saddle, the more padding it provides your horse, the more moisture it is capable of absorbing, and the more bulk you have under your leg. Most riders select the one-inch thickness, unless they're dealing with a problem back, in which case the horse's comfort takes precedence over loss of leg contact for the rider.

Density and absorbency principles apply to foam as to other materials. Large-pored foam is less dense. It compresses to provide less of a cushion under the saddle and less bulk under the rider's leg. Because it compresses, it holds less moisture. Of course, the thickness of the foam may offset its porosity. A two inch pad of large-pored foam may provide the same amount of cushioning as a one inch small-pored foam pad.

Foam rubber doesn't stand up well to machine washing, but it wipes clean and dries quickly. Used in direct contact with the horse's skin, without a protective cover of some sort, it is not particularly durable.

Riders who favor the cushioning properties of foam get around its drawbacks by using it in combination with other materials. For home schooling, some riders lay a foam pad over an acrylic-blend Navajo-style blanket. The machine-washable Navajo absorbs sweat and protects the foam from wear. The foam provides cushioning.

You can buy foam pads with *removable cotton covers,* and some riders make their own. The cover protects the foam, keeps it clean, and zips on and off for easy washing.

Some of the double-ply synthetic-fleece pads are available with *foam inserts* in the cantle; others can be specially ordered with foam padding. The foam provides extra cushioning for the horse's back without adding bulk under the rider's leg. The whole pad, foam included, is machine washable and dryable.

Cotton plays a role in the saddle-pad marketplace, but seldom as a solo. *Quilted cotton pads* don't provide much padding, but they keep whatever is above them clean and they're easily washable and relatively inexpensive. Some riders use them in combination with foam or fleece pads. Since repeated washing shortens the life of almost any pad, they wash the cotton pad and prolong the life of the other, more expensive one.

The *Navajo-style blanket*, so popular for schooling, is an acrylic (or cotton-acrylic) imitation of the Indian original, which was woolen. Like the quilted cotton pad, it provides more padding and more absorbency, but also more bulk under the rider's leg. It isn't suitable for English-style competitions but has quite a following among English riders for use at home.

Many saddle pads incorporate a device or design to keep the pad in place. Generally speaking, if a pad is thick and soft (like foam or Navajo) and the girth is pulled snug, the pad won't move. And if it doesn't move, it cannot bunch under the saddle. At the other extreme, lightweight pads such as single-ply acrylic fleece and quilted cotton are inclined to slide around. Pretty soon half the pad is out in front of the saddle flaps or bunched up under the cantle.

Double-ply synthetic pads are marketed with all sorts of *nonslip devices* in addition to billet loops: girth loops, saddle-skirt loops with Velcro closings, and pockets into which the entire bottom half of the saddle skirt fits. But the same pad is proclaimed "nonslip" even without these attachments, and many users claim that it does indeed stay in place. Whether a double-ply synthetic fleece pad slips or not may be due to the rider's mobility and the tightness of the girth. It doesn't seem to depend on the material or design of the pad.

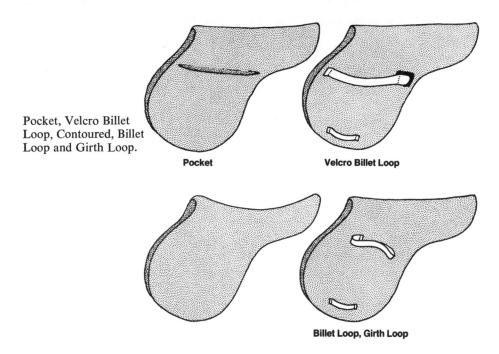

Pocket, Velcro Billet Loop, Contoured, Billet Loop and Girth Loop.

Pocket **Velcro Billet Loop**

Billet Loop, Girth Loop

If your saddle pad tends to move around, *billet loops* won't stop it. They'll simply keep it from falling off. *Girth loops* hold the center of the pad under the center of the saddle. The pad won't slip forward or back, but if the rear part really wants to bunch under the cantle, there's nothing to prevent it from doing so. *Loops and pockets* that hold the saddle skirts add stability. Since the pads equipped with these nonslip features are made of medium-weight materials at least, they tend to hold their position quite securely.

Another feature touted to prevent bunching and slipping is *contouring*. If you notice a curve in the folded edge when you fold your pad in half lengthwise, your pad is "contoured." In other words, its shape conforms to the curving underside of your saddle. Whether or not contouring really helps is an open question. Foam pads and Navajo blankets are not contoured and they stay put without the help of so much as a billet loop. But contouring certainly does no harm, and if the contoured pad does slip out of place, there is at least less material to bunch under the saddle.

In choosing a saddle pad, every rider has his own set of priorities and problems to consider. To give an idea of the various ways in which horsemen satisfy their individual needs, the following are the preferences of some successful riders who practice various equestrian sports.

STOREY JENKS (Three-Day Event):

The ability of a saddle pad to withstand pressure without collapsing is important in protecting the horse's back from the pressure of the saddle. Felt makes a good pad, because it is so dense that it holds the saddle off the horse's back and protects him where the saddle exerts the most pressure.

Foam pads look nice and soft, but they are too soft and compressible. This isn't so important with a perfectly fitted saddle, but most saddles have pressure points, often at the pommel, where the bars come together and bruise the horse's withers if they're not protected.

I've had success with my felt pad. It's covered with flannel to protect it and make it easier to keep clean, because I simply wash the flannel. On top of the felt, I use a Roma pad, made from cotton-covered foam, quilted like a bedspread. It adds cushioning and a little extra protection against pressure sores.

BARBARA NEWTON (Combined Training):

My main consideration in choosing a saddle pad is protection for my horse. Many of my Thoroughbreds have high withers and sloping backs, which require extra padding.

For flat work and jumping, I use an English-made pad called, coincidentally, the Newton pad; it is similar to American-made synthetic fleece pads except that it has a leather binding around the bottom, where the girth rubs, which protects the skirts and makes the pad last longer. It's a little thicker than other synthetic fleece pads and protects the high, thin withers of my horses. It might be too thick for a Quarter Horse, for example.

For all my conditioning work at the gallop, I ride in a steeplechase saddle, and with it I use a foam pad with a cotton-type material on the saddle side. I choose the thickness (one, one and one half, or two inches) according to the horse I'm riding: a thin pad on a broad horse, a thicker pad on a thin-backed, high-withered horse.

I use a pommel pad under all of them as extra protection for the withers. Under everything, I put a quilted cotton pad, primarily to keep the others clean and help them last longer. The quilted cotton is a lot cheaper to replace, easy to wash, and quick to dry.

LENDON GRAY (Dressage):

My Grand Prix dressage horse Beppo (winner of two reserve national championships) had some scar tissue on his back from old saddle sores when I bought him, so I looked around for a special protective pad. Linda Zang, whose own horse had back problems, suggested I try a "decubitus" pad, made of thick Kodel fleece and used by hospitals for bed sores. It works beautifully.

They come in three rectangular sizes, and I buy the smallest, thirty by forty inches, which hangs only about halfway down the saddle flaps, leaving me with a great feel for my horse's movements. Some horses might not like having the bottom edge of the saddle skirt right against their skin, but Beppo has not been bothered by this in the least.

Because of his particular problem, I use two pads back to back, so that one layer of fleece rests on his back and the other faces the saddle. It also looks nice for showing. I've used one pair of pads every day for over a year and they show no sign of wear.

For horses that don't have particularly sensitive backs, I use a commercial synthetic fleece pad over quilted cotton. I prefer the double-ply pads, as they seem to fit better and slip less. The thin quilted cotton pad is more to protect the fleece one than the horse, as it is easily washed and quick-drying. I sometimes wash it after each use, but the fleece one only every couple of months. For showing, I remove the quilted cotton and use the fleece pad alone.

WINKY MACKAY-SMITH (Endurance riding):

We used Navajo blankets on all our Endurance horses until we found a way to make a pad to suit our special needs. Our greatest concern, besides protecting the horse's back, is overheating. When you're in the saddle fourteen to sixteen hours a day, it's absolutely necessary to make sure the horse's back stays cool.

We make our pads from small-pored (very dense) foam. They are good shock absorbers, distribute the rider's weight evenly, and absorb sweat, keeping the horse's back cool. We test the foam by laying it on a hard surface such as a table and sitting on it. If we can feel the table, the foam is too porous. It's easy to confuse thickness and denseness. Dense foam need not be thick to give protection; ours is only one inch. We cut it to the exact shape of the saddle so that, unlike the Navajo, there's no extra material hanging down the horse's sides, and he stays cooler.

To protect the foam, we make a flannel cover with a zipper at the front edge. When the pad gets dirty, we take out the foam and throw the flannel cover in the wash. It also prevents the foam from scalding the horse's back and seems to hold its position better than a Navajo. It doesn't slip or bunch at all. Furthermore, these pads are easy to change during a ride, since there are no straps or billets. You just slip it off, remove the dirty flannel cover, and replace it with a clean one.

FITTING YOUR HORSE'S HALTER

Aim for a fit that is snug, yet not so tight as to suggest discomfort to the horse.

1. This is the trim, workmanlike fit appropriate for a show halter. The throatlatch rests above the prominence of the jaw, with no daylight visible. The noseband hangs at just the right height across the bridge of the nose. Only a small amount of daylight appears at the underside of the noseband.

2. The correct fit for a stable or turn-out halter. The noseband is a little roomier, allowing the horse to open his mouth comfortably. If you notice a crease across the bridge of your horse's nose, either his halter is too tight or the noseband droops to meet the nose with a slicing edge. Slip your thumb and first finger into the side of his mouth, between the upper and lower teeth, and separate his jaws to determine exactly how wide his noseband lets him open his mouth.

 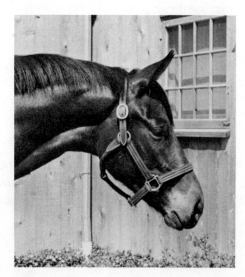

3. A halter so big that it's sloppy. The throatlatch falls below the prominence of the jaw, and the noseband droops low on the nose and shows too much daylight. This kind of fit is dangerous on a young horse or a mare with a foal at her side. A small foot could slip in between the noseband and the throatlatch.

4. This halter is too small in every respect. The throatlatch pinches, and the noseband is restrictively tight and too high on the nose. It will crease the hair across the nose and rub the jawbones raw underneath. The brass fittings on the noseband are rubbing directly on the cheekbones. Halters on foals and weanlings should be checked once a week for fit. On a fast-growing youngster, a correctly fitted halter can look like this in a matter of weeks.

SHOULD HORSES WEAR HALTERS IN THE STABLE?

It all depends . . . judging from the replies of three experienced equestrians.

> JOHN MANNING, director of the riding program at Stoneleigh-Burnham, a girls' prep school in Massachusetts, where he is responsible for the welfare of more than sixty horses and the riding progress of over a hundred students:

Until recently, our horses never wore halters in their stalls, but we've changed our policy as a result of a (fortunately false) fire alarm. Mass disorder! Now we leave the halters on.

We have a lot of beginning riders, and it's much easier for them to take a horse out of a stall if he's already wearing a halter. It's nicer for the horse, too, because he doesn't end up getting the crownpiece poked in his eye or the halter buckled on backwards.

I avoid nylon halters, because they rub hair off and if they snag on something they won't break. I buy the cheapest leather halters I can find, made in India. They hold up fine for normal purposes, such as leading and grooming in cross-ties. And if a horse gets in trouble, such as catching his halter on a bucket, the halter breaks, which suits me fine. There is an added benefit in our particular case. We number each horse's stall, and each halter carries the appropriate stall number. At the end of a lesson, every horse gets back to his own stall and his proper feed ration. It's easier than trying to remember what stall Snowflake lives in. Especially if Snowflake looks just like Snowball!

TOMMY MANION is one of the most respected Quarter Horse trainers in the country. His show stable in Springfield, Illinois, houses anywhere from twenty-five to forty horses in active training, among them numerous World Champions in both halter and performance divisions:

In my opinion, the chances of a horse's being trapped in a barn fire are a lot smaller than the chances of his getting caught up in his halter. A haltered horse can hurt himself in infinite ways. He can hang himself up on a post, catch his halter on a hook or bucket in his stall, put a foot through it, or injure himself or another horse roughhousing in the pasture. I don't leave a halter on any horse or broodmare, show or pleasure. It's just too dangerous.

When I do use a halter (for grooming, leading, or shipping), I don't want it to break. So I use expensive nylon halters with high-quality fittings. In these circumstances, the horses are never unattended, so if one gets into trouble there is always somebody present to get him out of it.

Our halters hang on the stall doors, handy for slipping on in order to groom, medicate, or lead out. Although safety is the primary consideration, our show horses stay nice and slick, without the bald marks that constant halter wear leaves.

STEPHANIE LLOYD helps her husband operate the Larry Lloyd Stables, in Santa Rosa, California, primarily a breeding farm from which have come many fine working hunters, stakes winners, show-ring stars, and road horse champions:

Even good-quality, correctly fitted halters tend to rub the hair if they're worn around the clock. When we leave halters on, it's primarily for convenience.

We use good leather halters with quality fittings. Nylon is dangerous, because it won't break, is stiff, and is impossible to remove if it gets wet. It's much more likely to rub and scald the skin than leather.

Almost all the horses that live in stalls—the stallions, the show and race stock, the visiting mares and foals—wear halters only when they're turned out or being handled. The rest of the time, their halters hang on their stall doors. Except for one difficult mare who wears hers all the time, it's easy enough to halter a horse in the confines of a stall.

HOW TO MAKE AN EMERGENCY HALTER

Tie a knot at the end of a piece of cord to make a small loop. We used clothesline, but baling twine is fine, or anything else you happen to have handy.

Slip the cord over the horse's neck.

Now you have him and you can take hold here if he starts to move off.

Pull a section of cord through the knotted loop.

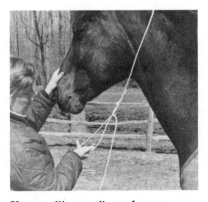

Keep pulling until you have a second loop about this size.

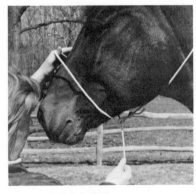

Slip it over the horse's nose.

After you have pulled it snug, a gentle tug puts pressure on the horse's nose, and a more forceful pull adds poll pressure.

Now you have a halter that can be used with a light touch on a quiet horse or very severely on an unruly one.

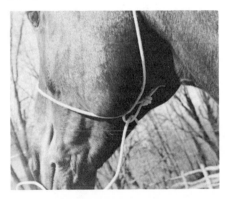

Mrs. Frank Chapot riding Shover in a standing martingale.

SPEAKING OF MARTINGALES

With the Trainers Who Win with Them

RONNIE MUTCH, owner of Nimrod Farm, in Weston, Connecticut, one of the leading training/teaching establishments in the East, is also a prominent hunter, jumper, and equitation judge.

If all those ostriches who condemn its use would look, they would see that 90 percent of the hunters and jumpers that are winning are using a standing martingale.

Over the average hunter-height fence, I find a standing martingale useful for controlling a horse's form. I particularly use them on horses that want to raise their noses on landing or descent. Over larger jumps, I find a standing martingale helps to stabilize the horse's approach and is less inhibiting than a running martingale, which tends to pull down on the bars of the mouth.

A young horse on the flat needs a standing martingale to help balance him, and it places the head where you want it, letting your signals get through to the horse much better. You can also bring down the heads of short-necked horses or those which tend to be ewe-necked, with the help of a standing martingale.

Adjustment is important. Half the horses shown in a standing martingale wear it so loose that it is simply swinging in the breeze. The textbook rule of fitting a martingale by the throatlatch is nonsense. I usually start a lot shorter. I adjust it so that as the horse stands naturally there will be a slight tension on the martingale. The only way there will be any looseness is if he brings his head in. But I think that proper adjustment requires a ground man. If I am the ground man, I put the martingale tight enough so that I begin to see the horse use himself and round himself. If I find that the martingale invites the horse to draw or swing its hind end, I loosen it or remove it entirely. If I find that it starts to inhibit a horse, I'll also take it off.

If you have the time, you can probably achieve some of the same results without a martingale. But in the real world we don't always have the time to devote months to getting a horse to lower its head and round its back over a fence. The use of martingales can be a shortcut and a training aid.

CARL KNEE, instructor/trainer, owner of Rock Bottom Farm, in Lagrangeville, New York, coach of many A.H.S.A. Horse of the Year titleholders and many famous jumpers:

The largest percentage of jumpers in all divisions go in running martingales because of the F.E.I. rules prohibiting standing martingales, although I'd say that more horses go without martingales in the Open division than with them.

For Junior and Amateur Owner horses, the standing martingale stabilizes the horse, keeps it in a frame with its head in place, and makes it easier to ride between fences. I also use standing martingales on the flat with green horses, although I'm prone to switch to a running martingale after the horse is trained.

I don't like to see a standing martingale adjusted tightly. I start by pushing it into the horse's throatlatch, and then adjust it tighter or looser depending on the individual horse.

I adjust the running martingale so that when you pick up the reins there is a line from the horse's mouth to the rider's hands when the horse's head is in a normal position. This is tight enough for Thoroughbred-type horses and temperaments, which is what we deal with mostly in this country. With the more cold-blooded European jumpers, and especially with the German Team horses, you see running martingales adjusted so tightly that there is a distinct V in the reins from the horse's mouth to the rider's hands. As far as I'm concerned, that's too much martingale for a hot-blooded horse.

Bea Perkins riding Dixie Grey in a running martingale.

PATTY HEUCKEROTH, a successful show rider and trainer and active fox hunter, operates a stable in Southern Pines, North Carolina, buying, selling, schooling, and campaigning hunters for field and show.

I use a standing martingale on almost everything I ride, both in training and in the show ring, except for hack classes, where martingales are prohibited.

On the other hand, I very seldom use a running martingale: I found some horses started balancing themselves on the reins, rather than relying on their natural balance.

A standing martingale is a big help on a green or a shy horse. If the shy horse shies or makes some other sudden move, I hold on to the neck strap instead of the reins to keep from grabbing its mouth and interfering with it. It keeps the green horse from raising its head to evade the bit. But the martingale must be loose enough so that if the horse raises its head and feels it, it won't panic and flip over backwards in fright. Once the horse is used to the martingale, I gradually tighten it. I like to see it adjusted on most horses so that it barely touches the throatlatch. If the horse throws its head or fools around, I'll make it a little looser.

BERNIE TRAURIG, one of the leading professional riders in America, is famed at home and abroad for his achievements with a dazzling roster of Grand Prix jumpers, including The Cardinal, Jet Run, Gozzi, and Eaden Vale:

A martingale contributes nothing to the horse's jumping effort. Its main purpose is to keep a high-headed horse's head in place and to protect the rider's nose if his horse throws its head a lot.

I like my hunters to go very relaxed, with their heads low and their noses stretched out. I can't help feeling that a tight martingale would interfere with this type of head and neck carriage, especially at a gallop.

However, some jumpers work better in a running martingale adjusted a shade tighter than normal. If the rider takes hold of the reins, the horse uses them for steadying as it raises its head on the approach, especially in time classes.

Adjustment varies. If you adjust a standing martingale to the horse's throatlatch and then ride around the warm-up ring over a few fences, when you recheck your adjustment you'll always find that the saddle has slipped back three or four inches, taking out any play in the martingale. So I recheck my martingale frequently, and if the saddle has slipped, I loosen the strap accordingly so that it is still touching the throatlatch.

You'll find that the same horse doesn't use the same adjustment all the time. Springer, a jumper I campaigned in 1975, could throw her head very high and took a long time to break. At first I had to use both a standing and a running martingale on her: the standing martingale to keep her head down, and the running martingale to catch her just before the other one did. But eventually she ended up going without any martingale at all. Jet Run was a rubbery-necked horse. At first we used a tight standing martingale on him, then switched to a tight running martingale. By the end of the New York National in 1974, he was performing in a very loose running martingale.

BUYING A BRIDLE

If you have ever taken home what you thought was a good-quality English bridle only to find that with use and cleaning the leather wrinkled and colored unevenly, you know that all bridle leather is not the same.

These tips on quality differences in leather bridles come from STANLEY ROSENFELD, assistant manager of Miller's, in New York, the country's largest wholesale/retail distributor of riding equipment. Mr. Rosenfeld knows a lot about horses (he was a bareback bronc rider at sixteen and is now an active fox hunter with the Smithtown Hunt), and all about bridles:

The two major English bridle makers are Barnsby and Crosby. Their bridles come in three qualities. Japanese bridles come in only one quality, coinciding with the lowest English quality. Maycraft is probably the best-known of the Japanese manufacturers.

From first-quality to third-quality, both the leather and the workmanship deteriorate. It is often quite obvious which is the third-quality bridle, but first- and second-quality are not always that easy to distinguish unless you know what to look for.

Leather. First-quality leather is butt stock, from the hindquarters of the animal. Second-quality comes from the shoulder, and third-quality from the belly. The lesser-quality leather lacks body. It feels spongy, porous. In the store, the best leather resists bending. It seems stiff and perhaps unap-

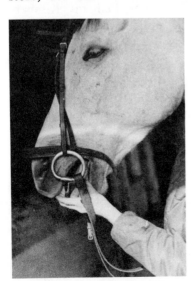

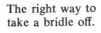
The right way to put a bridle on.

The right way to take a bridle off.

pealing, while the poorer leather is soft and pliant. But get the bridle home and, with use, the good leather softens while retaining its smooth, firm body, and the inferior leather wrinkles and goes limp. Better leather darkens evenly to a rich reddish brown, and poor leather turns yellowish and streaks.

Stitching. The better-quality bridle has more stitches to the inch. If you compare bridles side by side, you will see that the stitches on the poorer tack are fewer and larger.

Finishing. On better bridles, the edges of the leather are hand-rubbed to remove sharp corners and produce a smooth edge. The first-quality bridle will have more of the corners removed than the second-quality, and third-quality may not have the corners smoothed at all. On the best bridles, all corners are removed from the reins to give a comfortable grip, and the front edges are removed from the parts of the headstall. In second-quality, not as much edge is taken off. In third-quality, not only are the edges not removed, but the underside of the leather may be left rough.

All three grades usually have a groove stamped along the edges of the leather and a red stain applied to the edges. This is nothing more than window dressing. It makes no difference to the quality of the leather. First- and second-quality come with a protective coat of wax; third-quality may not.

ALL ABOUT BITS

Bitting is a subtle business with as many exceptions to rules as there are horses with differing mouths. Horsemen go to their graves without knowing all there is to know on the subject. In a few minutes, you can learn the mechanical principles governing the popular types of bits—how they function and why. The rules are simple and apply to most horses in most situations. When they don't, when a bit that should work doesn't, then you have to start experimenting with alternatives. The rest is experience.

If you ride in the so-called English style, which embraces everything but Western and Saddle-Seat, you're acquainted with snaffles, Pelhams, Kimberwickes, double bridles, bradoons, and curbs. The simplest approach to the subject is to realize that these are all variations of two basic types: the snaffle and the curb.

The Snaffle. Snaffle bits come in many styles and in a variety of materials. But all snaffles have in common a mouthpiece, which may be jointed or a straight bar, always with rings for the reins at either end. Because of the location of the reins in relation to the mouthpiece, a snaffle bit always exerts a direct pull on the horse's mouth equal to whatever force the rider uses on the reins, no more, no less (unless, of course, another piece of equipment, such as a running martingale, adds leverage).

The Curb. Although the curb bit is very popular with western riders, its only role in English riding is in combination with the bradoon in a double bridle. But the principle of the curb is embodied in both the Pelham and the Kimberwicke.

The mouthpiece of a curb is flanked, not by rings for the reins, but by vertical metal shafts called "shanks." At the top of each shank is a small ring that serves a double purpose: It attaches to the cheekpiece of the bridle, and it holds a hook for the curb chain. At the bottom of each shank is a ring for the rein. When you pull back on the reins of a curb bit, you pull not on the mouthpiece, but on the bottom part of the shank. As the bottom of the shank moves toward you, the top leans away, taking the curb-chain hooks with it and tightening the curb chain against the horse's chin. Your pull on the reins makes itself felt indirectly by leverage. The force of your pull is determined by the length of the lever. The longer the shank, the tighter the curb chain will squeeze.

The Pelham. A very popular bit for hunting and showing, the Pelham provides more control than an ordinary snaffle. Just how much control depends on the length of the shank and how it is used. The Pelham is a double-rein bit with the features of both snaffle and curb. In addition to the rings for the snaffle rein, it has rings at the bottom for the curb rein, and rings at the top for the curb chain.

Put pressure on the snaffle rein, and the Pelham bit acts like a snaffle. However hard you pull, the horse feels exactly that amount of pressure transmitted directly to his mouth. Pull on the curb rein, and the mouthpiece remains relatively still while the curb chain tightens. How much it tightens depends on the length of the shank. Pelhams come in a variety of shank lengths, from "Tom Thumb," with $3\frac{7}{8}$-inch shanks, to a severe bit with a 7-inch shank.

The Pelham is designed to be operated one rein at a time. It is difficult to combine snaffle and curb pressure simultaneously, because pressure on the snaffle rein tends to neutralize the effect of the curb. When you pull on the snaffle rein, you pull the entire bit closer to you, which automatically loosens the curb chain.

The Kimberwicke. A one-rein bit that combines the properties of snaffle and curb, the Kimberwicke gives more control than an ordinary snaffle. It is favored by riders who don't want to bother with two reins, but it is less popular than the Pelham, because it gives the rider almost no control over the amount of curb action that comes into play.

The Kimberwicke consists of an unjointed mouthpiece flanked by two fairly large D-shaped rings. The straight side of the D extends upward for a very short distance beyond the ring, providing an attachment for a curb chain and slots for the bridle cheekpieces.

A gentle pull on the reins of a Kimberwicke produces the same effect as a snaffle, but if the rider encounters resistance and pulls harder, the reins slide toward the bottom of the D-ring and the ring begins to act like a short shank. The rider is now pulling not so much on the mouthpiece as on the bottom of the ring. As he pulls the bottom of the D toward him, the top

METAL MULLEN

JOINTED RUBBER

LESS SEVERE

SOFT RUBBER

ROLLER-MOUTH

BREAKING BIT

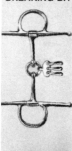

The curb. When the rider pulls the reins back, the tops of the shanks swivel forward, exerting downward pressure on the poll via the cheekpieces fo the bridle and tightening the curb chain against the chin groove. The horse is inclined to drop his head and flex at the poll, so that the mouthpiece works on the bars of the mouth.

Curb

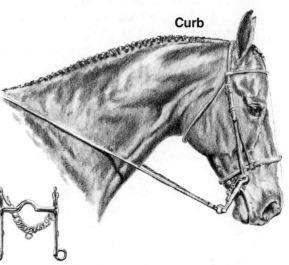

Pelham

The Pelham. A pull on the curb rein, alone, has the effect of a curb. A pull on just the snaffle rein duplicates the effect of a snaffle. If the rider pulls equally on both reins at the same time, the result still resembles the action of a snaffle, alone. The mouthpiece moves back in the horse's mouth, putting pressure on the corners or bars. The swivel effect is neutralized, rendering the curb action mild or nonexistent.

The double bridle. The horse carries two bits in his mouth, a snaffle-like bradoon and a curb. Since they function independently, the rider can produce a snaffle effect alone by putting tension on the bradoon reins; or a curb effect alone with the curb reins; or he can produce both effects simultaneously, using snaffle and curb reins together.

The Kimberwicke. A single pair of reins controls a straight bar mouthpiece with curb chain. The effect is like that of a snaffle since a pull on the reins moves the mouthpiece back in the horse's mouth and actually releases the curb chain. In a variation called the Uxeter, the reins are fixed near the bottom of the bit rings so that a pull back swivels the bit and exerts a mild curb effect.

SOFT RUBBER PELHAM

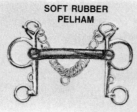

THIN RUBBER PELHAM

TOM THUMB PELHAM

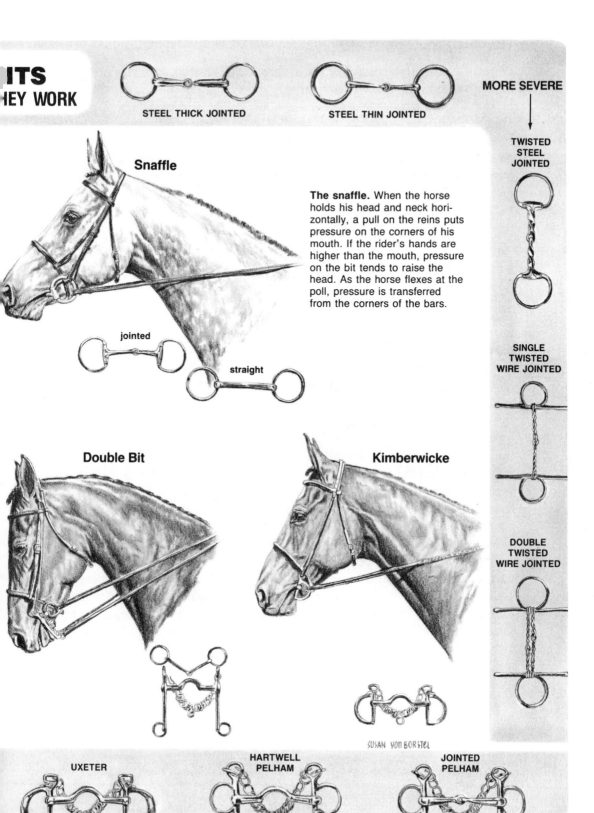

STEEL THICK JOINTED

STEEL THIN JOINTED

MORE SEVERE

TWISTED STEEL JOINTED

Snaffle

The snaffle. When the horse holds his head and neck horizontally, a pull on the reins puts pressure on the corners of his mouth. If the rider's hands are higher than the mouth, pressure on the bit tends to raise the head. As the horse flexes at the poll, pressure is transferred from the corners of the bars.

jointed

straight

SINGLE TWISTED WIRE JOINTED

Double Bit

Kimberwicke

DOUBLE TWISTED WIRE JOINTED

SUSAN VON BORSTEL

UXETER

HARTWELL PELHAM

JOINTED PELHAM

pivots forward, tightening the curb chain. The degree of force exerted by the curb chain is limited by the relatively short length of the lever.

The Double Bridle. When simultaneous snaffle and curb action is desirable, a double bridle gives the greatest scope. It consists of two separate bits: a narrow snaffle bit, known as a bradoon, and a curb bit. The bits can be operated separately or simultaneously. The double bridle is seen most frequently in the higher levels of dressage, where the curb action helps to achieve collection. It is not uncommon in the hunting field. In fact, it used to be the traditional hunting bit until the Pelham, which requires less finesse, surpassed it in popularity.

How Does the Bit Work?

It is generally said that the bit works on the bars of the horse's mouth, although this is not 100 percent true. First of all, if you look inside your horse's mouth when he is bridled, you will see that his lips fold in over the bars. The bit is actually resting on his lips.

When the horse is relaxed, with his head held more or less horizontally, and when your reins are slack, the bit rests on the lips covering the bars. When you pull on the reins, unless your horse raises his neck and flexes at the poll so that his head approaches the vertical, the bit slides back in his mouth, transferring most of its pressure to the corners of the lips. A horse that has been taught to flex at the poll in response to pressure from the bit holds the bit on the bars of his mouth by dropping his head into a somewhat vertical plane. But most horses do not respond to the bit this way, and so most horses most of the time carry the bit on the bars of the mouth only when the bit is passive.

Many bits also exert some pressure on the poll, just behind the ears. An ordinary snaffle won't, but Pelhams and Kimberwickes do. When you pull on the curb rein of a Pelham, you pull the bottom of the shank not only toward you but upward. You force the top of the shank away and downward. Since the top of the shank is attached to the cheekpiece of the bridle, it pulls the bridle with it as it goes down—hence, pressure on top of the horse's head. The amount of pressure varies according to the length of the shank and the adjustment of the curb chain. Once the chain is tight, the shank movement is arrested.

The shank portion of a Kimberwicke is much shorter than the Pelham, but the cheekpieces, because they are fixed in slots instead of rings, are quicker to follow the shank movement.

You can feel the amount of pressure your bit exerts on the poll by slipping a finger under the top of the bridle as you pull back on the reins with your other hand. It probably won't amount to much.

Mouthpieces. Mouthpieces are made in two basic styles: jointed and straight bar. "Straight" in this instance means "not jointed" but not necessarily straight. Usually a "straight" mouthpiece curves forward slightly and sometimes it has a little hump in the middle, called a "port," to make room for the tongue.

A jointed snaffle is more severe than a straight bar. When you pull back on the reins, the bit bends in the middle, relieving the tongue of all pressure but exerting a sort of nutcracker action on the corners of the mouth. The straight snaffle doesn't have this nutcracker effect; on the other hand, the harder you pull, the harder it presses on the tongue. Some horses relieve the pressure by pulling their tongues up out of the way and even by pushing against the bit with the tongue. A straight bar with a port gives the tongue a little more room.

Generally speaking, the smoother and thicker the mouthpiece, the milder it is. A thin mouthpiece cuts more sharply into the bars when you pull. Young horses with tender mouths are usually started in a thick, smooth snaffle. At the opposite end of the scale, a snaffle with a twisted or wire mouthpiece can be more severe than a long-shanked Pelham.

Most Pelhams have a straight bar mouthpiece, sometimes with a port. Jointed Pelhams are available, but they are less effective, because when you pull back on the curb rein, the mouthpiece folds and the curb chain falls away from the chin. Kimberwickes always have a straight bar mouthpiece with port for this very reason. The leverage on a Kimberwicke is so slight that if the mouthpiece buckled there would be no contact with the curb chain at all.

The severity of a mouthpiece is also affected by the material of which it is made. You can buy a very mild straight bar snaffle made of soft, flexible rubber, or a jointed snaffle covered with soft rubber. Jointed snaffles also come with a copper mouthpiece, which is supposed to encourage the horse to salivate. The saliva acts as a lubricant, cushioning the movements of the bit in the horse's mouth.

Pelhams and Kimberwickes are available with a choice of metal or vulcanite (hard rubber) mouthpieces. The latter is generally milder, not only because it has a little more give to it than metal but because it is a little thicker, too.

Cheekpieces. This is the only visible part of the bit, and so fit, comfort, and effectiveness move over to make a little room for personal taste.

Snaffles come in a variety of styles. The basic snaffle is a mouthpiece with a ring revolving freely at each end. The disadvantage of a plain ring snaffle is that the skin at the corners of the horse's mouth is sometimes pinched between the rings and the mouthpiece. The solution to this is an eggbutt snaffle, which puts a metal casing around the connection between rings and mouthpiece.

The D-ring snaffle is a popular racing bit. It is light and has a relatively small, D-shaped ring. The flat side of the ring is still, however, able to contribute to the steering power of the bit and to prevent it from being pulled through the horse's mouth.

The most effective steering bit is the full-cheek snaffle, which is particularly popular with dressage riders. The "cheeks" are two narrow bars inside the rings, at right angles to the mouthpiece. They prevent the bit from slipping through the mouth and are a significant steering aid on a green horse. The cheek may be fastened with a keeper to the cheekpiece of the bridle in order to hold it vertical.

Pelham cheeks are all designed alike, the only difference being length. The longer the shank, the more severe the curb action.

While most Kimberwickes come in a simple D-ring style, the rings of an Uxeter Kimberwicke have slots for the reins. You can set the position of the reins near the top of the ring or near the bottom in order to vary the amount of leverage.

Quality

For all practical purposes, bits come in two grades: Never-Rust and stainless steel. Stainless steel costs more but never tarnishes. Never-Rust is an alloy that requires polishing to produce a shine, while stainless steel needs only washing. There is an in-between called "Kangaroo Metal." It looks like stainless steel when new and costs almost as much, but it tarnishes like Never-Rust.

All bit styles are available in Never-Rust, but you can't find rubber and vulcanite models in stainless steel. A stainless steel bit usually comes with a stainless steel mouthpiece. If you favor stainless steel, you can make the mouthpiece thicker and softer by wrapping it with latex bandage.

The Right Bit for Your Horse

There are two questions to consider when selecting a bit for your horse:

1) Is it comfortable in his mouth?
2) Does it get the job done?

The first depends on the conformation of his mouth, while the second is a matter of his temperament, his schooling, and the kinds of riding you do.

Here is a test to help you determine whether your horse is comfortable with his bit. (We'll assume that his mouth and teeth are in good condition.) Choose a day when he's relaxed, and put him into a canter in a place where you know he will stop willingly—moving away from the barn, for example. When he's going fairly energetically, pull on the reins. If you give your horse no other clue by voice or shift of weight that you want him to stop, you should manage to get in a firm but not extreme pull before he stops. If he throws his head up or shakes it back and forth, pulls against you and keeps going, or in any way shows that he objects to the moderate pressure on his mouth, you can be pretty sure that his bit is causing discomfort. Now is the time to experiment with different types of mouthpieces and different

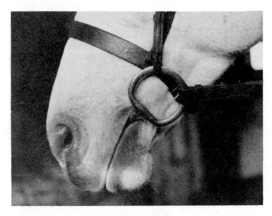

This is a correctly fitting snaffle, adjusted properly to produce two or three wrinkles in the corners of the mouth and, in the case of a gelding, with no danger of interfering with the tushes.

This Pelham is adjusted correctly to hang a little lower than a snaffle (but still safely out of reach of the tushes), so that the curb chain will meet the right spot on the horse's chin.

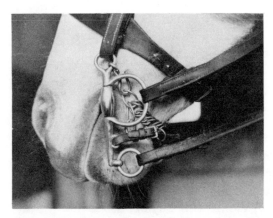

The curb action is most effective when the curb rein is used alone.

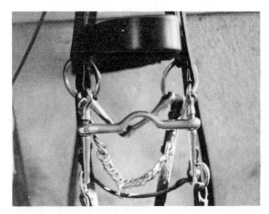

The double bridle consists of a curb bit (foreground) and a slender, jointed snaffle called a bradoon.

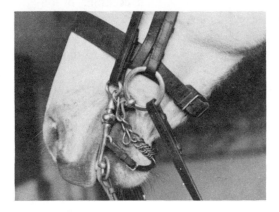

The bradoon should be adjusted to fit snugly, like a snaffle, while the curb hangs lower, like a Pelham.

The advantage of a double bridle is that snaffle and curb action can be effective simultaneously.

materials until you find one to which he responds comfortably—assuming that you're asking him to do something he's willing to do.

There are also times when you have to ask him to do something he doesn't want to do. You've found a mouthpiece with which he's comfortable. Now you have to put it in a bit that is severe enough to be persuasive.

Ideally, the bit operates as a signal. The horse reacts to a cue, not because it hurts but because he has learned its meaning and has been taught to respond correctly. However, even a well-schooled horse sometimes forgets his signals—in the hunting field, for example, or in other exciting circumstances. So there will probably be times when you will need to make your signals more forcefully in order to get them across to your horse.

The trick is to tread the thin line between enough and too much. Severity does not necessarily mean control. Your object is to create just enough discomfort to convince your horse that his best course is to obey. But as discomfort approaches the level of pain, fear is aroused, and the last thing a horse wants to do when he's frightened is to slow down or stop.

The solution is therefore the mildest bit that does the job, combined with a patient schooling program that clarifies the meaning of your signals while diminishing the need for discomfort.

FAVORED BITS OF FAMOUS RIDERS

JANET CARTER, with her husband, former professional steeplechase rider Raymond Carter, operates the Chartwell Stables, in Potomac, Maryland, where training, selling, and promoting show hunters and jumpers is a specialty, along with buying, schooling, and selling field hunters.

I would like every one of my horses to go in a snaffle if at all possible. We always try that first. If you could see our tack room, which contains probably fifty bridles, you would see nearly forty snaffles of various types and descriptions. Along with the traditional eggbutts and full-cheeks, there are copper-mouthed bits, hollow bits, wires, dangles, and Dr. Bristols, to name a few.

On the whole, with our show horses, we have found that by experimenting with these various types of snaffles, we usually come up with something that is effective, even with a real problem horse.

If a horse is getting really strong in an ordinary snaffle, the first thing we generally try is tightening the standing martingale and changing the noseband.

We would then try a narrower bit that will be more severe in the horse's mouth. Some horses respond well to copper-mouthed bits, which seem to make them salivate more and consequently keep them mouthing the bit and make them softer in your hands. Another bit we have used with great success is the Dr. Bristol snaffle, which is jointed in two places, allowing more play as well as leverage and control, without creating a lot of resistance. There is also, of course, the traditional wire snaffle, which, when properly used, is also a very effective deterrent. I would not like to see a rider with bad hands or an explosive temper abuse a horse's mouth by jerking and snatching with this type of bit, but for the sensitive, thinking rider it can be a good option on a strong animal. I also am very apt to keep changing bits around on a horse, going back whenever possible to an ordinary snaffle, particularly for work at home on the flat.

I have never particularly liked using Pelhams or full bridles on show horses unless it is strictly for the sake of tradition, as was customary in the under saddle classes a while ago. This is not to say that if a horse comes to me in a Pelham and goes well in that bit, I won't let well enough alone. I have found some horses that were strong in a snaffle and responded very nicely to a Pelham, particularly the Tom Thumb type, with the very short shank. However, I think that many horses tend to drop too far behind the bit in a Pelham and won't take enough of a contact to maintain a smooth, flowing picture between fences. The worst fault I find with a Pelham is that it causes many horses to get very stiff, with their backs, heads, and necks in the air over their fences, which under any circumstance is undesirable as well as being quite possibly disastrous.

An absolute no-no in our stable is the Kimberwicke. We feel that constant pressure of the curb chain is unavoidable with this bit and has a definitely detrimental effect.

All of this applies to showing and schooling. Fox hunting is a different thing altogether. Rarely have I found a horse, particularly a properly fit Thoroughbred, that didn't pull your arms out after a very short time hunting in a snaffle. Of course, you cannot tolerate this in the hunt field, where you must be in absolute control at all times, mainly for safety (of yourself as well as other members of the field) but also for the enjoyment of the sport. Nobody can have a good time out hunting if his arms, back, and shoulders are aching after the first half hour from doing battle with his horse. Consequently, when it reaches the point where a horse is lying heavy in my hands out there, as far as I'm concerned either a Pelham or a full bridle is just what the doctor ordered.

JIM WOFFORD has been one of the strongest assets of the U. S. Three-Day Olympic Team since 1965, thus carrying on a family tradition, since his father (first president of the U.S.E.T.), two brothers, and a sister-in-law have all been members of Olympic equestrian teams. Jim's first Olympic horse, Kilkenny, was retired at the age of twenty-three at his Fox Covert Farm, near Upperville, Virginia, while he campaigns with his 1984 Olympic hope, Carawich ("Pop").

I start my young horses in snaffles and train most of my made horses at home in one. The Fulmer snaffle has been the most satisfactory for me, because you have the horse's head framed between the cheeks of the bit. I take the keepers off the Fulmer, because this allows the action of the bit to slide up and down the bars of the horse's mouth, rather than acting directly against the bars. Hollow-mouth snaffles seem to move through the horse's mouth too much.

If I encounter difficulties with a horse during his training, I still don't change from a snaffle to a specialty bit, because the problems must be solved by classical means in order to achieve a lasting result. You must not substitute a sharper bit for a fuller technique, or you will prove the old adage of "more bit, less rider." An experienced rider can bring about quick results with a specialty bit, but an inexperienced one will bring about more problems than solutions. I try to leave myself a wide range of options with a horse, and for this reason I try to school the horse at home without martingales or specialty bits. Thus when I place the horse in a competitive situation, I still have artificial aids that I can utilize. If your horse has to be ridden in a double-twisted wire at home, yet is still a raving maniac, then you may be sure that the situation will not improve under competitive circumstances.

When I do change from a snaffle to some other bit, I first try to analyze what the horse is doing and what I am trying to accomplish. The most common reason for changing is that the horse is getting too strong. If this is the case, he will pull in one of three ways: up, out, or down.

A horse that hollows his back and pulls up will sometimes respond to a double bridle or a Pelham, coupled with a running martingale. This is because the lever action of the curb rein with the running martingale on the snaffle brings the horse's head down and in.

If he pulls straight out, many times a Kimberwicke or a Tom Thumb will convince him of the error of his ways. The more direct action of the single rein coupled with the port in a Kimberwicke will make the horse flex at the poll and contract his neck. The Tom Thumb depends more on the action of the curb chain, which also flexes the neck.

A horse that pulls down will respond well to a gag snaffle. The gag snaffle slides back and up in the horse's mouth as the rider applies pressure to the reins, so that the horse learns that in order to escape the pressure of the bit, he must raise his head and neck. People often fail to suit the bit to the problem, such as using a gag snaffle on a ewe-necked horse, or a Kimberwicke on a low-necked puller. By using a gag snaffle on a high-headed horse, all you accomplish is to pull his head up even higher and back over his withers. A Kimberwicke on a low-necked puller makes the horse yield at his poll and in his jaw without raising his head and neck, thus teaching him to pull with his chin against his chest, a common escape device.

Finally, you should remember that all these bits are like a razor blade in a monkey's hand. Solve your problems at home by perfecting your own technique, and not by some esoteric piece of equipment. In the long run you will derive more enjoyment from your sport when you convince your horse, and not compel him.

BUDDY BROWN won the A.H.S.A. Medal Finals on his jumper Sandsablaze, and the pair continued to excel on the U.S.E.T., winning an Individual Silver Medal in the 1975 Pan American Games along with the Team Gold Medal, as well as the Dublin Grand Prix that year. As a leading Grand Prix rider, he has won many important competitions with some of the country's most famous jumpers, including The Cardinal, Idle Dice, and Number One Spy.

I start a young horse off with some kind of rubber snaffle. I use the mildest bit that he'll respect. If he is sensitive and tends to back off the bit, he wears a straight bar rubber snaffle; if he leans, he wears a jointed rubber snaffle, which is slightly more severe because it squeezes against the horse's tongue.

A horse that steers well goes in a D snaffle. But when I have a horse that's hard to turn, I put him in a full-cheek snaffle. I prefer to use the D and full-cheek designs because they are easy on the corners of the horse's lips and won't pull through his mouth the way a ring snaffle does.

Most horses get a bit keener when they start to jump. Most stop paying attention to the fat rubber snaffle, and I have to exchange it for a jointed metal snaffle. I prefer the regular weight, neither too thick nor too thin. I stay away from the thick hollow-mouth bits; if a horse needs a bit that thick, he might as well stay in his rubber snaffle.

I get the most out of my bits by keeping the cavessons snug. A horse can evade the jointed snaffle's squeezing effect by opening his mouth. But why go to a harsher bit if a tighter noseband will do the trick? Some of my jumpers stay quite soft and controllable in a plain snaffle with a figure-eight or a dropped noseband.

If the horse needs a more authoritative bit, I use a twisted snaffle. Most of my open jumpers end up in them. The pressure of the little ridges on the horse's tongue reminds him that I'm boss. It's still a fairly mild bit, but it produces a crisper response.

Occasionally I use wire bits. Idle Dice, for example, goes in a double twisted wire snaffle. That's what he was wearing when he came to me, and who's to argue with success? The twisted wire bit has a very thin metal mouthpiece; the thinness and the small ridges make it a severe bit.

With a Pelham, I can keep a horse in a tighter frame. The Tom Thumb Pelham is less severe than a wire snaffle. The Pelham comes with a straight mouthpiece and a short shank in both rubber and metal versions, and it's less complicated to use than a double bridle, although its effect is similar. When I use the snaffle rein, the bit works on the corners of the horse's mouth; when I pull on the curb rein, the shank comes back and compresses the horse's chin between the curb chain and the mouthpiece of the bit. I could dispense with one rein by using a bit converter, but I prefer to use two reins so that I can apply the snaffle and curb effects separately. I find the rubber mouthpiece especially useful for long, galloping jumper courses, where the horse tends to get strung out. On the other hand, I never use a Pelham when I'm riding a twisting course in a small ring, because I find it difficult to turn quickly.

I've experimented with hackamores, mostly on the occasional crazy. The curb hackamore has shanks and a curb chain but no mouthpiece. When you pull back on the reins, the nosepiece presses on the horse's nose and the chain presses on his chin. Although it's easy enough to stop a horse in a hackamore, you certainly can't keep him in any sort of frame. And unless he neck-reins, you can't turn him, either.

I've had more success with a gag snaffle, although I use it mostly as a schooling device. It works well on a horse that's heavy on his forehand. The cheekpieces run down through the rings of the bit and back to the reins. When you pull, the bit rises and the horse feels pressure both on his poll and at the corners of his mouth. If he leans on the bit, the gag makes him uncomfortable; he soon learns to rock back on his haunches. Since it's hard to turn a horse with the gag alone, I like to attach an extra set of reins directly to the bit rings and use both the gag and the regular snaffle effect.

Some horses are real bit wizards. Whatever you put on them, they learn how to evade. One of my horses, A Little Bit, was sort of heavy and liked to lean. I tried a number of bits with only temporary success. Finally I put him in a roller-mouth bit. He played with the rollers on the mouthpiece and I thought I had the problem solved, until one day I realized that he had learned to lean on the cheekpieces.

JUDY RICHTER, A.H.S.A. Horsewoman of the Year in 1974, runs Coker Farm, a successful training and teaching stable in Bedford, New York, which is famous for its horses as well as for its riders. She is a sister of Carol Hofmann Thompson, former U.S.E.T. Team member, and a daughter of Philip Hofmann, generous patron of the equestrian sports and a renowned coaching enthusiast.

Most of my horses, whether they are equitation mounts, hunters, or jumpers, go in fairly mild bits.

For schooling I prefer a plain metal jointed snaffle with a loose ring. A loose-ring bit has more play; it encourages the horse to mouth and to relax his jaw. I use a thick mouthpiece for a horse that has a soft mouth, and a thinner mouthpiece for a horse that is less responsive.

If the horse is a little strong, I school him with a dropped noseband so that he can't evade the bit. Since a hunter can't wear a drop in the show ring, I'll show him in a bit with a little more authority, such as a full-cheek twisted snaffle. The twist's edge against his tongue and the corners of his mouth keeps the horse more in hand; and with his head framed between the cheekpieces, he's easier to turn.

When I put a really strong horse in a must-stop situation such as a Hunter Pace, I send him out wearing a Pelham or a double wire snaffle. Finesse is not the issue. I have to use whatever works. The double wire is actually less severe than the single wire, because it distributes the pressure over two points, rather than one. The double wire is considerably harsher than the twisted mouth snaffle, though, because the wire is thinner and has many more ridges. The double wire is a bit you have to use with care. In the wrong hands, it can cut up the corners of the horse's mouth.

If a show horse gets really strong, I'll go to a twisted wire or a jointed Pelham. The Pelham is less severe than the twisted wire. The mouthpiece is thicker, and it's smooth, rather than ridged, but the joint adds a squeezing effect on the tongue to the leverage of the curb.

I don't like to ride a horse in a Pelham all the time. A straight bar Pelham, especially, deadens the horse's mouth and he ends up lying in the rider's hands. But if I school in the snaffle and save the Pelham for showing, I minimize the Pelham's bad effects.

The Kimberwicke has all of the disadvantages and none of the advantages of the Pelham. When you pull on the reins of a Pelham, the shanks move back, pivot the bit in the horse's mouth, and press the curb chain into his lower jaw. This lever action encourages the horse to soften his jaw and bend at the poll. Since a Kimberwicke has no shank, the bit does not pivot and the curb chain does not do its job. The rider pulls, the bit deadens the horse's mouth, and the horse pulls back.

Although I prefer to use snaffles and the occasional Pelham, I've had good luck with both gags and hackamores in special circumstances. The horse that pulls like a train often goes well in a gag. When the rider pulls, the gag puts pressure on the horse's poll as well as on the corners of his mouth. The more the horse pulls, the more pressure he feels on his poll. The horse usually provides his own solution: He stops pulling and the pressure eases.

When a horse can't wear a bit for some reason—say he has a sore mouth from losing a tooth—I've used a hackamore with good results. The bosal type of hackamore, which works primarily on the horse's nose, is quite mild. I've had more experience with the curb hackamore, which works on the nose and jaw. Adjusted loosely, it is as mild as a thick snaffle; adjusted tightly, it is as severe as a wire bit. Although it's pretty hard to turn a horse with a curb hackamore, it's easy enough to stop him.

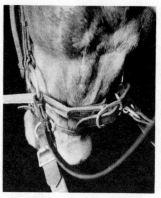

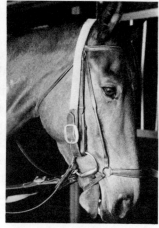

Longeing cavesson equipped with bradoon strap and snaffle bit to accommodate side reins.

Without a cavesson, the longe line passes under the chin . . .

. . . or over the poll.

To keep the reins out of the way, make a single knot . . .

. . . slip it over a tuft of mane, and pull it tight.

Or twist the reins and slip them over your horse's head.

To keep the stirrups from flapping, run them up, thread the leathers from front to back . . .

. . . then back to front and through the loop.

Finally around to the rear and through the loop again.

Dressed for longeing.

TACKING UP

Schooling at Home

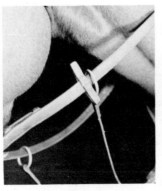

Checking the running martingale.

Position of the rein stops.

A gag snaffle with an extra pair of reins added.

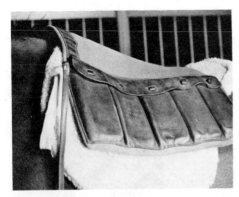

The front of the weight pad rests just behind the peak of the withers.

Turn the bell boots inside out and work the toe first.

Hampa boots in front let the horse feel the rails; ankle boots behind.

The jumper ready for action.

Show Jumping

First the polo breast-
plate, looping around
one billet only . . .

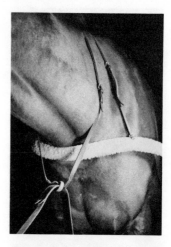

. . . then the martingale.

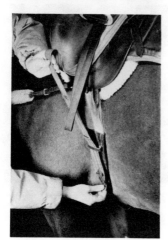

The overgirth slips
through loops on the
girth . . .

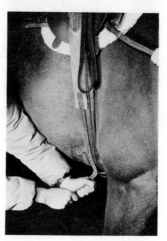

. . . and fastens on the
offside.

Ready for cross-country.

Combined Training

  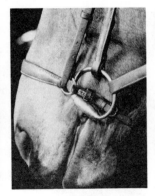 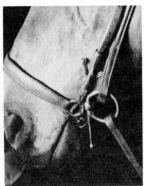

A dropped noseband properly adjusted.

Wrong.

Wrong.

The nose strap is too long.

 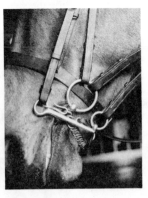 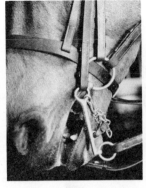 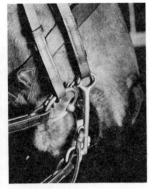

The double bridle correctly worn.

The curb chain is too loose; the bit "falls through."

The curb chain is too tight; the bit shank locks at less than 45 degrees.

The curb chain is out of place.

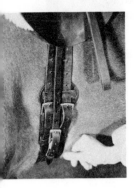

The short girth properly centered and the saddle flap buckled down.

The dressage horse, attired.

Dressage

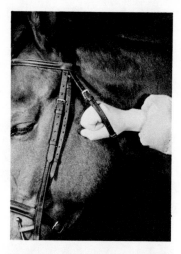

One fist under the throatlatch.

A finger under the noseband.

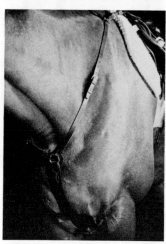

The ring of the breast-plate falls at the base of the neck.

Checking the martin-gale strap.

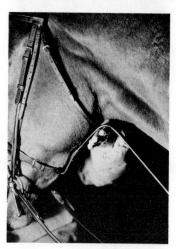

Correct show hunter attire.

Hunting

Chapter 3

FEEDING

PASTURE PSYCHOLOGY

Making the most of your pasture is basically a matter of understanding the simple life plan of the grass plant and turning it to your advantage.

Pasture grass, on the scale of living things, ranks low in its ability to adapt its life-style to unfavorable conditions. Each variety of grass is programmed to perform a simple function on a timetable, and given the proper conditions of soil, climate, and pasture management, all goes smoothly. But if there exists a flaw somewhere in its environment, the little grass plant doesn't roll with the punches. If the mower is broken, for example, it doesn't say, "Oh, well, I'll postpone going to seed for a week or two." It doggedly pursues its life plan, and if conditions aren't right, it surrenders to the consequences.

Since the life plan is simple and the plant can be depended upon to adhere faithfully to it, the pasture owner knows exactly where he stands. By meeting a few simple demands, he can put the grass plant's determined nature to work for him; or, with equal effort but less attention, he can pit himself in a struggle against a stubborn plant-creature that evidently functions on the premise that it has less to lose than he.

Grass life accepts input from three sources: climate, soil content, and management procedures such as mowing, harrowing, and pasture rotation. These three are grass language, and if you want to wheedle maximum performance from your grass, you have to use language your grass understands.

Climate

You can't manipulate your climate, but what you can do, if you're starting from scratch, is to plant a kind of grass that does well in your climate.

For example, *blue grass* is wonderfully suited to horses. It's nutritious, they love it, and it forms a good, durable sod underfoot. But blue grass becomes unproductive when the weather turns hot and dry. An ideal pasture, where the spring is cool and wet but the summer hot, combines blue grass for spring and fall production with a plant that does well in the summer.

Timothy will help stretch the grazing season into summer. It's nutritious and palatable, but not durable. It requires reseeding every few years.

Orchard grass is nutritious, palatable, and has a deep root system that withstands dry weather well. But instead of forming a smooth, tough sod, it grows in clumps. Unless your orchard grass is very closely seeded, your horses will tend to dig it up when the ground is wet.

Fescue, like orchard grass, has a deep root system, which helps it along through dry weather. It's a very productive growth, but horses don't relish it as they do blue grass and seem not to do well on it. According to Dr. Robert C. Buckner, professor of agronomy at the University of Kentucky and research agronomist for the U. S. Department of Agriculture, some grasses may have toxic qualities. "We don't really understand why animals perform better on blue grass than fescue," he says, "except that fescue contains an alkaloid that may inhibit digestibility." Although Kentucky is the "Blue Grass State," blue grass flourishes in only about ten counties, in which the soil is rich in phosphorus. Fescue grows well elsewhere. Dr. Buckner has succeeded in developing a variety of fescue with a low alkaloid content.

For almost every climate, there is a grass that will do well. The problems are palatability and nutrition. Given no alternative, a horse will learn to forage almost any green plant, but the owner must be aware of the nutritional content of his horse's grazing so that he can supplement the diet appropriately.

Soil Nutrition

If you have the climate and reasonably appropriate drainage, you can grow the grass of your choice simply by supplementing soil minerals. In addition to water, grass pulls nitrogen out of the soil, along with four major minerals: calcium, magnesium, phosphorus, and potassium. A shortage of any one ingredient becomes the limiting factor in grass production. An abundance of water, nitrogen, calcium, magnesium, and phosphorus is no abundance at all if potassium is lacking. Pasture grass performs only as well as its weakest component permits. If an important mineral is in short supply, the result is twofold: less grass, and grass that is deficient in that mineral. Calcium and phosphorus deficiencies are especially significant in horse pasture grass, since these are the two major bone-building ingredients.

Joe Alexander, manager of Mrs. Peggy Augustus' Keswick Stables, which annually sells high-priced youngsters at the Saratoga Yearling Sales, stresses the importance of balanced soil minerals: "In Virginia, the soil is very low

Identifying your pasture

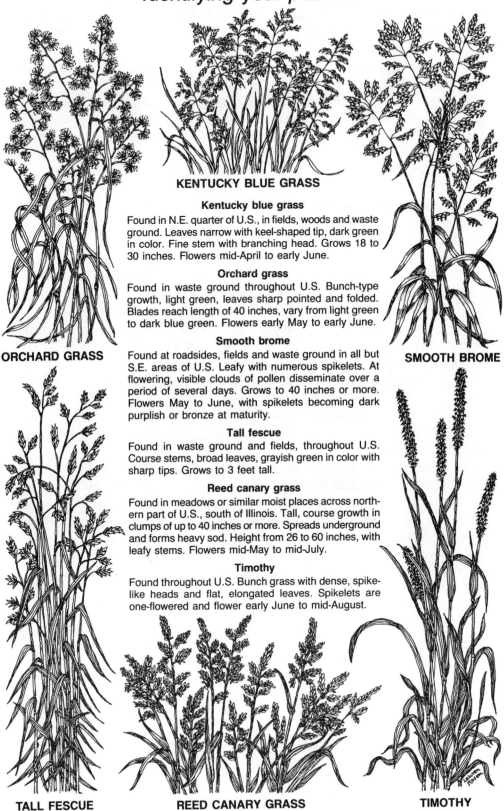

KENTUCKY BLUE GRASS

ORCHARD GRASS

SMOOTH BROME

Kentucky blue grass
Found in N.E. quarter of U.S., in fields, woods and waste ground. Leaves narrow with keel-shaped tip, dark green in color. Fine stem with branching head. Grows 18 to 30 inches. Flowers mid-April to early June.

Orchard grass
Found in waste ground throughout U.S. Bunch-type growth, light green, leaves sharp pointed and folded. Blades reach length of 40 inches, vary from light green to dark blue green. Flowers early May to early June.

Smooth brome
Found at roadsides, fields and waste ground in all but S.E. areas of U.S. Leafy with numerous spikelets. At flowering, visible clouds of pollen disseminate over a period of several days. Grows to 40 inches or more. Flowers May to June, with spikelets becoming dark purplish or bronze at maturity.

Tall fescue
Found in waste ground and fields, throughout U.S. Course stems, broad leaves, grayish green in color with sharp tips. Grows to 3 feet tall.

Reed canary grass
Found in meadows or similar moist places across northern part of U.S., south of Illinois. Tall, course growth in clumps of up to 40 inches or more. Spreads underground and forms heavy sod. Height from 26 to 60 inches, with leafy stems. Flowers mid-May to mid-July.

Timothy
Found throughout U.S. Bunch grass with dense, spike-like heads and flat, elongated leaves. Spikelets are one-flowered and flower early June to mid-August.

TALL FESCUE

REED CANARY GRASS

TIMOTHY

in *phosphorus*. We used to add a mineral supplement to the horses' feed, but it didn't amount to a thing. For the last three or four years we've been soil-testing spring and fall and putting the phosphorus right on the pastures. Blood phosphorus levels are up and it seems to me that we have bigger bone on the horses."

Nitrogen is the dynamic ingredient, the growth pusher. The more nitrogen applied to the soil (within usable limits), the more grass production, provided all other essential ingredients are present. However, the more growth you coax out of your grass, the more minerals will be depleted from the soil. And so nitrogen applications must be coordinated with mineral applications.

Fortunately, *fertilizer* formulas also contain phosphorus and potassium. One application provides all three ingredients in the ratio of your choice. For example, 10–20–10 fertilizer contains 10 percent nitrogen, 20 percent phosphorus, and 10 percent potassium (potash). One hundred pounds of 10–20–10 supplies ten pounds of nitrogen, twenty pounds of phosphorus, and ten pounds of potassium. You would accomplish the same thing with two hundred pounds of 5–10–5, but the more concentrated products are usually more economical. Not only do the concentrations vary, but the ratio of ingredients varies too. If you have plenty of grazing in relation to the number of horses on pasture, but low soil mineral content, 0–20–20 will raise the phosphorus and potassium levels of your soil and probably increase production, too, by providing a proper mineral balance.

Calcium is applied separately in the form of limestone, and where magnesium is deficient, a *magnesium limestone* supplies both nutrients in one application.

To bring your pasture soil up to maximum productivity, have it tested. Most states provide a *testing* service, usually performed by a state-funded university laboratory. Some fertilizer manufacturers perform soil testing in their own laboratories. You can either have the commercial firm through which you plan to purchase fertilizer take soil samples and arrange for testing, or you can do it yourself using a kit purchased for a few dollars from your county agricultural extension agent. Each pasture requires a separate kit.

The important thing is to provide a representative sample for testing. If you do it yourself, make a small hole with a sharp shovel. When the hole is big enough to accommodate the shovel to a depth of six inches, take a thin slice of earth from one side the full depth of the hole. Depending on the size of the pasture, take ten to twenty samples from scattered spots to give an average picture of the full range of conditions. Use a clean bucket for each pasture. Put in all your samples, mix them thoroughly, and from that mixture fill the kit bag.

When the report comes back (you may have to wait two or three weeks during the peak spring planting season), it will include mineral analyses, the pH factor (which indicates the need for limestone), and a specific recommendation for liming and fertilizing as needed.

This recommendation is designed to do two things: to bring any deficiencies up to requirements, and to provide enough soil nutrients for one season's output. You should retest every three to five years, and in intervening years nourish each season's grass crop with an application of five hundred pounds of 10–10–10 to the acre. Every other year, spread one ton of lime per acre.

You can apply *lime* at any time of the year except when frozen ground prevents penetration. Lime works slowly and over a long period. Its effectiveness has approximately a one-year half-life. In other words, half of the benefits of an application are experienced in the first year, one quarter in the second year, one eighth in the third year, and so forth. Do not apply more than two tons to the acre in any one application. Any more is likely to wash away and go to waste. If tests show that your soil is very low in calcium, continue to apply two tons per acre annually until you meet the basic requirements before switching to the maintenance recommendation of one ton every other year.

Fertilizer acts more promptly than lime. Given necessary moisture, you should see growth stimulated within a week or two.

Time your applications to maximize the growth-boosting power of the *nitrogen*. Apply either in early spring, before the start of the growing season, or, if your pastures tend to produce an abundance of grass early but run short later in the summer, hold off your fertilizer application until late spring. For good fall grazing, come back with fifty pounds of nitrogen to the acre toward the end of summer.

You should not turn horses out onto freshly limed and fertilized pastures. Fertilizers contain some toxic elements, and although limestone is fed to horses in small quantities as a mineral supplement, limestone with every mouthful of grass is too much of a good thing. Time your applications for a dry day but at a time of year when rain is frequent. A good rain will soak the chemicals into the ground and your pastures will be ready for use. But if the grass is wet when the chemicals go on, dust particles will stick to blades of grass, burning the leaves and delaying absorption. Ideally, it will rain soon after your application, soaking chemicals into the ground and producing a day or two of fresh, clean growth before you turn your horses out again. But if rain fails to materialize, you should keep horses off fertilized fields for at least a week in order to minimize the risk of nitrate poisoning. You can schedule liming and fertilizing consecutively, so as to tie up pastures only once. But if you do, avoid urea and ammonia-type fertilizers, which tend to release their nitrogen to the air when brought in direct contact with lime.

Management Practices

The timing of your *mowing* makes all the difference in the productivity of your pasture. The grass plant seems to be programmed toward one objective: reproduction. It lives to produce seed, and once that function is performed, it shuts down productivity. After the leaves are up in the spring, you will see a tightly rolled cluster of seeds begin to emerge from a leaf sheath. This is the *boot stage*. The seed head emerges from the sheath on a lengthening stem, flowers, and goes to seed. From the time of the boot stage, leaf production slows and the plant becomes stemmy, fibrous, and unpalatable, and loses its nutritional value.

The mare is not the only organism whose reproductive cycle awakens in response to lengthening daylight hours. Every variety of grass marches to a time schedule of its own.

For blue grass, fourteen hours of daylight is the turning point. Through the spring, as the days lengthen, the plant is programmed to work toward seed production. If you mow at any time before fourteen hours of daylight, the plant simply renews its efforts. From the time the days reach fourteen hours or longer, the plant automatically switches to a new program. Any plant mowed past its turning point (each variety having its own timetable), calls off seed production and remains in the leaf-producing stage throughout the remainder of the growing season. This is the objective to aim for. Grass remains nutritious and palatable, and you have only to mow if you wish to control leafy growth—or weeds.

Ideally, you should time your mowing to coincide with the boot stage, the moment at which the seed head begins to emerge from the leaf sheath. You mow once, you preserve the plant in its vegetative state, and yet you permit the scattering of some seed, which perpetuates the pasture. In practice, this is difficult to accomplish. Most pastures consist of two or more varieties of grass, which head out at differing times. And if you have a large pasture, or if you have bad weather, you may not be able to time your mowing as precisely as you'd like. The alternative is to mow early in order to postpone the heading out of early varieties, and then repeat once or twice more, as necessary, preventing any heading out until the turning point for all varieties has come and gone.

In old pasture, where *weeds* threaten to become a problem, you will have to continue mowing throughout the growing season to prevent weeds from going to seed and reproducing themselves. Weeds taken as a group have a survival edge over grass. While your pasture may contain two or three varieties of grass, the variety of weeds is infinite, with the collective ability to survive under a wide range of conditions. While your grass all heads out in the spring, your weeds take turns heading out all summer long.

Harrowing helps too. A chain harrow dragged over a field works up matted grass from the previous year's mowing and helps aerate the soil. And it converts accumulated manure from an undesirable to a useful commodity.

Manure, rich in nitrogen, is a natural fertilizer. Where it falls, it encourages lush, green growth. But unfortunately, if left concentrated in spots it seems to taint the grass in a way that makes it unpalatable to horses. It is frustrating for the owner of limited grazing to see areas of pasture eaten to the ground while lush green grass stands all around. Harrowing spreads manure so as to distribute its fertilizing benefit while apparently eliminating the palatability problem. At the same time, it fills an important parasite-control function by exposing eggs to air and sunlight.

Pasture rotation is admittedly a luxury that few farms can afford. Like a stable with an empty stall, it's a rare farm that has an empty pasture. Yet, heavily grazed pasture needs a chance to bounce back undisturbed. Agronomists suggest that pasture be subdivided into grazing units in order to maximize productivity. A five-acre field will produce more forage in a season if fenced into five one-acre plots that are grazed down in turn, than if steadily grazed as a whole by the same number of horses. Fencing is expensive and you may not care to subdivide to that extent. But at least fencing is a variable, whereas available acreage is fixed. The principle to keep in mind, if you would like to maximize your pasturage, is to subdivide into the smallest practical units and graze in rotation.

For better or for worse, grass marches on, the dogged little plants doing what they have to do. You can't alter grass behavior the way you can train a horse, but with a little attention you can understand it and turn it to your advantage. If you meet and recognize its life-style, it will flourish for you. If not, it will go down just as cheerfully, taking your most valuable feed resource with it.

IN OR OUT FOR FITNESS?

The Question: In order to keep a horse fit and conditioned, should he be kept stalled most of the time, or turned out to pasture? Does the type of pasture make a difference? The sport I have in mind is Eventing at the training level.

The answer, from MARY BACON, a jockey who is also a riding instructor, dressage judge, and Combined Training competitor:

Keep him stabled. A few hours on pasture is fine for mental health, but all-day grazing will make him fat and soft.

Mixed grass is best. Alfalfa or clover pasture will produce a butterball or, worse still, a case of founder. Keep a check on your horse's girth and his respiration when at work. If he shows signs of a big belly or if he's huffing and puffing, cut back on the amount of turn-out time.

A Thoroughbred with a typical Thoroughbred temperament keeps himself fit. Two or three hours of pasture a day will help relax him and keep him in a happy frame of mind. A half-bred turned out on lush growth for the same amount of time will probably get too fat. Half-breds need more work, more grain, and less grass to keep them fit and hard. Some horses fret when they're out. They walk the fence and get themselves too fit. If you have a horse like this, you should turn him out only very briefly, or you won't be able to keep any weight on him.

Many horses, in fact, have this problem in the summer. Flies and heat drive them to distraction. They do very poorly turned out in the hot part of the day.

The Nutrients in One Pound of Feed

	Lbs. Digestible Protein per lb.	Mega-calories per lb.	Lbs. Calcium per lb.	Lbs. Phosphorus per lb.
HAY				
Alfalfa				
Early bloom	.134	1.10	.017	.003
Mid bloom	.116	1.04	.015	.003
Late bloom	.101	.98	.013	.002
Clover				
Crimson	.131	.98	.014	.002
Red	.100	.98	.015	.003
Lespedeza	.093	.94	.012	.003
Timothy				
Pre-seed	.072	1.00	.005	.003
Head	.048	.90	.004	.002
Brome	.050	1.08	.003	.002
Orchard grass	.061	.94	.004	.003
Coastal				
Bermuda	.042	.90	.004	.002
GRAIN				
Oats	.105	1.51	.0007	.0037
Corn	.085	1.75	.0005	.0060
Barley	.114	1.63	.0005	.0037

Daily Nutritional Requirements for Horses

HORSE	Digestible Protein lbs.	Mega-calories (Digestible Energy)	Calcium lbs.	Phosphorus lbs.
Mare, Last 90 days of pregnancy	.86	18.36	.075	.05
Lactating Mare	1.85	28.27	.110	.07
Weanling (6 mos.)	1.14	15.60	.075	.06
Yearling	.99	16.81	.068	.05
Adult Maintenance	.64	16.39	.050	.03
Horse in Light Work (1 hour slow trotting some cantering)	.76	18.92	.057	.038
Horse in Medium Work (1 hour fast trotting, cantering, some jumping)	.92	22.63	.069	.046
Horse in Intense Work (1 hour cantering, galloping, jumping)	1.12	27.94	.084	.050

Balancing Your Horse's Diet
Sample Chart

	Digestible Protein	Digestible energy	Calcium	Phosphorus
1. Your horse's requirements *(medium work)*	.92 lbs.	22.63 mcal.	.069 lbs.	.046 lbs.
2. Nutritional composition per pound of test hay *(mid-bloom alfalfa)*	.116 lbs.	1.04 mcal.	.015 lbs.	.003 lbs.
3. Your horse eats 15 pounds, which provide how much of each nutrient?	1.74 lbs.	15.6 mcal.	.225 lbs.	.045 lbs.
4. Leaving a nutrient deficit of	– lbs.	7.03 mcal.	– lbs.	.001 lbs.

If you're figuring on grass hay and you're short on protein, switch to a legume.
If you're figuring on a legume, and you're short on protein, supplement with oats, barley, or a high protein commercial mix.
If you're short on energy, supplement with corn.
If you're short on calcium, you must be feeding a grass hay. Cut back the amount and supplement with a legume.
If you're short on phosphorus, supplement with corn.

	Digestible Protein	Digestible energy	Calcium	Phosphorus
5. Nutritional composition per pound of the supplemental feed CORN (only for deficient nutrients)	____ lbs.	1.75 mcal.	____ lbs.	.006 lbs.
6. Number of pounds required to satisfy deficit (line 4 divided by line 5)	____ lbs.	4 mcal.	____ lbs.	.16 lbs.

HOW TO BUY HAY

The quality of the hay you give your horse is as important, if not more so, than the quantity.

It takes only a little experience to be able to evaluate hay quality and maturity (the best stage of maturity corresponding roughly to mid bloom), if you know what to look for. Here is a checklist you should run through mentally every time you go hay shopping.

When was the hay cut and baled? Unless you are an experienced judge of hay or have an ironclad money-back guarantee in your agreement, don't buy hay that has been baled for less than six weeks. Hay must cure, and until this process is completed, there is always the possibility of its becoming moldy.

Where is it stored? If you're shown a pile of bales stacked on an earth or cement floor or piled up against the stone wall of a barn, specify that you want inside bales only. Hay stored in contact with damp surfaces becomes moldy.

Color. Hay should be green, the brighter the better. Don't worry if the outside of the mow is faded, but if the exterior of bales extracted from the mow are faded too, the hay may have overdried in the field or been rained on or simply cut at an advanced stage of maturity. It has lost some of its nutritional value.

Purity. Mixed hay is very nice feed as long as the price is right. But if you're paying for alfalfa, you shouldn't see a high proportion of grass plants. No harm in a few weeds, but keep in mind when you're discussing price that 10 percent weeds means 10 percent less nutritional value. Clumps of weeds tend to hold moisture and form pockets of mold during curing in otherwise well-made hay.

Texture. The more leaves you see in proportion to stem, the more nutritious is the hay. Leaves and blades contain most of the nutrients. And as the hay matures past its peak in the field, the stems become coarse, woody, and unpalatable. Feeding value plummets and percentage of waste rises.

Flowers and seeds. The primary role of the hay plant is as a seed producer. Once the survival of the species is assured, the parent plant goes downhill fast—hence the expression "going to seed."

Grass hay produces its seed in heads, legumes in flowers. If the seeds come free when you rub a seed head between your fingers, the hay has peaked in nutritional value and is on its way down. Legume hay loses its punch shortly after it begins to flower. The presence of a few flowers in a bale is no cause for concern, but past the mid-bloom stage (when more than half of the plants are in flower), the nutritional quality is declining significantly. Grass hay heads out only before first cutting. To judge the maturity of subsequent cuttings, you have to go by stemminess alone.

Weight. Pick up a bale. Is it heavier than you expected it to be? It might be that it's baled extra tightly, which is fine, or it might be heavy with moisture, which may culture mold. If you are surprised by its lightness, it may have been loosely baled. That's not necessarily bad unless you're buying by the bale. It means that the farmer baled the hay while it was a little damp, perhaps rain was threatening, and he packed it rather loosely in order to let it dry. As long as it has dried without molding, that's fine.

If your criteria have been met so far, it is time to open a bale.

Critical mold test. All other shortcomings you have found to this point you can live with if the price is right. But mold, even a trace of it, is grounds for immediate rejection.

Mold dissipates quickly when exposed to the air, so you must work quickly with a freshly opened bale. The center sections are the slowest to dry and so the likeliest to mold.

Take a flake from the center and look closely. Is the color clear and pure, or do you detect a faint gray film? Hold it to the light and pull it apart. Does the dust rise in clouds? It might be mold. Any dust is an undesirable irritant to your horse's respiratory tract. But you can live with ordinary field dust if you must, by wetting your horse's hay.

You can't tell mold from dust by sight. In fact, you can't always see mold. The one surefire detection method is scent. Mold has a distinctive odor. Once you know it, you'll never miss it. Good hay smells sweet. Ordinary hay sometimes has no smell at all. But moldy hay has an unpleasant acrid odor, like something that came out of a factory, rather than a field.

While other flaws in your hay can be offset by supplementary feeding, mold is a fatal flaw. Some molds (and there's no way to distinguish one from another) are toxic, causing colic and even death.

WHEN THINGS GO WRONG WITH HAY

There are good years and bad years for hay crops. In a bad year, such as an excessively rainy one, you will either have to pay more, for good-quality hay, or settle for a lesser quality—in other words, make a compromise. These are some of the things that go wrong with hay, and some guidelines to help you decide where you can afford to give a little and where you'd better stand firm.

Stemmy. The longer a crop of hay grows in the field, the coarser and woodier the plant stems become. The older the plant and, in legume hay, the higher the proportion of stem to leaf, the lower the food value.

Stemmy hay looks coarse. In timothy bales, the heads are long. In legume, the proportion of stem to leaf is high. You see a lot of stemmy hay. Some farmers deliberately let it grow a little beyond its peak because the yield is greater. Some years, farmers are forced to let it grow because of rain.

A little stemminess is not the worst thing that can happen to hay. Just be aware that the nutritional value drops proportionately.

Faded. Bright green hay is the ideal, but color isn't necessarily a measure of quality. Green signifies the presence of carotene, a source of vitamin A. Since horses exposed to sunlight can manufacture their own vitamin A, the absence of carotene does not make or break hay quality. It depends on how the color was lost.

If only one or two sides of the bale are faded, you can be pretty sure that the bale was stacked on the outside of the mow or the load where the light hit it. As long as it's green on the inside, a little bleaching at the edge is insignificant. If, when you open the bale, you find it uniformly faded throughout, it was probably overdried. The leaves of a legume crumble and turn to powder during raking and baling. Some nutritional value is left in the field. Still, overdried is better than underdried.

But when fading is in streaks or layers in the bale, you should beware. The hay was probably rained on in the field—not soaked, but wet on the surface of the raked rows. The farmer gave it a little extra drying time in the field and baled it anyway, feeling that it would still cure properly. At best, the effect of rain and sun have leached out some of the nutrients. At worst, the hay was too damp for baling and is now moldy.

Weedy. This is a relative term. If you're talking about a crop of alfalfa, clover, or timothy, orchard grass is technically a weed. However, a part-grass mixture can be a very nice hay, as long as you're aware that the grass content lowers the average feed value of the hay somewhat.

On the other hand, broadleaf weeds such as thistles spell trouble. Not only are they low in nutritional value and often unpalatable, but they hold water, too. In the field they dry more slowly than the hay. The farmer has to either overdry the hay or bale it while the weeds are still damp. He usually chooses the latter course, with the result that you'll find moldy sections where weeds are clumped together in the bale. They're easy to spot, obviously different in consistency from the rest of the bale—dark, matted sections, with the characteristic odor of mold. They're also easy enough to eliminate from the feed ration, as long as the person who does the feeding knows what to look for and as long as they're not too numerous. But weeds are pure waste and potentially dangerous, so hay with a high proportion of them should be avoided.

Dusty. Dusty hay is not necessarily moldy. It may simply be dirty from one cause or another. Say the crop is growing beside a dirt road where dust rises in dry weather. Another common cause of dusty legume hay is over-drying. The leaves become brittle and turn to powder. Clover hay is especially susceptible, and in fact, clover hay that is not at all dusty is the exception, rather than the rule.

Dusty hay is undesirable. A horse that inhales a lungful of dust every time he puts his nose in his hay is a candidate for respiratory troubles and possibly heaves. And for a horse that already has respiratory problems, dusty hay can make matters much worse.

You have to open a bale to determine whether or not it's dusty. Pull apart a flake in the light, and the dust will rise. Take a whiff and, if it makes you cough, you can imagine what a steady diet of it can do to a horse.

Avoid dusty hay if you can. But if you're stuck with it, wetting it down before feeding may help to limit the ill effect of it.

Moldy. Moldy hay is invariably dusty. What is worse is that some kinds of mold are toxic, even fatal. Compromise, if you must, in other respects, but never buy moldy hay. If you discover moldy bales or sections, throw them away.

You almost always have to open a bale to detect mold. There are many varieties, some light, some dark, some visible, some invisible, depending on the color of the hay itself. To check for mold, go right to the center of the bale, which is always the last to dry. Any discoloration other than fading is probably mold. A bale or section that is unusually heavy is very likely moldy. Dust may be mold, but not always. The only sure test for mold is smell.

Leafy hay is much more likely to mold than grass or timothy, because its leaves hold water and cure more slowly. Faded grass and old timothy may not look very appetizing, but the leafiest deep green bale of alfalfa is the prime target of mold, so beware.

The hay cost situation is increasingly bad, and it's unlikely ever to get a lot better. So there's every reason to buy your hay wisely, especially when you have to compromise.

There's also a wonderful opportunity for some enterprising individual to invent a technique for spinning out synthetic protein in long green strands suitable for baling, nourishing, palatable, and fun to chew.

WHERE TO BUY HAY

Direct Marketing. The buyer purchases hay directly from the grower, who is usually a nearby farmer. This is not always satisfactory, because when the grower has livestock of his own, he may keep the best hay for his own use and sell the poorest.

Contract Arrangements. A large hay buyer contracts to buy hay from the grower either directly or through a custom harvester. Chemical analysis of nutritional values will usually be used to determine the price.

Hay Dealer or Broker. The true dealer makes a profession of hay and buys wherever the values are best. He generally has facilities for storage, where the customer can examine the hay and purchase it. The trucker, as distinguished from the dealer, often sells hay as a sideline. Rather than buying it himself and reselling it, he may take it on consignment, sell it to the buyer on behalf of the grower, and take a percentage. The buyer sees the hay for the first time when the trucker delivers it to him.

Public Auctions. The buyer conducts his own transaction and has an opportunity to examine what he's getting, although he may be deceived if he relies solely on the appearance of the outside bales. There is no guarantee of price until the hammer falls, and the auction takes a cut based on weight, not price.

Farmer Cooperative Associations. Producers and/or consumers may form a group to encourage reliability and price stability in a hay market. It is effective in proportion to the strength of its leadership.

FALSE FEARS ABOUT FEEDING HAY

The idea of encouraging a horse to fill up on hay may be contrary to life-long beliefs of some horse owners. But almost without exception, it is good feeding practice. Many long-standing fears about hay feeding are without foundation. For example:

Ponies founder on alfalfa. Ponies shouldn't be fed alfalfa anyway. Besides, it is throwing money down the drain to feed alfalfa to a pony or horse that is easy to keep. A pony will do fine on grass hay, far better than on grain. He may not need as much as he'll eat, but a steady supply will entertain him, prevent stall vices and fence chewing, and do him no harm.

A horse that eats a lot of hay won't eat his grain. The reasoning is backwards. If a horse is willing to eat a lot of hay, you won't have to feed much grain, if any. A high-hay, low-grain diet is more healthful for your horse and cheaper for you.

A lot of hay gives a horse a "hay belly." Horses need to have a generous supply of food in their bellies at all times in order to keep the digestive bacteria alive and well. One of the nice things about hay is that it provides an all-day supply of food, while the grain meal is a once-and-done affair, allowing bacteria to die off, thus lowering digestive efficiency. The horses that acquire hay bellies are those that do nothing but stand around all day and eat. Their bellies are full and their muscles slack. If you want your horse to have a streamlined silhouette, put him to work. His muscles will tighten, his shape will improve, and if you actually get him pretty fit, he won't want a lot of hay. Horses at the racetrack have hay nets in front of them all day long and they don't have hay bellies.

Alfalfa is too rich for horses. It's true that the legume hays are more concentrated in nutrients than the grass hays. But as long as you're feeding your horse the nutrients he needs, it is no more dangerous to feed them in alfalfa form than in grass-hay form or in grain form. And, naturally, you want to avoid feeding him nutrients he doesn't need in any form.

HOW TO FEED HAY:
ON THE GROUND OR IN A RACK OR NET?

RALPH MCILVAIN, expert trainer and conditioner of racehorses, manager of Alfred Gwynne Vanderbilt's Sagamore Farm, in Glyndon, Maryland:

Preferably and naturally, the way horses eat would be from the ground. However, since they are confined to a stall for long periods of time, I don't believe that it's too healthful to feed hay on the ground, where it gets mixed up with their bedding. This means that they have to pick through what you could call a messy feeding.

Feeding from a rack is difficult, for the simple reason that it is seldom done in the proper manner. The hay ought to be pulled apart and shaken out before it is put into a rack, but all too often this is neglected and the horse pulls it down in the same clumps in which it was placed in the rack.

At the racetrack, where a great deal of activity is going on that the horse can see, the horses seem to be quiet and content to eat from a hay net hung outside the front of the stall. You figure that a net will hold approximately twenty-five pounds of hay and that a horse will consume between five and ten pounds during the day and waste another three to five pounds. At "do-ing-up" time, around four o'clock, you can't hang the net inside the stall, because of the danger of the horse's getting hung up in it, and you don't want him hanging his head out of the stall all night, so the best thing to do is to empty the net in a back corner of the stall so that he will have some-thing to pick at during the evening.

At the farm, we feed in racks, not because I like to but because it is what you must do. Even with the racks, horses tend to pull down a large amount of hay, which gets mixed in with their bedding and soiled and is then com-pletely wasted. This means that in order to ensure that a horse gets as much hay as he needs (and I feel that good hay is the most essential part of a horse's diet), you have to overfeed hay to allow for waste. Of course, this means that hay is the most expensive item in the budget, but it is also the most important.

MICHAEL WETTACH, co-owner and manager of Merryland Farm, a breeding and training establishment in Hydes, Maryland; he is also a famous rider who was twice the leading amateur steeple-chase jockey of the year on the major racetracks:

By preference and practice, we feed all our horses hay on the ground, with the exception of those in one yearling barn, which are fed from built-in racks filled from the loft. These racks were already installed, so it would be foolish not to use them, but by and large we feed hay on the floor.

At the racetrack, all our horses are fed this way, because, first of all, we feel that this is the natural way for horses to eat. Then, we feed two kinds of hay: timothy, with a little alfalfa, and it is easier to mix this on the ground than layering it in a net or a rack. Also, by putting hay on the floor we feel that the horse is encouraged to drop his head, which is especially helpful if he should come down with a cold or a sinus problem. Otherwise, a horse would have no reason to hang his head for any length of time during the day, so in such cases it might be considered a part of the treatment.

A hay net or rack that is fixed in one place doesn't seem to encourage a horse to move around at all. Particularly at the track, where horses are confined most of the time, we feel that feeding on the ground gives the horse a little more inclination to move around as he eats—perhaps picking through the straw or peering through the door between times—instead of just planting himself by the door for hours on end.

At the farm, we feed hay on the ground except in the one barn I mentioned, and although it may seem a minor point, another aversion I have to overhead feeding is that the horses tend to get covered with chaff and seed and look as if they've never been groomed. It always seems to follow that just when they look their worst is when their owners arrive to see them.

I have seen some bad accidents resulting from a hay net hanging in a stall after the horse has emptied or partially emptied it, when the animal was caught by his halter or a tooth or put a leg through it and then fought in a panic. For this reason, I guess I'd prefer a rack to a net if I had to make a choice, but as far as I'm concerned, the only way to feed hay is from the ground.

MARIE MOORE, owner of High Hopes Farm, in The Plains, Virginia, and breeder of successful racehorses in the United States, in England, and in Ireland, has produced numerous stakes winners, many of them from a line based on Gallorette, whom she purchased when that fabulous race mare was retired from competition:

All my horses are fed hay from the ground. I believe that this is the most natural way for a horse to eat. After all, he grazes this way. Feeding from the ground keeps the chaff and tiny particles of leaf and seed from being drawn into the horse's nostrils or falling into his eyes when he is eating.

Some people feel that feeding hay on the ground increases the incidence of foreign matter and/or parasites, which the horse may pick up as he eats. I do not think this is a real problem, because, as a rule, horses are pretty selective about their feed and parasites are not present in clean stalls. In addition, most farms have a program of parasite control, which eliminates all danger of parasite transmission in the stalls.

Aside from falling chaff, which is unavoidable, I have found that horses that are fed hay from overhead racks or nets tend to pull it down or drop it and then eat it from the ground anyway. So it might just as well be put there in the first place. Furthermore, you always run the risk of a horse's getting his foot, leg, or halter (if he wears one in the stall) caught in a net or rack and seriously damaging himself.

I don't feel that there is anything economical about feeding in a net or a rack, either. A horse that wastes his hay will do so no matter how he is fed, and in my opinion the hazards involved in using nets and racks far outweigh any possible saving.

ALL ABOUT GRAIN

Grain is one of the major variables we work with in feeding our horses. It is also one of the major expenses of horse maintenance. To grasp the function of grain in the horse's nutrition, you must consider it in relation to the contribution of forage (grass and hay): what grain can do for your horse that forage can't, and vice versa.

Nutrients are packed into grain in a particularly concentrated fashion. You know that the space occupied by two 50-pound bales of hay is greater than the bulk of a 100-pound bag of feed. Moreover, of that 100 pounds of grain, your horse will digest 72; whereas your horse benefits from only about half of the hay he eats. So it follows that if you want to get the nutrients into him fast or in large quantities without distending his belly, you feed lots of grain. If you want your horse to have something to chew on, to keep him occupied and content, while restricting his intake of nutrients, then forage should be his mainstay and grain a negligible part of his diet.

Aside from being more concentrated than forage, grain possesses unique nutritional characteristics. It supplies energy more efficiently than forage. Hay and grass, especially the legumes (alfalfa and clover) are superior sources of protein.

So for work energy and weight gain, grain is the feed of choice. But, for growth and reproduction, forage is a very important feed. For maintenance, grass forages that are not particularly high in either protein or energy are often adequate.

The two other nutrients horsemen usually consider when they balance a ration, aside from calories and protein, are the minerals calcium and phosphorus. Again, grain and forage play complementary roles: Grain supplies greater amounts of phosphorus; forage supplies calcium.

Visualize a spectrum of nutritional needs bounded at one extreme by an orphan foal and at the other by a foundered pony. Somewhere along the spectrum lies your own horse's need for grain versus forage.

The foal needs large quantities of nutrients to fuel his rapid growth, but there's not much room in his belly. At three weeks of age he will do well on a diet of milk-replacer pellets and water. The pellets are a highly concentrated grain feed. He eats almost no hay or grass. They simply don't supply the nutrients in a sufficiently concentrated form.

Next come such hard workers as racehorses and Three-Day Event horses, which expend tremendous amounts of energy. There aren't enough hours in the day for a racehorse in training to fill his energy needs by eating hay. He eats some hay, but his diet is primarily based on grain. (A racehorse might well eat fifteen pounds of hay per day and fifteen pounds of grain, but when we say that he eats large quantities of grain in relation to hay, remember that a pound of grain contains more nutrients than a pound of hay and that his hay-grain ratio is lower than for most of the other horses on the spectrum.)

In the center of the spectrum are the performance horses, the show horses, the hunters, and the pleasure horses. Along the performance-horse segment, hay and grain requirements are roughly equal, unless the needs of the individual animal dictate otherwise. A Thoroughbred field hunter working three days a week might match the high-grain requirement of a racehorse. The grade pleasure horse, whose owner rides only on weekends, might subsist perfectly well on pasture alone. But within this category are the majority of horses for whom forage and grain play equally important roles. A typical show horse, for example, may eat ten pounds of grain a day and fifteen or twenty pounds of hay, which amounts to just about equal nutrients from the two sources.

A producing mare eats large quantities of grain at certain times of the year. During the last three months of pregnancy and during lactation, the demands of the foal she is nourishing require a greater concentration of nutrients than can be supplied by hay alone. Even so, forage is of vital importance in feeding broodmares. Protein is growth food. Large amounts of calcium are essential to the development of the fetus and of the nursing foal. These nutrients are supplied more efficiently by forage than by grain. Another practical consideration in favor of forage is that broodmares stand around all day long. If they have a steady supply of low-octane food, they are safely occupied chewing hay instead of fences.

To the foundered pony, grain is poison. There are also pony-type horses, individuals with slow metabolism and a tendency to get fat, who simply cannot handle significant amounts of grain. Some merely get fat. In others, the ill effects are vastly disproportionate to the degree of overfeeding. Grain triggers a chemical response and internal systems go haywire. The horse founders. He experiences severe and sometimes permanent pain. All because of a little too much grain.

As you ponder where your horse fits in the spectrum, you'll consider his work and his type: whether he holds his flesh easily or is hard to keep weight on. And as in any matter requiring judgment, you'll feel a bit uncertain. Don't try to silence your qualms by throwing in a little extra grain for good measure! When in doubt, err toward the low-grain end of the spectrum.

Look at it this way: Horses in their natural state survive on forage alone. They eat no grain at all. But they also do no work. The more work demands you make, the more feed you have to provide and the more you deviate from the life-style that nature intended for the horse. You pay for increased work output with increased risk.

Your management role thus becomes trickier. Something you now have to worry about is tying up. A fit horse on a high grain ration is very likely to tie up if he misses a day's work. You must be a skillful manager and alter the grain ration as the work schedule changes. And the higher your horse's grain ration, the smaller is your margin for error.

Meanwhile, as you feed more grain, your horse begins to neglect his hay, and he may become a candidate for colic. The bacteria in his intestines which activate digestion require an almost steady stream of nutritional material. However, on his high-grain diet your horse eats two big meals a day and very little in between. During the long stretches between meals, intestinal bacteria start dying off. By the time they're faced with the next big digestive job, their numbers are reduced.

With hay, on the other hand, you have a built-in margin for error. It's difficult to overfeed hay. If worse comes to worst, your horse can convert the protein in his hay to meet unsatisfied energy needs. This isn't a recommendation. Protein is an inefficient and expensive source of energy. But it's reassuring to know that the protein is there and available for conversion to energy if your calculations are off. Also, your horse can handle an excess of calcium if you feed him too much hay. But the high phosphorus intake that can accompany an excess of grain could get him into serious trouble.

Which Grain to Feed?

The choice boils down to three popular horse feeds: oats, corn, and barley. Each has its own distinct set of characteristics that make it better suited to some feeding programs than to others.

Oats. A good source of protein, as grains go. Like all grain, oats supply more phosphorus than calcium, but the ratio is closer than it is in corn or barley. When you're feeding grass hay, or when your horse is on pasture without much clover, oats will help you to meet his protein and mineral requirements.

Corn. The most energy-intensive of the grains. Relatively low in protein, with a high ratio of phosphorus to calcium. When you're feeding high-quality legume hay or you know that your pasture is rich in clover, you'll probably save money by meeting your horse's energy needs with corn instead of oats.

Fallacy: "Corn is a heating feed." Corn doesn't spontaneously raise body temperature. It is rich in calories, which in winter can be converted to body heat as necessary. In summer, the same calories, if not burned up in work, will be converted to fat. And when you work a fat horse he becomes hot sooner than a lean horse. But if you feed corn appropriately, taking into consideration the horse's caloric needs, he won't become fat and he won't overheat.

Barley. A nourishing grain, almost as high in protein as oats, and approaching corn in its energy yield. The only drawback is that the hull is too hard for horses to chew. Barley must be processed commercially, which increases its cost. Still, if you have a horse in poor condition, the concentrated nutrition supplied by barley may be worth the extra expense for a limited period of time.

If you find that more than one of these grains will meet your horse's needs adequately, let economy be the deciding factor. Select the grain that is the most economical source of the nutrient in shortest supply. For example, if you feed high-quality alfalfa hay, you're probably meeting protein requirements comfortably, and you're buying grain as a source of energy. So select the grain that represents the best energy buy. If your forage is poor, on the other hand, you may need grain as a source of protein. Shop for the most cost-effective variety in terms of protein.

Buying Top-quality Grain

When you've seen one oat, you haven't seen them all. Oats grown on various plants, in various soils, under various conditions, cannot be expected to develop identically. Some oats are bigger than others, and some (here's where you have to be sharp) are emptier than others: big hull, small kernel. This is also true of corn and barley.

The other important quality consideration is cleanliness. When grains are picked in a dusty field on a summer day, dirt and debris are mixed in. So the grain must be cleaned before it is sold, mechanically filtered through large screens. One cleaning is standard, but a second and sometimes even a third improve quality. Dirty grain is not only uneconomical (since you are paying for dirt), but harmful to your horse.

You buy your grain by weight, in hundred-pound bags. But your feed dealer buys it by the bushel, a volume measure. Grain is graded by the federal Department of Agriculture on the basis of weight per bushel, percentage of foreign material and broken grains, and in some cases, percentage of moisture.

The higher the grade, the more your dealer pays. This makes sense. Your dealer doesn't want to pay for dirt, for water, or for empty hulls. Neither should you.

Therefore, when the dealer quotes you a price on grain, ask him what grade he's quoting and compare it to other dealers' prices for the same grade. Ask him how many cleaning processes the grain has undergone, and compare with other dealers. Ask to see the grain. Develop your own eye. It doesn't matter so much whether the grains are large or small, but they should be firm. You shouldn't be able to crush a whole oat. Open the hull to see whether the kernel fills it. You can't do that with corn and barley, so take a handful of them, heft it, try to remember the feel so that you can make comparisons. Reach deep into the sack of grain, take a handful, and let it run through your fingers. Do you see significant amounts of foreign material? Is your hand dirty? Does dust rise?

Since you buy grain by weight, be suspicious of extra volume. If a new shipment of grain fills its sacks fuller, if it rises higher in your feed bin, check the grade. You may be paying for empty hulls or debris.

To Crimp or Not to Crimp?

Every additional processing stage costs money, and guess who pays in the end? Cleaning is essential. You'll probably want your corn shelled (removed from the cob). Barley must be processed, because of its hard hull. But before you pay for crimping, flaking, cracking, rolling, and steaming, consider whether the extra expense is justified.

The purpose of all these procedures is to render the grain more digestible. Infirm horses and very young ones may have difficulty chewing whole kernels of corn. If your horse tends to leave his corn, or if you see a quantity of whole kernels coming through in his manure, try cracking. If your horse swallows grain without chewing it, either because he cannot chew or because he doesn't bother, the oats, whose hulls remain unbroken, will pass through his body undigested. If significant quantities of oats appear in the manure, try having them rolled or crimped, and watch to see whether your horse makes better use of them.

However, if your horse is able to digest his grain whole, there is no sense in paying a premium for processing.

Precision Feeding

The only intelligent way to feed grain is by weight. Your feed scoop is a volume measure. To know what nutrients it contains, you must know what its contents weigh. As you now know, weight depends not only on the type of grain but also on its quality.

If you are feeding your horse two 6-quart scoops of oats per day and you decide that you can feed him just as well and for less money by switching to corn, be sure to make your switch on the basis of weight, not volume.

Storing Your Grain

After you've determined a ration that meets your horse's requirements while saving you money, don't lose the advantage with poor storage methods.

You'd be surprised how expensive mice are as pets, especially a well-nourished, fast-growing colony of them. Store your feed in rodent-proof containers, either trash cans or metal-lined feed-storage bins. Not feed bags.

Whatever your storage container, raise it about six inches above the ground. Otherwise, ground moisture will accumulate and your grain will begin to mold from the bottom up. Feed bins should have legs. Wooden shipping pallets make good platforms for feed stored in trash cans.

Maintain two storage containers for each kind of grain you buy. Fill them both. Feed to the bottom of one, clean it, and order more grain. You'll never run out of grain with this system and, more important, you'll always feed relatively fresh feed. Never let your feed dealer dump new grain on top of old. Eventually, the bottom layer will spoil and contaminate the entire contents of the bin.

ALL ABOUT COMMERCIAL FEED

If you were buying a box of cereal for yourself, you'd pick your favorite brand from the shelf without even slowing down the forward movement of your shopping cart. But here you are shopping for your horse, in a dim and dusty storeroom, on your hands and knees, wrestling with feed sacks, peering at labels, trying to make sense of them all. There's an ache in your knees, a crick in your neck, and despite the ray from your flashlight, you're in the dark.

Is 2-percent-more crude protein worth the extra cost? Should you favor the feed with wheat middlings over the one with corn gluten? And what about the feed with the processed grain by-products?

You are determined to provide a feeding program that meets all of your horse's nutritional requirements amply, yet without waste, without a costly shotgun program that rains down random nutrients whether they're needed or not. But trying to match your horse's needs to the information you find on the manufacturers' labels is proving to be a frustrating business.

Why bother with commercial feed at all? Why not feed grain, mix your own feed, and save yourself the headache of deciphering the label codes? There are indeed certain advantages in mixing your own grain. You save the cost of mixing, packaging, and advertising, which the commercial feed manufacturer must pass on to the buyer. You know exactly what goes into your horse's stomach, and you can make minor variations according to his needs.

On the other hand, there is much to be said in favor of commercial feed. If you're not a nutrition expert yourself, or if you haven't time to juggle with the charts and tables you need in order to formulate your own ration, you would be better off relying on the expertise of a reputable manufacturer than cooking up your own, hit-or-miss formula. Commercial feeds save time and space. You take home one sack of feed. You feed from one bin. You don't have to measure spoonfuls of supplements. If someone takes over for you at feeding time, the proportions of your horse's diet will remain the same. The manufacturer has done the mixing for you.

And his machinery mixes evenly. The vitamins and minerals are uniformly distributed throughout the feed. In a sweet feed, the molasses holds them in place. In a pelleted feed, they are trapped in every pellet. There is no risk of losing valuable nutrients at the bottom of the sack or the bottom of the feed tub.

Even though you pay for the manufacturer's overhead, commercial feed won't necessarily cost more than straight grain in the end. This is because 1) the manufacturer can buy ingredients more cheaply than you; 2) he can obtain ingredients not available to you, such as brewers' dried grains; and 3) he can use low-cost components with high nutritional value that would not be palatable without a molasses coating or concealment among components of a pellet. You might pay more for a hundred pounds of good-quality racehorse oats than for a hundred-pound bag of a commercial sweet feed. If you examine the sweet feed closely, you'll find that the oats it contains don't match the quality of the racehorse oats, but that is to be expected. Something has to give. The oats are only one element (often a minor one) contributing to the nutritional value of the feed. Whether or not the oats are of high quality, the feed must contain the nutrients claimed on the label. And that brings us back to the major problem: how to decipher the information on the label.

The Language of the Label

No federal law governs the labeling of horse feed packages. But almost all states have enacted model legislation produced by the Association of American Feed Control officials, together with the Feed Manufacturers' Association. Under the bill, labels must include five categories of information to help evaluate what is inside the bag. These are as follows:

1) Brand name and product name of the food. Example: Purina (brand name), Omolene (product name).
2) The name and address of the company that makes or distributes the food.
3) The net weight of food in the bag.
4) The manufacturer's guarantee for the food. Example: Min. crude protein: 12 percent.
5) The ingredients.

Each state department of agriculture has decided which portions of the AAFC model legislation it will adopt. State feed control officials carry out spot-check programs, periodically testing samples taken from feed on sale at dealerships throughout the state.

Only those statements on the package that can be substantiated by laboratory testing are required, because they are the only ones that can be verified. This is one reason why feed package labels tend to be uninformative.

The Guaranteed Analysis

Each state's feed control officials decide which statements are required, but all agree that the following three items must be declared in a "guaranteed analysis" section on the label, or on a separate ticket sewn into the seam:

The minimum percentage of crude protein;
The minimum percentage of crude fat;
The maximum percentage of crude fiber.

Since items expressed in minimums are expensive, and items expressed in maximums tend to be cheap fillers, the percentage figures given in the guaranteed analysis are pretty close to the actual proportions in the product.

Crude protein in commercial feed ranges from 10 percent to 16 percent. Fat is a pretty standard 2 percent to 4 percent. Fiber runs from 6 percent to 20 percent in a grain-type feed. In a pellet feed combining hay and grain, fiber is frequently as high as 25 percent.

The percentages of the three components in the guaranteed analysis usually add up to about 25 percent. Add 10 percent as the probable moisture content of the feed. Virtually the entire balance, around 65 percent, is carbohydrate, the primary source of energy.

The Ingredient List

This follows the guaranteed analysis. The catch here is that manufacturers are not required to list ingredients by name. They can lump categories of ingredients together under officially recognized generic terms. Oats, corn, and barley become "grain products." Protein meals, cottonseed, linseed, peanut, soybean, and safflower are lumped under the term "plant protein products." "Processed grain by-products" includes bran, brewers' dried grains, grain sorghum gluten feed, and wheat middlings. These are by-products of other industries such as brewing and flour milling. All of these low-cost nutritious products are available to feed manufacturers, but not to the private horse owner.

This use of catchall generic terms allows the manufacturer to vary the ingredients as the prices of raw materials fluctuate, without having to print new package labels. When the price of a component rises, he switches to another of comparable nutritive value and so manages to hold the price of his product steady. If an expensive ingredient goes down in price, he uses more of it and so maximizes his profit. Naturally, he must always maintain the values guaranteed in the analysis.

Nevertheless, unannounced changes in the recipe may make the feed less nourishing to your horse by making it less palatable. The horse eats less of it. One week, you're feeding him a sweet feed with a high proportion of oats. The next week, you open a new bag and stare down at corn. If it's a pelleted feed, you may never notice the difference except perhaps for a slight change in color. But your horse may gaze disparagingly at his feed tub and walk away.

The list of ingredients goes on and on, through forage products if any, molasses, salt, and a bewildering litany of chemical compounds, most of which are vitamin and mineral supplements, for which the following mini-glossary may be useful.

Deciphering the Ingredients List

Grain products. Corn, oats, barley, wheat, and/or grain sorghum; primarily sources of energy. The whole grain must be present in the feed, although it may have undergone processing of some kind. In sweet feed, the grains are usually rolled or crimped, but you can still recognize them. In a pellet you won't, of course, see them, but you know that the entire kernel was used in the production. For example, ground grain sorghum is the entire product made by grinding the grains of sorghum.

Plant protein products. These meals are primarily protein sources. Finely or coarsely ground, they include cottonseed, linseed, peanut, soybean, and safflower.

Processed grain by-products. Primarily energy sources left over from flour and beer manufacture, they include wheat bran, brewers' dried grains, grain sorghum gluten feed, wheat middlings, and wheat mill run.

Alfalfa meal. A high-protein and high-fiber ingredient. It may be sun-cured (dried naturally by the sun) or dehydrated (dried by thermal means). Supplies a crude protein between 13 percent and 22 percent, and a crude fiber between 20 percent and 33 percent. The higher the protein, the lower the fiber.

Cane molasses. The thick, dark, viscous by-product of refined sugar, used in both sweet feeds and pellets primarily as a binder. Reduces dust. Makes the food palatable, and manufacturers claim that horse owners like to see it in the feed. High energy, calcium (.7 percent), and iron content.

Beet molasses. Similar value to cane molasses.

Salt or sodium selenite (sodium salt). Essential for regulating your horse's water metabolism and the passage of nutrients into the cells.

Lignin sulfonate. A binder holding the ingredients firm in their pellets. No nutritional value. Shouldn't exceed 4 percent of total amount.

Brewer's yeast. A good source of B-complex vitamins, a dietary essential.

Forage. Provides fiber and protein. In general, it is higher in protein than roughage. It appears in almost all commercial feeds, roughage only in complete hay/grain feeds. Chief sources are alfalfa, sun-cured and dehydrated, which may be chopped or finely ground, and any of thirteen other items ranging from dehydrated corn plant (the entire corn plant, ear, leaves, and stalk, which has been artificially dried and ground) to ground peanut vine.

Roughage. Provides the necessary bulk in a complete feed. Has a high fiber value and, depending on the quality of the fiber, may be convertible into energy. Sources include ground corn cobs, oats, soybean and cottonseed hulls, beet pulp, and citrus meal.

Calcium carbonate. Supplies calcium from several sources, including ground limestone, dicalcium phosphate, and legume forage products.

Calcium iodate. Another calcium source, with iodine, which is required for the function of the thyroid gland. A deficiency leads to weak or stillborn foals.

Calcium pantothenate. Pantothenic acid is a B vitamin. The calcium compound keeps the vitamin stable.

Defluorinated phosphate. Phosphorus source essential to bone development and maintenance and to many enzyme systems. The fluorine is removed because it is toxic to horses.

Manganous oxide (or magnesium oxide). A version of manganese. A small amount is known to be a necessary part of body tissue.

Copper sulfate. Copper builds healthy blood cells. Sulfur is used in tissue formation, especially of the hoof wall.

Cobalt carbonate. Cobalt is used by the horse to manufacture the vitamin B_{12} needed to nourish his blood.

Iron sulfate, ferrous carbonate, and iron carbonate. Mixed iron sources essential to healthy blood and body-tissue formation.

Zinc oxide. Mineral; minimum dietary requirements unknown.

Vitamin A supplement. Necessary for normal vision, growth, reproduction, and lactation. In natural form, found in green forages, yellow corn.

Vitamin B_{12} supplement. Derived from cobalt carbonate. Mature horses synthesize their requirement, but some respond well to a supplement. Foals, especially, are known to benefit from receiving B_{12}.

D-activated animal sterol. Vitamin D aids absorption of calcium and phosphorus. Deficiency leads to rickets in foals and osteomalacia in mature horses. Sunlight and sun-cured hay supply the natural form.

Choline chloride. Required amount is not known, but other species are known to grow abnormally without it.

Vitamin E supplement, or di-alpha-tocopherol. No deficiency of vitamin E proved in horses under normal feeding conditions, but its presence prevents sweet feed from turning rancid.

Niacin. Contained in soybean meal, linseed meal, and molasses. Requirement unknown.

Riboflavin. Vitamin B_2. Naturally supplied in alfalfa hay and other green, leafy forages. Essential for normal growth and efficient use of feed.

Potassium iodide. Source of potassium, believed essential to body tissue, and of iodine, required for thyroid function.

Soy lecithin. Derived from soybean oil by a degumming process. Helps fat digestion and absorption.

Making Sense of What You Read

Now that you speak the language of the label, how do you apply what you see on the label to your horse's needs? Let's begin with the manufacturer's name. You are at the mercy of the manufacturer and of his integrity more than you realize. A reputable name on the label is a plus.

The presence of the address as well as the name enables you to write for information that does not appear on the label. Manufacturers can supply you with the results of feeding trials they have conducted. Any reputable manufacturer should be willing to supply you with a figure for digestible energy and the calcium and phosphorus percentages of his feed. If this information is refused, look for another feed.

The net weight figure is important only when bags of similar appearance actually contain slightly different amounts of feed. Most feeds are sold in quantities of fifty or one hundred pounds. A few are marketed in seventy- or seventy-five-pound packages, but that doesn't happen very often. Variation in weight naturally affects the cost per pound.

The guaranteed analysis provides an index for comparison with other feeds, which is only very roughly helpful. You can be reasonably sure that the minimum crude protein guarantee is pretty close to the actual crude protein found in the feed. The trouble lies in the word "crude." Not all of that protein is digestible by your horse.

Crude protein is listed on the bag because only crude protein can be verified in a laboratory. You're left to determine what portion of that crude protein is digestible, and here you're on your own. Even the major manufacturers admit that they cannot supply a definite digestible-protein figure.

A wide range of protein sources appears in horse feed. Some, like soybean meal, are highly digestible, high-quality protein. Others, like linseed meal, provide relatively small amounts of digestible protein. In most cases there is no way to tell, either from the label or by sight, what proportion of the guaranteed crude protein is digestible. As a very rough rule of thumb, when considering the product of a reputable manufacturer, figure that 75 percent of the crude protein is actually digestible. If the label states, "Crude protein not less than 15%," assume that your horse is receiving about 11.2 percent of digestible protein.

Fat is valuable as a very concentrated source of energy. Linseed meal and corn gluten meal are good fat suppliers. Until recently, nutritionists placed more emphasis on carbohydrates as the chief energy source for horses, but new studies have suggested that fat may be a useful component in the diet of high-performance horses. At the moment, fat content varies little from one feed to another. It won't be a major consideration in your choice.

Fiber is the scaffolding that holds the plant together. It is what remains after the sugar has been extracted from sugar beet, the hull that holds the kernel or grain, the shell that holds the nut in place on the plant.

If the horse eats the plant in an early stage of its maturity, he can convert some of its fiber content into energy. But as the plant continues to mature, the digestible portions become bound up with indigestible material that renders the whole of the fiber useless. Since there is no reason to assume that the fiber content of the feed you are considering is digestible, assume that it is not, and shop for a feed with a relatively low fiber content, or else for a reduced price. As fiber percentage rises, so, proportionately, does the amount of grain you must feed. If a commercial feed has more than 15 percent fiber, do not buy it, unless the manufacturer assures you that a portion of the fiber content is convertible to energy. An exception to this advice is the case of a complete hay/grain feed, with which fiber may be your horse's only source of roughage, and so is acceptable up to about 25 percent of total weight.

The list of ingredients generally gives energy and protein sources first, vitamin and mineral sources last. Don't assume that ingredients are listed in quantitative order. Many manufacturers list first the items they believe their customers most appreciate.

If the manufacturer uses the generic terms, make sure that one primary energy source is present, either grain products or processed grain by-products. If he itemizes ingredients, look for at least one popular horse grain as the primary energy source.

Make sure that there is a good protein source on the list, either one of the generic terms such as "plant protein products" or "forage"; or a good protein source by name, such as "alfalfa meal" or "soybean meal." Check for sources of calcium, salt, phosphorus, and any vitamins or trace minerals that your horse isn't obtaining from natural sources.

This chart shows just what he needs:

What Your Horse Needs In His Feed

	Crude Protein %	Digestible Protein %	Digestible Energy Megacalories (per 100 lbs. of feed)	Calcium %	Phosphorus %	Fiber %
Mare						
Last 90 days of pregnancy	14	6.9	1.0	.38	.29	12
— Lactating	14	8.3	1.21	.47	.37	12
Weanling	18	13.0	1.4	.78	.48	12
Yearling	14	9.6	1.21	.43	.28	12
Adult maintenance	9	5.3	1.0	.33	.25	15
Performance horse						
— Moderate Work	9	5.3	1.2	.33	.25	15
— Intense Work	9	5.3	1.3	.33	.25	15

Figures given for horses of 1100 lbs. mature weight

Feeding Trials

At some point, you're going to have to buy some feed, take it home, and try it. Label study will put you on the right track, but you still have to find out 1) whether your horse will eat the feed; and 2) whether he will do well on it.

If there are too many feeds in the running to take home and test, there are other criteria you can apply in order to narrow the field. Cost, for one. Ease of handling is another. To decide between sweet feed and pellet form, you can weigh the following pros and cons:

PRO	CON
Sweet Feed	
More palatable	Shorter shelf life
Ingredients partly recognizable	More vulnerable to heat and cold
Easier to add worm powder or drugs	Horse can sort feed
Manufacturer less likely to change ingredients	
Pellets	
Usually less expensive	Less palatable
Longer shelf life	Ingredients unrecognizable
Horse cannot sort feed	Manufacturer more likely to change ingredients. You won't know it, but your horse will.
Makes possible combination of hay ration with grain in a single pellet	
Eliminates hay belly	
Eliminates dust	
Eliminates hay storage problems	

Testing Palatability

Now it is time to bring your horse in on the decision. The simplest way to establish your horse's preference is to select two of the feeds on your preferred list and offer both, side by side. Put two feed tubs in your horse's stall, and in each tub put the total daily amount you would normally feed, so that you're offering two full meals at one time. (If your horse immediately gobbles up both of them, you don't have to worry about palatability and can make your selection on the basis of nutritional performance.)

After the meal, remove, weigh, and record the uneaten portion from each tub. Follow this procedure for five days. Finally, for each feed, add up the total amount your horse ate and figure out what percentage of his total diet this represents (by dividing the amount of each feed by the total amount consumed).

If one feed accounts for at least 60 percent of the five-day trial diet, that is the one your horse definitely prefers. If neither accounts for more than 60 percent, he will probably do well on either of them. If he consumes less total feed than on his accustomed diet, you can assume that neither test feed is particularly palatable to him.

If you are considering more than two feeds, test the third feed in the same way in competition with the winner of the first trial.

Testing Nutritional Performance

There may be several feeds that seem to meet your horse's nutritional needs and that he eats willingly. But which will serve him best nutritionally? This is, of course, the crucial question, and you can test to find the answer.

Each trial requires at least three weeks, in order to establish a trend. Begin by offering exactly the same amount that your horse eats of his old feed. Determine his weight at the beginning of the trial with a weight tape (available free of charge from most feed stores). Measure your horse, at exactly the same time of day, once a week until the end of the trial. (It is assumed that he is in good health and neither underweight nor overweight.)

If your horse eats all of the feed offered every day and

1) loses weight for three consecutive weeks, eliminate the feed as being incapable of maintenance;
2) maintains his weight within 3 percent of its total over the three-week period, the feed is adequate;
3) gains weight for three consecutive weeks, reduce the amount fed and extend the trial to determine the exact quantity required for maintenance;
4) gains or loses one week and then reverses the next week by an amount greater than 3 percent, feed for two additional weeks to see if you can establish a trend. If reversals continue, eliminate the feed from your list on the basis of nonuniformity.

If your horse does *not* clean up his feed every day and

1) loses weight for three consecutive weeks, eliminate the feed as unpalatable;
2) maintains or gains weight for three consecutive weeks, reduce to just the amount the horse will clean up and feed for two more weeks to confirm that the feed is capable of maintenance in the amount the horse will eat;
3) gains or loses one week and then reverses the next week by an amount greater than 3 percent, continue the trial for two more weeks in order to establish a trend. If reversals continue, eliminate the feed on the basis of nonuniformity.

ALL ABOUT VITAMIN AND MINERAL SUPPLEMENTS

Conventional wisdom has it that a healthy horse, fed a commonsense diet of good-quality grain and hay, doesn't need supplements. This may not always be true.

Take the example of a mature thousand-pound horse, not in work, receiving twenty-five pounds a day (half oats, half good-quality timothy hay), with free access to trace-mineralized salt. It sounds like an adequate diet and, in fact, it is more than adequate in many respects. But this horse is probably running a deficit in two trace minerals—zinc and copper—and he's cutting it close on calcium, too.

Let's take another example: the same horse but on a corn-alfalfa diet, still a half-and-half mixture, totaling twenty-five pounds a day, with free access to the trace-mineralized salt. Copper is sufficient now, but the zinc deficiency persists, we're running low on manganese, and in the vitamin category, thiamine (vitamin B_1) is in short supply.

These aren't fad diets. They're sensible, middle-of-the-road rations that any conscientiously cared-for horse might receive. These are maintenance diets for simplicity. But if the horses went to work and the rations were increased proportionately, the deficiencies would persist.

Deficiencies like these are not the end-all and be-all of successful horsekeeping. Horses have thrived on similar diets and less. Our knowledge of the horse's trace mineral requirements is only sketchy. Perhaps the requirements for certain substances are not as high as researchers today believe them to be. However, anyone who has given stable-space to a wood chewer or a dirt eater now has cause to credit the researchers and to suspect the diet. And if horses favored with good health and good feed harbor minor deficiencies, horses maintained in less than ideal circumstances are probably running substantial deficits.

Help is here. Dozens of commercial vitamin/mineral supplement manufacturers clamor for a crack at your horse's dietary deficiencies. They promise everything from improved health to cleaner stalls and increased riding pleasure. All you have to do is choose. But this is not as simple as it sounds.

In the first place, there are many products on the market, and various products in various areas of the country. They all contain vitamins and minerals but not necessarily exactly the same ones or in the same amounts. All the ingredients are listed on the label, in the guaranteed analysis, but you would need a computer and a chemical dictionary in order to interpret and compare them.

To make your product comparison a little easier, here is a Glossary of the Most Common Terms and Measures:

Amino acids. The components of protein: arginine, cystine, glysine, histidine, isoleucine, leucine, lysine, methionine, phenylalanine, threonine, tryptophan, tyrosine, and valine.

Ascorbic acid. Source of vitamin C.

Biotin. A B vitamin.

Chelation. Process of applying amino-acid coating to trace minerals, which may aid absorption.

Choline. A B vitamin.

d-pantothenic acid. A B vitamin.

Folic acid. A B vitamin.

IU. International unit. A measure of vitamin activity. One IU equals one USP.

Mcg. Microgram. One thousandth of a milligram.

Mg. Milligram. One thousandth of a gram. There are 453,000 milligrams in a pound.

Niacin. Also nicotinic acid, a B vitamin.

Para-amino benzoic acid. A water-soluble vitamin.

Pyridoxine. Vitamin B_6.

Riboflavin. Vitamin B_2.

Sequestering. Similar to chelation, but trace minerals are coated with polysaccharides to aid absorption.

Sodium chloride. Salt.

Thiamine. Vitamin B_1.

USP. United States Pharmacopeia. One USP equals one IU.

Vitamin D_2. A plant source of vitamin D.

Vitamin D_3. An animal source of vitamin D.

What is the importance of these elements? What are their benefits and potential dangers?

On pages 168 and 169 in chart form, is a summary of what the knowledgeable, practical horseman ought to know about vitamins and minerals.

Which Ones to Worry About

HORSE NEEDS			DOESN'T NEED
Synthesized in Intestine	**Supplied in Feed**		
Vitamin D	Vitamin A	Magnesium	Vitamin C
Vitamin K	Vitamin D	Sulfur	(mature horses)
Niacin	Vitamin E	Iron	
Vitamin B_{12}	Thiamine	Zinc	
Pyridoxine	Riboflavin	Manganese	
Folic Acid	Pantothenic Acid	Copper	
Biotin	Calcium	Cobalt	Fluorine
	Phosphorus	Iodine	Lead
	Salt	Selenium	
	Potassium		

With the basic schooling behind you, now it is time to consider your horse and his individual needs, and to look for products that seem tailored to his situation.

Unless your horse has a specific known deficiency (for example, your veterinarian has diagnosed a nutrition-related disease or you know that your soil is lacking in some vital element), you should select a supplement as you might buy insurance. You don't have to take every coverage available, but you do want to protect your horse from the major risks.

Horses fall into general categories of mineral/vitamin needs. See where your own horse fits into this range of hypothetical situations, and estimate his potential for deficiency accordingly:

Situation I: Healthy horse, good-quality feed. (Suspect possible deficiencies of zinc, manganese, copper, and thiamine.)

Does this surprise you? The following table will show you why this risk exists:

The Risk of Deficiencies in a Standard Diet

This table shows how four commonplace diets measure up to maintenance requirements for feed-supplied vitamins and minerals. The figures in the four right-hand columns give the multiple of each requirement supplied by each diet. Numbers greater than one indicate surpluses; numbers smaller than one indicate deficits. For example: the timothy-oats diet supplies 2.8 times the iron requirement but only .6 of the zinc requirement. These calculations include amounts of trace mineral consumed by the horse as he obtains the balance of his sodium requirements from iodized trace mineralized salt offered free choice.

Requirement for Horse at Maintenance on 25 lb. Total Daily Ration		Multiple of Requirement Supplied by Iodized Trace Mineral Salt Free Choice and:			
		25 lbs. Alfalfa	25 lbs. Timothy	25 lbs. Timothy-Oats (half & half)	25 lbs. Alfalfa-Corn (half & half)
Vitamin A	16,250 IU	9.5	3.25	1.7	5.2
Vitamin E	170 mg.	6	4.2	2.7	3.9
Thiamin	34 mg.	1	.58	1.5	.88
Riboflavin	25 mg.	4.8	5.6	3.2	2.7
Pantothenic Acid	170 mg.	*	*	*	*
Calcium	30,618 mg.	5.6	1.5	.9	2.9
Phosphorus	20,412 mg.	1.4	1	1.6	2.4
Sodium	39,690 mg.	1	1	1	1
Potassium	45,360 mg.	4.8	4	2.6	2.8
Sulfur	17,010 mg.	1.9	.86	1.7	1.4
Magnesium	10,206 mg.	3.2	1.4	1.9	1.8
Iron	454.5 mg.	4.6	3.6	2.8	2.7
Zinc	454.4 mg.	.6	.14	.6	.7
Manganese	454.5 mg.	.9	1.3	1.2	.6
Copper	102.25 mg.	1.5	.6	.7	1
Cobalt	1.14 mg.	1.5	1.2	1.2	1.8
Iodine	1.14 mg.	1.5	1.2	1.2	1.8
Selenium	1.14 mg.	*	*	*	*

*Information not available

What You Should Know About Vitamins

VITAMINS		DAILY REQUIREMENT		CONTRI-BUTES TO	EXCESS DAMAGING	RICH NATURAL SOURCES	COMMENT
		MAINT.* (1100 lb. mature weight)	GROWTH**				
Vitamin A	Maint: 11.36 IU/lb body weight Growth: 18.18 IU/lb body weight Lact: 22.73 IU/lb. body weight	12,496 IU	9,199 IU	Epithelial tissue which wards off infection	Yes, prolonged overfeeding can cause bone fragility	From carotene in green grass; legume hay	Unstable in stored feed sources; horse can store excess
Ascorbic Acid (C)	Not essential for mature horse			Absorption of iron from the intestines	Not demon-strated to date		
Vitamin D	3 IU/lb body weight believed adequate	3300 IU	2211 IU	Bone growth and maintenance	Yes, at 68.181 mg/lb of diet causes calci-fication of soft tissues and bone abnor-malities	Sunlight; sun-cured for ages	Affects absor tion of dietary calcium and phosphorus
Vitamin E	6.81 mg/lb feed believed adequate	170 mg.	114 mg.	Muscle main-tenance and pre-vention of white muscle disease in foals	Not demon-strated to date	High-quality forage	Combined wi selenium treats tying-up syndrome. No evidence for fertility improv ment in horse
Vitamin K	Not established			Blood clotting in the bleeder horse	Yes		Assumed ade quately syn-thesized by intestinal micr flora
B-complex vitamins:							
Thiamin (B¹)	1.36 mg/lb of diet believed adequate	34 mg.	23 mg.	Energy release	Not demon-strated to date	Grains and forages	Used to treat tying-up in race horses
Riboflavin (B²)	1 mg/lb of feed adequate for maint.	25 mg.			Not demon-strated to date	Green leafy forages, brewer's yeast; skimmed milk	
Niacin	Not established			Growth and func-tioning of all living cells	Not demon-strated to date	Protein supple-ments: forages; most grains	Synthesis by horse possibly eliminates a dietary need
Pantothenic Acid	6.8 mg/lb of diet believed adequate	170 mg.	114 mg.		Not demon-strated to date	Most feeds	
Vitamin B¹²	Not established			Prevention of anemia	Not demon-strated to date		Believed syn-thesized in suf ficient amount in intestine
Pyridoxine (B⁶)	Not established				Not demon-strated to date		Synthesized i lower digestive tract
Folic Acid	Not established. 20 mg. may be beneficial to stabled horses.				Not demon-strated to date		Synthesized in lower di-gestive tract
Biotin	Not established				Not demon-strated to date		Synthesized in lower di-gestive tract

*Maintained on 25 lbs. total daily ration
**Calculated for 506 lb. weanling on 16¾ lbs. daily ration

hat You Should Know About Minerals

INERALS	DAILY REQUIREMENT	MAINT.* (1100 lb. mature weight)	GROWTH**	CONTRI-BUTES TO	EXCESS DAMAGING	RICH NATURAL SOURCES	COMMENTS
cium	Maint: 0.27% of diet Growth: 0.80% of diet	30,618 mg.	60,782 mg.	Maintenance of bones; fetus development; milk production	Possibly when fed in ratios greater than 6:1 with phos-phorus	Legume hay	Proper utiliza-tion dependent on intake of phosphorus and vitamin D
osphorus	Maint: 0.18% of diet Growth: 0.55% of diet	20,412 mg.	41,789 mg.	Same as calcium	Yes when fed in ratios greater than 1:1 with calcium	Legume hay; grain	Proper utiliza-tion dependent on intake of calcium and vitamin D
dium Chloride (Salt)	0.5%-1% of diet believed adequate	56,700 mg.	37,989 mg.	Prevention of heat stress	Yes but un-likely under normal cir-cumstances	Most hay-grain diets require supplemen-tation	When offered free choice, horses regulate their own intake
assium	Maint: 0.4% of diet Growth: 0.5% of diet	45,360 mg.	37,989 mg.	Essential for carbo-hydrate meta-bolism	Not demon-strated to date	Forages	Diets containing 35% forage should be adequate
fur	0.15% of diet be-lieved adequate	17,010 mg.	11,397 mg.		Not demon-strated to date	Molasses	
gnesium	Maint: .09% of diet Growth: 0.1% of diet	10,206 mg.	7,597.8 mg.	Development of bones and teeth; nerve impulse transfer	Not demon-strated to date	Forages	Rations of 50% hay generally adequate
n	Maint: 18.18 mg/lb of diet Growth: 22.73 mg/lb of diet	454.5 mg.	381 mg.	Prevention of anemia	Not demon-strated to date	Most feeds	Adequate supply in most feeds; the body con-serves it
c	18.18 mg/lb of diet	454.5 mg.	305 mg.	Adequate weight gain and maintenance of normal stores	Yes, at 4090 mg/lb feed	Wheat bran	
nganese	18.18 mg/lb of diet believed adequate	454.5 mg.	454.5 mg.	Bone formation and growth	May produce anemia	Clover and lespedeza	
pper	4.09 mg/lb of diet	102.25 mg.	69 mg.	Assimilation of iron	Not demon-strated to date	Molasses	
balt	.045 mg/lb of diet	1.14 mg.	.76 mg.	Bone marrow formation	Not demon-strated to date	Beet sugar	
ne	.045 mg/lb of diet	1.14 mg.	.76 mg.		Yes, at 2.18 mg/lb feed	Kelp	Excess in pregnant mares harmful to foals
enium	.045 mg/lb of diet	1.14 mg.	.76 mg.	Prevention of white muscle disease in foals	Yes, at 2.25 mg/lb feed	Forages	Toxic in forages containing as little as 2.72 mg of selenium per lb of dry matter
orine	Not established			Bone and teeth development in some species	Possibly, in amounts over 22.73 mg/lb daily diet	Forages	
ad	Not essential				Yes, at 36.36 mg/lb of feed		

*aintained on 25 lbs. total daily ration
*alculated for 506 lb. weanling on 16¾ lbs. daily ration

Situation II: Healthy horse, good-quality feed, last year's hay. Green hay is the chief source of vitamin A in the form of carotene. As hay ages, carotene decomposes, and color fades proportionately, signaling the loss of vitamin A.

(Suspect possible deficiency of vitamin A, also of zinc, manganese, copper, and thiamine.)

Situation III: Last year's hay, horse confined to stall. He's constitutionally healthy, but let's suppose that he has fractured a cannon bone and is spending six months indoors. Sunshine is the primary source of vitamin D, but he's not in the sun. Sun-cured forage is the next-best source, but vitamin D, like A, is unstable, and your hay is old.

(Suspect possible deficiency of vitamin D, plus vitamin A, zinc, manganese, copper, and thiamine.)

Situation IV: Healthy horse, poor-quality hay. While horse grain doesn't fluctuate a great deal in terms of feeding quality, the vitamin and mineral content of hay is highly sensitive to conditions of harvesting. As hay matures in the field, it increases in nutritionally valueless fibrous material, while vitamin and mineral content drop proportionately. If rain falls between cutting and baling, nutrients leach away. Since you don't know which nutrients have been affected (unless you submit a sample for laboratory analysis), you have to assume that the entire spectrum of hay-supplied vitamins and minerals is involved.

(Suspect possible deficiences of vitamin A, vitamin E, thiamine, riboflavin, pantothenic acid, calcium, phosphorus, magnesium, sulfur, and iron.)

Situation V: Hay's okay, but now the horse is sick. His feed is doing its job, but the horse may not be doing his. A new concern arises, this time for the vitamins that he synthesizes himself. If he is seriously ill, his digestive functions may be compromised. In this predicament we would, of course, consult a veterinarian.

(Suspect possible deficiencies of vitamin A, vitamin D [because he's in a stall], riboflavin, pantothenic acid, calcium, phosphorus, magnesium, sulfur, and iron, plus zinc, manganese, copper, and thiamine.)

You may have noticed that several minerals were never suspected of deficiency. Even Situation V, despite the severity of the problem, doesn't cause concern in regard to the horse's potassium needs. This is because almost any reasonable feeding combination supplies potassium in surfeit. Nor is there concern for deficiency in salt, iodine, or cobalt, because it is assumed that a trace-mineralized salt block is available to each of these horses. By voluntarily consuming enough salt to meet his needs, each horse has automatically covered his requirements for iodine and cobalt at the same time.

When it comes to matching your horse to the proper product, consider the nutritional categories above. If your horse is healthy and well fed, you probably have only four potential deficits to worry about: zinc, manganese, copper, and thiamine, and very likely small ones at that. Just be sure that the product you select contains moderate amounts of these elements. Portions of them are already supplied by his diet.

For a Situation II horse, add vitamin A to your shopping list, even though the compound supplement may contain it. This vitamin is just as unstable in the commercial product as it is in the bale of hay.

For a Situation III (last year's hay and confined to stall), expand your list to include vitamin D. The same instability problem exists here as it does with vitamin A.

In Situation IV, with a poor-quality hay diet, the list of vitamins and minerals to be ensured grows considerably longer so as to include all the nutrients normally supplied in the horse's feed. Since good hay is a major source of protein, this horse is a likely victim of protein deficiency, too. If protein were your only concern, there would be less-expensive ways of providing it. But while you're buying vitamins and minerals anyway, you can probably add protein supplements at little or no extra cost.

Make sure that a substantial amount of calcium is present in the product you select and that all the other feed-supplied elements are well represented. Check the vitamins (the list now includes the B vitamins riboflavin and pantothenic acid, in addition to A, D, and thiamine), allowing a margin for perishability. Don't worry about the vitamins your horse can synthesize for himself.

In Situation V, when the horse is seriously ill, he could have a deficiency in virtually any area. The wisest course is to bring your veterinarian into the picture to help you choose a complete supplement.

Once you've found several products that provide ample amounts of the elements your horse's diet lacks, study the feeding instructions. If you need a pound of the stuff to provide a reasonable level of, say, zinc, and the instructions tell you to feed three ounces—look elsewhere. Even though there's a large margin for error built into every over-the-counter product, it's not a good idea to exceed manufacturers' feeding instructions.

Having eliminated any products that require overfeeding, now consider the price. How much will it cost per day to maintain your horse on this product? Bear in mind that there's nothing wrong with underfeeding to manufacturers' instructions, if you can cut back and still deliver the desired level of the elements you're trying to supply.

Once you have narrowed the field, run a final check. Have you allowed for vitamin perishability? Are calcium and phosphorus, if included, present in a safe ratio to each other? A calcium/phosphorus ratio is acceptable within a range of 1:1 to 2:1. If you're feeding a poor-quality grass hay, a calcium content at the upper end of the acceptable range is advisable.

Look at the figure given for salt (sometimes termed sodium). Since you're providing salt free-choice in the form of a trace-mineralized brick or block, you don't need salt in your supplement. In fact, the more salt in the supplement the less your horse will consume free-choice, and the lower will be his intake of the accompanying trace minerals.

Check the iodine content. Of all the elements incorporated into vitamin/mineral supplements, it is the only one even remotely likely to cause problems. Iodine is believed to be toxic to horses when fed in concentrations as low as 2.18 milligrams per pound of feed. There are a few supplements on the market that might be capable of producing toxic concentrations of iodine if fed in combination with very small amounts of feed.

As for overdosing other elements, the theoretical possibility exists with regard to the fat-soluble vitamins A, D, E, and K (the body easily disposes of excesses of the water-soluble, B vitamins), as well as with zinc, manganese, and copper. But danger levels are either believed to be remote, or known to be hundreds of times the recommended dosage.

MIND YOUR P'S

When Buying Vitamin/Mineral Supplements

PERISHABILITY. There is no way to determine from the appearance of a product how much vitamin potency has survived shipping and storage. The best way to ensure relative freshness is to buy a popular product from a high-volume dealer, so that you can assume rapid merchandise turnover. When you get the product home, keep the package tightly closed, dry, and out of direct sunlight.

PRICE. Don't try to compare price, component for component, unless you're shopping for only one component. Calculate total cost per day for the product as a whole, based on the quantity you will have to feed in order to provide a sufficient amount of the element in shortest supply. Remember to allow for perishability of vitamins.

PALATABILITY. A great buy is no bargain at all if your horse won't eat it. Once you've narrowed the field to several serviceable products in an acceptable price range, let your horse be the final judge.

MEGADOSING

Horses in high-stress sports operate in the world of "jugs," B_{12} shots, and electrolytes.

Horses lose minerals through sweating. Normally the loss is very small, but in some sports it becomes significant. Endurance horses, racing twenty-five miles or more, especially in hot weather, sweat a great deal and lose minerals so fast that they exhaust body stores, and performance suffers drastically. Sophisticated Endurance riders often carry mineral supplements, in the form of electrolytes, with which they dose their horses at intervals throughout the ride.

A jug is a whopping dose of protein and energy food as well as vitamins and minerals, administered by IV drip (intravenously), usually to racehorses. The merits of the jug are controversial. Its vitamin/mineral content can be presumed useful only to the extent that a deficiency exists.

The giant doses of vitamin B_{12} administered to racehorses by injection are also controversial. Healthy horses synthesize enough vitamin B_{12} to meet their requirements. Horsemen who favor the injections claim that they produce euphoric "highs" that contribute to improved performance. No one has ruled out the possibility that they may contribute in some way which is not yet understood.

FEEDING HORSES ON A BUDGET

WILLIAM TYZNIK, Ph.D., professor at Ohio State University's Department of Animal Science, is one of the nation's foremost nutritionists working specifically with horses. He is also an active Standardbred racehorse owner, feed-company consultant, author, and lecturer.

Traditionally, horsemen believed that timothy and oats went together like love and marriage. Today, we seem to be seeing a lot of the latter broken down. I am looking forward to the same thing happening with the former.

Feeding with hay. If good hay were always available, 95 percent of our feeding problems would be solved. But hay, for the most part, is not good nutritionally, because horsemen don't demand that it be. The standard horse hay is timothy. There is nothing wrong with timothy if you cut it at the boot stage, which is when the head is just beginning to peek through the blades. But there's not much tonnage in this early stage, so the farmer lets it go until the nutrient value is greatly reduced or gone.

Alfalfa in all stages is by far the better hay around today as far as nutritional value goes, but most horsemen are afraid of it. Because alfalfa increases protein intake, the horse will urinate more frequently. The same thing happens to humans when they take more protein than they need into their systems. But when a horseman sees his horse urinating a lot and notices damp straw in the stall, he immediately thinks of kidney problems. This is a myth. I'd much rather see horses overfed protein than have it underfed, but it happens all the time.

The only problem we face with alfalfa is expense. Alfalfa is the best kind of protein you can get, but who can afford to pay the prices they're asking for it today?

Feeding on pasture. Pasture is another ideal way of supporting a horse, but it is as unrealistic for most people as getting good hay is. It's easy to be deceived about the amount of pasture you have for your horse. Horses refuse to eat the grass around the spots where they urinate and defecate. A horseman looks at what he thinks is a green pasture and would be surprised to learn that his horses consider most of it inedible. However, if the pasture is mowed and dragged on a regular basis in order to distribute droppings, horses have no other choice but to eat what's there. It's perfectly healthy for them, and you're getting the maximum use from your pasture. Most pastures benefit from being mowed and dragged on a monthly basis, and people find it a good method of weed control too, since the weeds don't have time to seed down when they're cut back regularly.

What makes pastures uneconomical is the amount of land it takes to support a horse. For one horse during the summer, you need two acres. Ideally, you'd want two separate pastures of an acre apiece, so that you could rotate them every four weeks. The unused pasture would be clipped and dragged and would grow back to a really lush condition after four weeks. Then you'd repeat the process with the other pasture.

A pleasure horse on good pasture doesn't need to be fed grain or hay at all. On a lush pasture, he needs nothing else in the way of nutrients aside from a free choice of mineral supplements such as limestone for calcium, phosphates for bone structure, and trace mineral salts for enzyme reaction. What your horse looks like should always be your prime guide when keeping him on pasture. Let his condition tell you if the pasture is insufficient to support him. To me, a horse is in good condition if he has no visible ribs, yet you can run your hand across his side and feel them right below the surface. If you have to dig for them, you've got a fat horse.

The best pasture is always the one that grows best in your area. Around my part of the country (Columbus, Ohio), we have luck with alfalfa-and-orchard-grass combinations. I'd suggest calling your local county extension office and telling them what you intend to do. They can suggest the best grasses for your area, climate, and soil.

I've found that there are usually two kinds of pasture: pretty pastures and useful pastures. Kentucky blue grass makes a pretty pasture, because people think that blue grass and white fences were made for horses, but this is one of the poorer grass choices in our area. It matures too quickly, its nutritional value goes down too quickly after maturity, and it can't withstand droughts.

Money-saving grains. Assuming that you do not have adequate pasture for support and that you must pay a lot for alfalfa hay, the most economical way to feed is with a grain ration supplementing the cheapest mold-free hay available, even straw if necessary, to give your horses something to chew on.

With good grain, horses don't need hay. But they do need something to combat boredom. The way we treat our horses is atrocious. We keep them in a stall all day and don't even give them the chance to decide whether they'd like to stand out in the rain or not. If you made a shed available to your horses and let them go in and out at will, chances are you'd see them standing out in the worst weather. I've yet to find a horse that has been harmed by this behavior. So we find that we have to give stalled horses some fiber in order to eliminate boredom. A horse that stands in without diversion soon learns to chew wood, and all of our technology and modern stable-management methods haven't found a way to stop this.

It doesn't matter what you feed your horse as long as you formulate a feed that meets his nutritional requirements. Just remember, when you substitute one kind of grain for another, to do it by weight. One of the greatest detriments to good feeding is the coffee-can measuring scoop. Horse owners feed by volume and end up foundering their horses, because they don't realize how much they're giving them. Feed should always be measured by weight.

Oats is the standard feed, but few horsemen realize that there are more-economical alternatives. There is a great deal of inconsistency in oats. A standard thirty-two-quart bushel can weigh anywhere from twenty-two to forty-four pounds. For some reason, much of the oats we feed goes right through the horse into the manure. Often you'll notice oats growing in a field where manure has been spread, because the oats weren't digested.

Nutrients are all relative, and I like to use corn as the standard. If corn has 100 percent nutrients, then good oats have 90 percent digestible nutrients and bad oats have 60 percent nutrients, by weight.

A bushel of corn weighs fifty-six pounds. No horseman in his right mind would consider doubling his horse's oats intake in a day, and yet you'll find that people will switch from feeding oats to feeding corn and still use the same two or three coffee cans as a measure. Since corn is twice as heavy as oats, they're doubling their horse's intake. Feeding half as much corn as oats will give you more nutrients than the oats. Since corn costs half as much as oats, it is obvious that you can cut grain costs by 25 percent if you switch to corn and halve the ration.

A misconception is that corn is hot feed. This, again, is due to the fact that most people feed by volume. A horse in cold weather will use a tremendous amount of energy just to keep warm. If you continue feeding the same amount of corn in the summer as you feed in the winter, pretty soon he'll put on a lot of weight, and when you try to work him he'll start to sweat because of the extra weight. It's nonsense to blame the corn for this. I would give a good ration of corn all year round, increasing it in the winter. The only thing that makes a horse fat is giving him more energy food than he needs.

A lot of people like to feed molasses with their grain, and in the South, where molasses is made, this may be an economical way of feeding. Molasses has 80 percent nutrient value compared to corn, but there's no magic to it. We use it to stick pellets together and to keep down dust in the food. While you can use mineral oil or water for the same purpose, molasses has nutritional value, which is an added bonus.

Feeding various age groups. Here at the Department of Animal Sciences at Ohio State University, we use a pelleted feed for horses in various stages of growth that has proved very successful and economical for us. We feed weanlings the greatest amount of protein, 20 percent to 22 percent, and the least protein, 10 percent to 12 percent, to horses over the age of three.

I personally like to use pellets. Each individual pellet is like a tiny energy capsule with all the vitamins and minerals incorporated. When you're feeding grain, the vitamins have a tendency to separate and end up at the bottom of the feedbox. Horses like to eat the larger chunks of corn and oats, and they frequently miss their vitamins and minerals entirely.

When a horse becomes a yearling, he no longer needs the 22 percent protein he has been getting, and we switch mixtures at this point to one with 16 percent protein. We take out most of the soybean meal and increase the oats and corn, leaving the minerals essentially the same. Two-year-olds are fed a ration of 14 percent protein pellets. In the third year, we switch to a diet of 10 percent to 12 percent protein, consisting of a grain mix containing corn and soybeans with molasses to stick it together and free choice of minerals. If the horses are not turned out regularly, we supplement with vitamins A, D, and E in crystalline form.

Vitamins and supplements. You hear a lot of talk about supplements. None of them are made of magic. I think some horsemen spend 90 percent of their time and money on exotics and forget to feed the horse.

Vitamin B_{12} is the one vitamin normal horses do not seem to need, and yet you see it mentioned again and again in tonics and supplements. B_{12} is given to horses as a treatment for anemia. Someone apparently came up with the idea that if you give a healthy horse B_{12} you will increase his blood count and therefore increase the oxygen in the bloodstream and somehow make him perform better. You can also increase a horse's blood count by scaring him, but I don't see anyone using that as a training method. If a horse is not anemic, there is no reason to increase his blood count and it doesn't seem to help his performance, either.

There are many commercial coat conditioners designed to put a shine on a horse, but the best of all is a tablespoon of Mazola oil, or any vegetable oil, in the feed twice a day. When you buy a commercial product, you are paying for a lot of processing that changes the oil into a granular or powder form. People don't think it is attractive to pour Mazola into the feedbox.

Horses that graze on a lush pasture are getting all the A, D, and E vitamins that they need, but these can be added to the horse's grain if you keep him in. The cost of vitamins A, D, and E in crystalline form is prohibitive, but the same vitamins are sold in a preparation for cattle at one quarter the price. Horses need 2,000 to 5,000 international units of vitamin A a day, 200 to 500 units of vitamin D, and 20 to 50 units of vitamin E. You can simply blend it in with whatever grain you're feeding so that each day's ration contains that number of units. All the B vitamins a horse needs can be obtained from brewer's yeast, which can also be mixed in with the feed. The one vitamin that can cause trouble in overdoses is vitamin D, too much of which results in excessive calcification of the soft tissues.

FEEDING GRASS

The Question: Is it all right to feed a horse grass clippings?

The Answer, from DR. MATTHEW MACKAY-SMITH, noted equine practitioner as well as active Endurance rider and fox hunter:

Fresh grass clippings, spread out so that they will not get moldy or heat up, are fine. However, extreme care must be taken to see that the grass is not left lying around in clumps or piles, because the possibility of mold or fermentation is tremendous. Just from fermentation, without mold formation, grass clippings can give a horse a bellyache within twelve hours. For example, wet grass clippings that are piled and left in the sun at eight o'clock in the morning will be well into the process of fermentation by suppertime. If you have a grass catcher on your mower and you shake it out so that the clippings are in a thin layer, it's all right. The horses either eat it up at once or it dries out, just like fresh hay.

Grass clippings are no different from any other lush vegetation and should be regarded as such. Hay, for instance, is clipped, and crimped to break the stems; some of the water is crushed out of it and it is fluffed up so that it will dry without fermenting or molding. Thus it follows that *any* vegetation should either be fed in the fresh state or else care must be taken to give it an opportunity to dry in such a fashion that it will not ferment or mold.

This brings to mind a word of caution on excessive changes in a horse's diet. If a horse has been on dry feed and you suddenly turn him out on very lush pasture, he may get what I call "pizza colic." This is because the grass is rich, and the other feed has been very bland and the large intestine is full of this relatively slow-moving material.

HOT MEALS FOR HORSES

Cooking feed for horses isn't widely practiced in the United States, but it is a faithfully respected element of stable management in the British Isles. The English cater to their horses in a way perhaps made possible by an abundance of youthful and enthusiastic stable help. Cooking feed may be too time-consuming for the large commercial stables in this country, but a private owner caring for his own horse will find that a hot meal once or twice a week is well justified in terms of the results it produces.

Why cook for horses? Cooked grain is more easily digested than raw. It's good for old horses and horses with tooth problems and digestive problems. Boiled barley is a very fattening feed. It's an efficient means of putting weight on poor horses and keeping weight on show horses without engendering the excess energy produced by a heavy oat diet. Boiled linseed is a fatty feed excellent for putting a shine on the coat and is soothing to the digestive tract. Boiled feeds, especially bran, have laxative properties helpful for the horse that stands in for a day or for a long period of time.

Feed swells when it is cooked (increases in volume and so goes farther). An appetizing warm meal encourages a shy feeder to eat and can be used to disguise medicine. On a cold day, warm food helps horses in the field or stable to maintain body temperature as a substitute for exercise and a high-carbohydrate diet.

What kinds of grains to cook. Oats, whole or crimped, barley, linseed, and bran lend themselves to cooking. Crimped *oats* cook more quickly but are less economical than whole oats. Oats are done when the husk cracks, exposing a grayish kernel. It takes about three to four hours of simmering for whole-grain, forty-five minutes to an hour for crimped.

Oats lend themselves to boiling or steaming. Steamed oats don't stretch as far as boiled oats, but they have a lovely aroma and are better suited than boiled oats for horses in hard training, when bulky feed is undesirable.

Barley is a wonderful feed for fattening horses without making them high and is an economical substitute for oats in areas where it is grown. Whole-grain barley is unsuitable for horses unless it has been properly cooked, and only whole barley should be used for cooking. Barley flakes, when boiled, are transformed into an unappetizing mush.

Like oats, barley should be cooked until the husk cracks, exposing the gray kernel. Barley will expand to about two and one half times its original volume. Cooked barley is not heating and makes a very good feed for show horses all through the summer. It is not suitable for feeding on a regular basis to fit horses, because it tends to make them fat and a little thick in the wind.

Bran is the basic ingredient of the famous bran mash, which, due to its laxative properties, is often fed in the evening when a horse is to stand in the next day, or with regularity to horses that are confined to their stalls. Dry bran is highly absorbent and is often added to other cooked grains to take up excess moisture.

Bran is a bland feed. Some horsemen add a handful of oats, salt, or bits of carrot and apple in order to increase its palatability.

Linseed is the seed of the flax plant. It is high in protein and fat content, which makes it fattening as well as an excellent coat conditioner. Horsemen often feed linseed in the spring and fall in order to put a bloom on the new coat. Its oil content is soothing to irritated intestines.

Whole linseed must be thoroughly cooked or it can actually be poisonous to horses. When quite done, the husk cracks, exposing a yellow kernel, the seed expands to about two and one half times its original volume, and the liquid thickens to a gray, jellylike gruel.

Cooked linseed is not a feed but a supplement that is added to the regular feed or mixed with bran in order to absorb the moisture.

Linseed is also available in meal, oil, or cake form, none of which requires cooking.

The equipment you need. If you are cooking for only a few horses, you can use an ordinary saucepan on a hot plate or stove coil. If you have a flame gas burner, even a galvanized stable bucket will do, since you adjust the flame to reach the indented bottom of the bucket.

Better still, a double boiler will guard against burning at the bottom of the pan. The upper element holds grain and water, and the boiling water in the lower part protects the mixture from direct heat.

Commercial cookers are available for preparing large quantities of stable feed, but they are hard to find. Hunt kennels usually own large cookers. Lobster and clam steamers—large enameled vessels sold for clambakes—may be adapted to stable use by replacing the steam rack with a container suitable for holding the grain-and-water mixture.

Whatever cooking arrangements you make, remember that there is always the danger of the grain burning unless it is stirred frequently. Most important of all, never leave grain cooking unsupervised in a stable. If you forget it, you may end up with a stable fire on your hands.

Recipes

Cooked Oats

1½ pounds of oats, whole or crimped
2 pints of water

Put the grain and water in a saucepan and bring to a boil, stirring frequently in order to prevent burning. Turn down the heat and simmer, adding water as long as the oats will absorb it, and stirring from time to time. Water should be just at the brink of a boil. Continue simmering until the husk has broken open, exposing the kernels (3 to 4 hours for whole oats, 45 minutes to an hour for crimped oats). Let it cool for ½ hour before feeding. May be fed alone, combined with dry grain, or with one pound of dry bran. (Feeds 2 to 3 horses.)

Steamed Oats

Steaming increases the palatability and digestibility of oats, while producing a less bulky feed than boiling. Place oats in a fine mesh container over but not touching boiling water. Cover and steam until the husks open. Cool before serving.

Boiled Barley

1 pound of barley
1 gallon of water

Combine grain and water in a saucepan and soak overnight. Bring slowly to a boil, stirring frequently. When the water is boiling, reduce the heat and simmer for 45 minutes or until the husk opens. (As a substitute for overnight soaking, you can simmer the mixture for 2 to 3 hours.) Mix with bran or other dry feed in order to absorb the moisture, let cook for 30 minutes, and feed. (Feeds about 3 horses.)

Bran Mash

3 pounds of bran
1 ounce of salt
Boiling water

Add as much boiling water as the bran-and-salt mixture will absorb until the bran is damp but not runny. Stir well with a wooden spoon or stick, and cover with a burlap feed sack in order to hold in the steam. Let stand for 15 to 20 minutes, until cool enough to feed. (Feeds one horse.)

Optional: to increase laxative properties, add a fistful of Epsom salts; for picky eaters, stir in a handful of oats or chopped apple and carrot.

Instant Bran Mash

When time is short or where facilities to heat water are unavailable, hot tap water may be substituted for boiling water in the above recipe. Add just enough water to the bran to dampen down the dust, and stir until cool enough to feed.

Linseed Jelly

1 pound of linseed
water

Place linseed in container, cover well with water, and let soak overnight. In a separate saucepan, heat one gallon of water to a boil and stir in the soaked linseed. Add a little cold water, stir, bring to a boil again, and continue boiling for about 20 minutes, stirring occasionally until a gray jelly is formed. Stir jelly into dry grain or bran, and feed. (Feeds one horse.)

Linseed/Bran Mash

1 pound of linseed
water
2 pounds of bran

Soak linseed overnight, as for linseed jelly, in enough water to cover completely. Heat the soaked linseed to a gentle boil and boil very slowly for 2 to 3 hours. Stir frequently. Linseed burns easily. Remove from heat, add bran, mix thoroughly, and cover with a burlap feed sack in order to retain the steam. Cool for ½ hour and feed. (Feeds one horse.)

Linseed Tea

½ pound of linseed
2 gallons of water

Combine linseed and water in a large saucepan, heat to boiling point and simmer for 2 hours. Strain out the seeds, let the liquid cool, and serve in place of water as a digestive aid. (Feeds one horse.)

Recommended frequency. Because of the high moisture content and relatively low energy value, boiled feeds are fed to horses in hard work not more often than once a week. After a hard hunt or a tough competition, a fit horse which is to stand in the next day benefits from the laxative effect of a bran mash.

Boiled oats may be fed every night during the winter to breeding animals —to horses standing in or to animals that have been let down. Barley, a richer feed than oats, is given to horses in need of fattening, up to three times a week. Linseed is fed once a week as a coat-conditioning supplement, often in combination with the weekly bran mash.

Will your horse eat it? Horses are creatures of habit, and any change in feed takes getting used to. Your horse may not dive into his first warm meal, but if you leave it in front of him, he'll eventually clean it up and gradually come to relish it. In the meantime, you can tempt him by adding handfuls of grain or of treats you know he likes. Another tip: Make sure that cooked feed is moist but not runny. The thicker its consistency, the more readily your horse will eat it.

Chapter 4

GROOMING

THE IMPORTANCE OF GROOMING

Your horse's hide is something more than just a wrapper for the package. If you think that a shiny coat does not in itself justify the time and effort required to achieve one, you should be happy to know that your elbow grease also contributes to a variety of vital functions.

The horse's skin and coat are his means of temperature control. When he sweats, the evaporation of moisture from the surface of his skin lowers his body temperature to within a normal range. His coat also insulates him from cold by trapping air between the hairs.

The long coat he grows in winter protects him from both cold and damp. When you bring in a horse on a snowy winter day, you will find that the outer coat is wet and cold, while the hair next to the skin is dry. These short, fluffy, inner hairs provide an insulating layer, while the coarse, outer hairs conduct moisture away from the horse's body. Moreover, when a horse is cold, his hair stands up, increasing the air space around each hair and thus providing better insulation. A sick horse also may have a "staring" coat, which stands up. This is nature's effort to help him conserve body heat.

Most horses have a fairly greasy, shiny coat. The grease is sebum, an oil secreted by the skin pores which more or less waterproofs the coat. Sebum combines with dandruff and flakes of dead skin to produce the grayish scurf you labor to eliminate.

When a horse is living outdoors and doing no work, nature usually provides adequate skin care. Like birds, horses groom themselves by rolling in dust or sand, thus breaking up dried mud on the coat. Left to himself, a horse seldom works long or hard enough to sweat through his coat.

When we bring the horse into a stall or use him for fairly demanding work, grooming becomes essential in order to help his skin and hair cope with this new way of life. The grease and scurf, while increasing insulation, interfere with the evaporation of sweat. In fact, they mix with the sweat to form a thick, gummy lather that is slow to dry. In hot weather, an unfit, ungroomed horse that works hard will lather profusely and may overheat. In cold weather, sweat soaks the coat from the skin out, robbing the hair of its insulating properties and conducting heat away from the body, where it is needed. Grooming reduces grease and scurf, so the horse sweats a thin, watery sweat that dries quickly. This is the basic purpose of grooming.

There are, of course, other purposes. Cleanliness certainly promotes good health, and daily grooming gives an opportunity to spot and treat minor injuries and abnormalities before they have become serious. Grooming also enhances beauty. In fact, really expert grooming can give the impression of more beauty than actually exists.

GROOMING THE GOOD OLD-FASHIONED WAY

There's more to grooming than knocking mud out from under the saddle and brushing straw from the tail. Before the era of the horse vacuum cleaner, a good grooming not only cleaned the horse right down to the skin; it toned his muscles too.

Modern horse owners often don't have time for a real old-fashioned grooming job. Fortunately, coat gloss comes in a spray can, but there's still no way to spray on health and muscle tone. There is no shortcut to the physical well-being that good grooming brings about. If you don't have time for the full routine, you can borrow parts of it to supplement your usual daily grooming procedure. But a word of warning: Don't try to take on the whole program the first day. A complete grooming job requires a fit groom!

The traditional thorough grooming starts with:

Picking out your horse's feet while he's still in his stall (so as not to clutter up the aisle).

With a rubber currycomb, curry the body, using a circular motion, breaking up mud and loosening surface dirt. You may use a rubber currycomb on the legs and head, but with extra care. It's uncomfortable for the horse, and bone near the surface is easily bruised. Never use a metal currycomb on any part of the horse's body. You can damage the coat and even injure the skin.

With a dandy brush, remove the dirt the currycomb has loosened. Work in the direction the coat grows, with short strokes ending with an upward flick. Brushing downward will only return the dirt to the coat.

The dandy brush can be used all over the horse's body. It's a handy tool for removing mud from heels and pasterns and other areas where it is difficult to use a currycomb. First employ a scrubbing movement in order to loosen the dirt, then work with the lay of the hair in short flicks, in order to remove the dirt.

Use the body brush after all the surface dirt is gone, to work up deep-seated dirt and grease that collect near the skin. Work the body brush over the whole body in a circular motion, as if you were currying. Hold a metal currycomb in the other hand and scrape the body brush against it occasionally in order to clean it.

Still with the body brush, go over the horse again, using straight strokes in the direction of the hair in order to remove the dirt you've brought to the surface. After each stroke, scrape the body brush against the metal currycomb in your other hand. To make sure your horse is really clean, rub hard with your fingertips. His coat may look clean, but if your fingers are coated with white, it means that dirt and grease still lurk.

For wisping, you can use a folded towel, although the correct way is with a real old-fashioned hay wisp (which you can make yourself). Holding the wisp in one hand and a towel in the other, you slam down the wisp and then swipe in the direction of the hair with the towel. When the wisp hits, the muscle underneath tenses. While you swipe with the towel, it relaxes. Wisping does away with any remaining dust, but primarily it's a muscle toner.

If wisping is new to the horse, start gently to avoid scaring him. Eventually you want to bring the wisp down with as much force as you can muster. To do it properly, you have to learn to put your body weight behind each stroke. You can't do it with your arm muscles alone, because they will tire too quickly.

The areas to wisp are the neck, the shoulders, the barrel, the hindquarters, and the muscular part of the hind legs. You can wisp the loins, but this must be done gently in order to protect the kidneys, which lie near the surface. You probably won't be able to do more than ten strokes in each area when you start out, but gradually, as your own fitness develops, you should aim for fifty.

Wash the eyes and nose with a damp sponge. Use a second damp sponge to wash underneath the dock.

Now the tail. Never use a dandy brush here. It breaks the hairs and pulls them out. Groom the tail by separating all the hairs with your fingers. Then you can safely use a comb to straighten the short hairs at the top and comb out the long hairs at the bottom. While you comb the bottom, take hold of the tail about a third of the way up with your other hand, in order to make sure you don't pull out any hairs. Even though all the tangles may be gone, never risk combing through the entire tail from top to bottom.

In winter, when you cannot wash the tail and you still want to remove all the dirt and grease that accumulates near the tailbone, part the hair at intervals and scrub in between them with a body brush. Then brush in the direction of the hair to remove the dirt you've loosened.

Lay the mane. If it lies on the right side of the horse's neck, brush it first from the left side, and then from the right, with a damp brush.

HOW TO MAKE YOUR OWN GROOMING WISP

Lay down a small section of hay in a long, narrow row. Grass hay or timothy with long fibers is best. Straw is too brittle. Sprinkle a little water on the hay.

Pick up a handful at one end and give it a half twist to start a half-inch-thick rope. Too thick, the wisp will be too bulky; too thin, the rope will break.

If it starts to break, untwist and add a little extra hay to the weak spot. While a helper holds the end taut, keep twisting until you have a rope six to seven feet long.

With your helper still holding one end, make two loops in the other end of the rope.

Pass the loop in your right hand under the rope.

Hold it in your left hand while you reach over the rope with your right hand . . .

. . . and bring the loop back over the top of the rope to your right.

Now do the same thing with the loop in your left hand, passing it under the rope . . .

. . . and bringing it back over the top of the rope to your left.

Continue almost to the ends of the loops, and pass the tail end of the rope through what remains of the loops.

Now weave the rope back under itself to make it secure.

Trim off the tail and the bristles, and you have a wisp that should last two to three weeks with daily use.

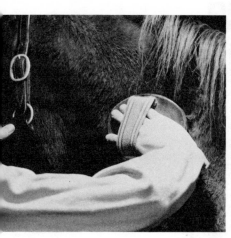
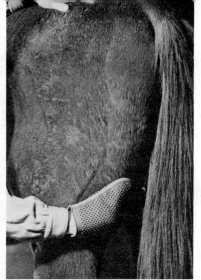

1. Steady your horse's head with your left hand on his halter while, with your right hand, you curry in circular strokes, beginning behind the ear and working down the neck and over the entire body. Work gently over sensitive areas like the belly while your other arm, resting on the withers, alerts you to sudden tension.

2. A flexible rubber grooming mitt works well behind the hind legs and over sensitive bony contours. Place your free arm on the croup and stand close, so that if your horse kicks, he won't catch you with the full force of an extended leg.

3. For elbows, use your grooming mitt or a cactus cloth rolled into a wad for scrubbing.

GROOMING TECHNIQUES

Captions by Susan Harris

Currying

4. Or loop it around the elbow and pull it back and forth like a shoeshine cloth. Work your way down each leg in turn, to break up caked mud.

5. Rub the cloth up and down the leg, gently poking the fingers of both hands into the grooves formed by the tendons. With one finger, scrub lightly on the backs of the pasterns.

6. Currying is complete when you can run your fingers over the entire coat without encountering bits of caked material. Don't forget to check the elbows, the girth and saddle areas, and the insides of the hind legs.

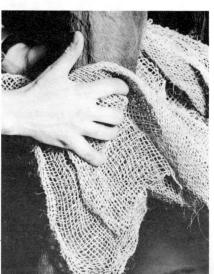
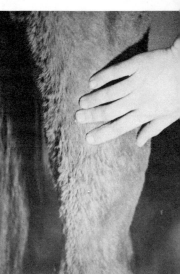

 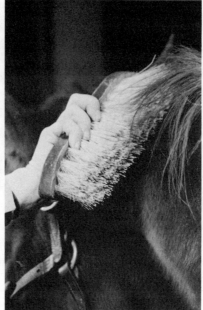 

1. Begin again behind the ears and work over the body, using short, brisk strokes.

2. End each stroke with an upward flick of your wrist to bounce the particles of dirt and dead skin out of the coat.

3. If your arm tires, hold the brush in both hands and . . .

Dandy-brushing

4. . . . flick it toward you.

5. For maximum effect from each stroke on the legs, hold the brush lengthwise. (Also, brushing crosswise wears out the center bristles.) Do the leg surfaces that face you from one position, and finish the legs when you move to the other side of the horse.

6. Stand close to the hind leg and keep your free hand on the hock to steady your horse and sense his movement.

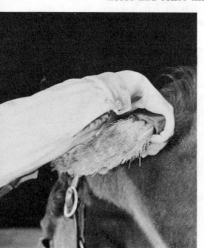 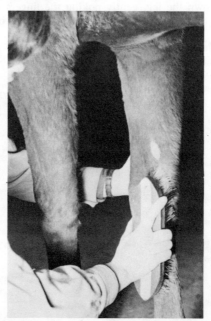 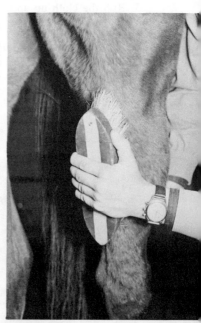

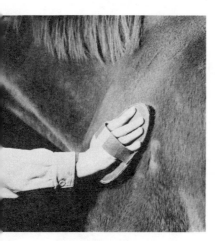
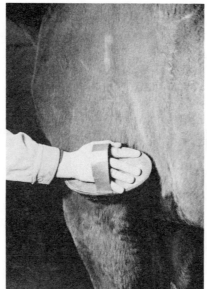
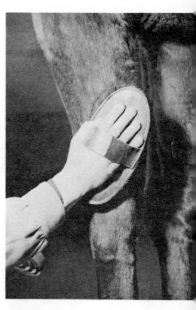

1 and 2. Lean your weight on the brush, pushing the bristles down through the hair, and cover the horse's body in long strokes. The first two photos show one stroke. Hold a metal or plastic currycomb in your other hand and scrape the body brush over it after every couple of strokes, to clean the brush.

3. Hold your brush diagonally, fingers pointing upward, to do the legs.

Body-brushing

4. Hold it diagonally, fingers downward, to penetrate the many crevices of the hock.

5. Hold the brush horizontally to do the pasterns and coronary bands. Always stroke in the direction of the hair.

6. If the croup is higher than your shoulder, stand on a stool to lean into your strokes; or bang your brush down at the beginning of each stroke to drive it well into the coat. After six strokes of the body brush, the dust is gone from the surface. Any fine gray particles still clinging to the roots of the hair will have to be removed by bathing or hot toweling.

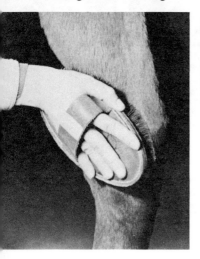
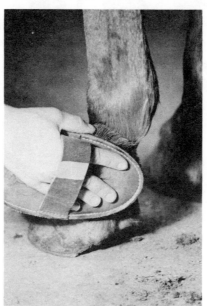
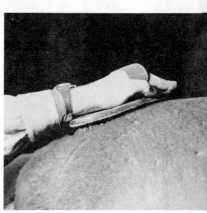

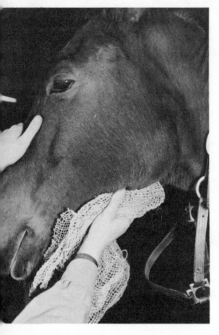

Grooming the Head

You can use a dandy brush to take mud off, but a cactus cloth works as well and is more comfortable for the horse. Slip the halter off his nose (he's still restrained by the crownpiece around his neck) and steady his head with your free hand.

With the body brush, work outward from the base of the mane.

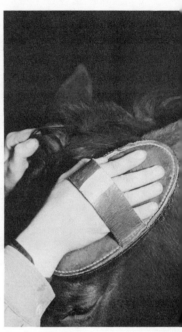

Grooming the Feet

1. Pinch the tendons with your right hand while your left hand rests on the front of the pastern, ready to support the hoof when the horse lifts it.
2. Insert your pick between the bulb of the heel and the end of the shoe and work quickly, levering out the dirt.
3. If you use hoof dressing strictly as a conditioner and you're in a hurry, you need only apply it to the bulbs of the heels . . .
4. . . . and in a strip around the coronary band.

Grooming the Tail

Use a regular hairbrush with natural bristles, brushing the bottom of the tail first and working up so that you're less likely to snag a tangle and break off hairs.

Hold the bulk of the tail in your left hand and gently brush out a small section at a time.

Grooming the Mane

With the body brush, first brush the underside of the mane up, then brush it down again, a section at a time, standing on a stool if necessary so that you force the bristles right to the roots of the hair.

Lay the mane flat with a dampened water brush.

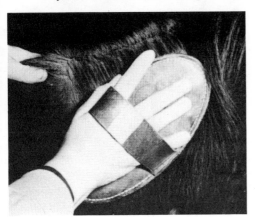
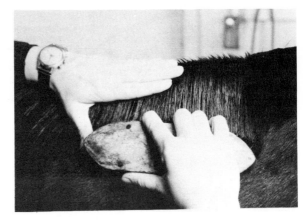

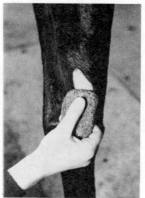

The Finishing Touches

1. To neaten the legs, cut the chestnuts flush with the hair.

2. Sand them smooth. The commercial bot-egg remover being used here works well. Then darken them with a little Vaseline.

3. Pat cornstarch onto stockings to whiten them. Brush off the excess.

4. Apply hoof dressing.

5. Pour a little baby oil into the palm of your hand and rub it over the ears, the muzzle, and the skin around the eyes.

Final Inspection Zones

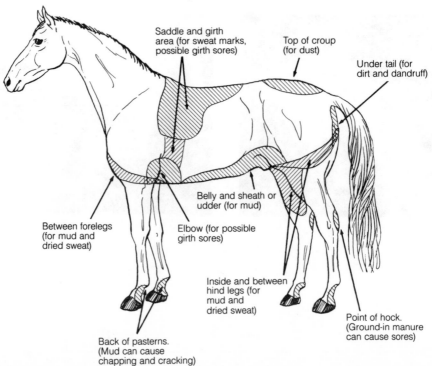

Saddle and girth area (for sweat marks, possible girth sores)

Top of croup (for dust)

Under tail (for dirt and dandruff)

Belly and sheath or udder (for mud)

Between forelegs (for mud and dried sweat)

Elbow (for possible girth sores)

Inside and between hind legs (for mud and dried sweat)

Point of hock. (Ground-in manure can cause sores)

Back of pasterns. (Mud can cause chapping and cracking)

HOW THE EXPERTS GROOM THEIR HORSES

ROBERT HALL, trainer of the British Olympic Dressage Team for four Olympic Games and founder of the Fulmer School of Equitation, is an international equestrian authority and a renowned dressage coach.

We groom our horses for three reasons: to stimulate circulation and promote health, to prevent disease, and to ensure cleanliness and improve appearance. We stress that our students must have the proper instruments at hand before they begin a grooming routine. These include a hoof pick, a dandy brush or a rubber currycomb for removing heavy dirt and caked mud, a body brush for dust and scurf, a metal currycomb for cleaning the body brush, a banger or wisp to promote circulation, a water brush for use on the mane, tail, and feet, two stable sponges for the eyes, muzzle, and dock, and a stable rubber for the final polish. Plaiting and trimming equipment (thread, needles, mane comb, and scissors) are necessary extras, along with Vaseline, insect repellent, bucket and water, hoof oil, and tail bandages.

"Quartering" is a ten-minute grooming performed to make the horse tidy before exercise. We pick out the feet; sponge the eyes, muzzle, and dock; and remove any stable stains. We then give a quick brush-down with the body brush. If the horse is blanketed at the time, the rug can be undone in front and turned back so that we can groom without undoing the roller or surcingle or stripping the blanket if the horse is not to be ridden immediately. I always stress that keeping a horse blanketed, even with a light sheet in the summer, does wonders to keep the coat clean and in good condition.

Strapping is a longer procedure best done after exercise, when the pores of the horse's skin are open, the skin loosened, and the horse relaxed. First, we tie the horse securely and pick the feet out carefully with the hoof pick, checking for any signs of thrush. While picking the feet, we always move the pick from heel to toe to avoid damaging the sensitive parts of the frog. We run our fingers over the shoes and hooves to make sure no clenches have risen and that the shoes are secure. We remove the heavy dirt or caked mud with the dandy brush or rubber currycomb, a procedure usually necessary only for horses kept on grass. We start at the poll on the near side and work backward, using the brush with a to-and-fro motion, and repeat on the off side. We are careful not to use this brush on the tender parts of the horse's body, and try to avoid using it on horses with sensitive skin as well.

The major part of the grooming is done with the body brush and a metal currycomb, always used together. The short, close-set hairs of the body brush are designed to reach right through to the skin below. We use the brush in short, circular strokes, always in the direction of the coat, drawing the body brush briskly across the teeth of the currycomb every four or five strokes to dislodge any dirt from the brush. So that we do not dirty a part of the horse already cleaned, we start with the mane and then work from the face backward. When dealing with the face on some horses, we may have to dispense with the currycomb in order to hold the horse's head steady. Finally, we brush out the tail, a few strands at a time.

The next step is the optional use of the banger or wisp on the neck, quarters, or thighs, to help develop the muscles and stimulate the skin. Then, working with the sponges, water brush, and a bucket of water, we gently clean the eye and muzzle regions with a damp sponge and follow with the second sponge under the dock. We then lay the mane with a dampened water brush, wash the feet with the brush, and oil them with a hoof preparation. We finally wipe mineral oil on the skin around the eyes, the muzzle, and inside the ears, which makes the skin a little shinier when we get ready to go into the show ring.

> WENDY WATERS, as head groom for Rodney Jenkins's Virginia stable, Hill Top, has prepared some of the nation's top hunters and jumpers for the show ring, including Idle Dice, Icey Paws, and San Felipe.

You can't make a horse shine at the show. It takes long hours before. Day-to-day care. Every day.

One of the most important conditioners of a horse is a regular schedule. The horses at Hill Top are fed at 7 A.M. and 4 P.M. on the dot. Like a factory with a time clock. Once they settle into a routine, they know exactly what to expect, and they don't fret away condition wondering when the next meal is coming.

After the horses have eaten in the morning, we turn them out in paddocks. We pick out their feet and boot them up. They all wear bell boots to protect the coronary bands of the front feet from heel grabs. The young horses that are inclined to play around and run a lot wear shin boots as well, to give them a little extra protection.

After each horse has been out for thirty or forty minutes, I bring him in and groom him thoroughly.

I go over the horse with a medium-stiff brush to take the loose dirt off. Then, if the weather is too cool for a bath and the horse is damp, I rub him out with a rag. I may go through several rags on one horse, rubbing in a circular motion, wherever the coat is damp with sweat. As I dry his coat, I'm also removing the grime that has worked to the surface during exercise. If his legs are muddy, I use a stiff brush. Finally, I take a dry towel and smooth the hair in the direction it grows to lay it flat. I walk him until he's cool and put him in the cleaning rack to do him up.

On warm days, instead of rubbing him dry I give him a bath, sponging him off from a bucket. After a hard workout, I add a brace to the water. But I don't use it regularly, because it dries the coat. I turn the hose on his legs if they're muddy, letting the water pressure take the mud off. I sponge out his nose and dock, then I squeeze all the water from the sponge and run it down his legs. If you leave the legs wet, you're encouraging infections, such as "scratches," at the back of the pasterns.

When he's dry and cool, I do him up. First I curry him vigorously with a round rubber currycomb. The rubber comb has more give than plastic. It's easy on the horse's skin and its shape lends itself to the circular, sweeping motion I make when I use it. I start on his neck, work around his ears, down to his knees, over the back and rump, loosening dirt and dead hair. Then I brush him off with a medium-stiff brush, using short, quick strokes. I use the brush all over his body, including his face and lower legs.

Next is the rub rag. The secret here is to rub, not just pat. I go all over the horse in the direction of the hair, really putting some effort into it. The rag takes off the fine dust left by the brush and puts a shine on his coat.

I pick out his feet again. I brush the soles clean with a stiff brush. Then I paint the walls and soles with hoof dressing. I use a mixture of one-third pine tar and two-thirds peanut oil. It seems to be the best conditioner of soft, shelly feet, and we never have a horse with thrush.

If the horse is to be ridden (we don't ride every horse every day), I tack him up. If not, he goes back to his stall.

When he comes in from his work, I repeat the grooming procedure.

I bathe him or, in cold weather, I rub him dry. I cool him out and do him up. I take a careful look at his legs. If they're hot or filled, or if he's had a hard work, I may massage them with one of a variety of medications. A few minutes of vigorous up-and-down rubbing with both hands helps restore circulation.

I may bandage his legs before I put him away. I do not follow a rigid procedure. I use whichever ointment a particular horse needs. I may use something different on each of his legs if they feel different. Leg treatments either cool a leg out, like a poultice; increase circulation, like a whirlpool; or sweat a leg, like glycerine. I might poultice a horse that has worked hard if I feel heat in his legs, or I might use white lotion or simply alcohol if they feel normal. An alcohol-and-water mixture under bandages is fine for most horses.

I bandage routinely at shows. The horses are working harder. They need the extra support. And when we're in temporary stalls with gaps between the boards, I wrap the legs so they can't fit between.

The day before we leave for a show, I give the horse a soap bath with a gel-like shampoo. After shampooing the tail, I rinse it with a mixture of vinegar and water, about three-fourths of a cup of vinegar to a bucket of water. The rinse cuts the suds and separates the snarls. When I'm washing a gray horse, I add some blueing to the final rinse water, about one capful to three gallons of water or two capfuls to five gallons. I use the rinse very sparingly; too much and the horse turns blue.

If the weather is cool, I use warm water for the bath, of course, and walk the horse dry under a wool cooler. Then, with trimming clippers, I trim his whiskers, his fetlocks, and the edges and insides of his ears. I also trim a one-inch "bridle path." I use scissors if the horse violently objects to clippers.

Most of the shows we go to last at least several days and we're stabled on the grounds. I try to maintain the home routine, except that I feed at 5 A.M. so that I have enough time to prepare horses for the early classes.

Six grooms travel with us to the big shows. When the horses finish eating, someone starts the longeing while I begin braiding. Meanwhile, a couple of other people are mucking out. Each horse gets about fifteen minutes on the longe line to save Rodney time. When he gets on, the horse is warmed up and ready to school over a few fences before going into the ring.

It takes me about twenty minutes to braid each horse. I use acrylic yarn, because it doesn't stretch like wool, navy blue for all the horses. It's a quiet color. I put in twenty to twenty-five braids, each about two and one half inches long.

I'll usually finish braiding about forty-five minutes before the first class. I assign people to groom and tack up.

Before a horse leaves the barn, we paint his feet. I take him to the ring about twenty minutes before Rodney needs him. This leaves me time to check his tack and give him a few more minutes on the longe line if he's been standing for a while.

I take a rub rag and a cooler or a fly sheet. Depending on the time of year, the cover keeps the horse warm or it protects his coat from sunbleaching. It also keeps the flies off.

When I reach the ring, I tighten the girth, tuck loose leathers into keepers, and check the martingale length.

When the horse comes out of the ring, if he had a good trip and it looks as if he may be called back to jog, I take his saddle off and dry his back with the rag I've brought with me. I rub him until the saddle and girth marks are gone, cover him, and walk him if he's warm.

Back at the barn, I take the braids down and do the horse up once again before he goes to bed.

PULLING THE MANE

Brush the mane flat on the right side.

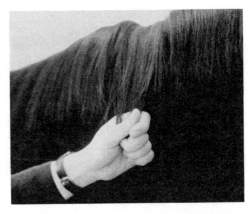

Grasp a small bunch of the longest hairs.

Comb sharply upward and away from you. The hairs should fan out from an area an inch or two long at the base of the mane.

Give a sharp jerk downward and toward you, keeping the teeth pointed in the direction of your pull.

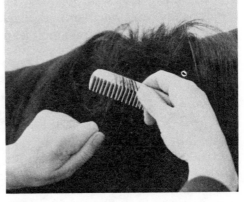

With the comb still up near the roots, wrap the hairs around it.

Some hairs will break, some will pull out from the roots. But you shouldn't come away with more hairs than this in any one effort.

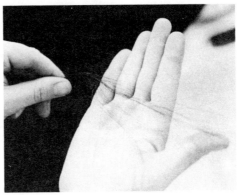

BRAIDING THE MANE

Braiding Equipment

A fine-tooth comb for parting off sections to braid.

A large, hinged hair clip, as used in beauty parlors, to keep the nearby mane out of the way while working.

A sponge to wet down the mane.

A braid puller (made by doubling a short piece of baling wire and leaving an oval loop at the end so that the wire looks like a needle with an oversized eye) for pulling the yarn through the braids.

A pair of scissors.

Yarn or rubber bands.

A large-eyed yarn needle.

A seam ripper for unbraiding without cutting the hair.

You might also want to invest in a grooming apron to keep your materials handy while you work, although many seasoned braiders find it just as easy to stuff their tools into their jeans pockets.

Start with mane and forelock pulled to a good braiding length.

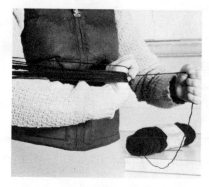

Make ten loops of the yarn and . . .

. . . cut the loops in h

Wet the mane with a damp sponge.

Use a comb to part between braids.

Check that the braiding sections are of uniform width, about two fingers.

  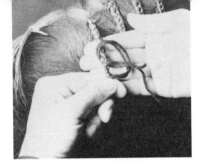

raid, keeping the hair close to the horse's neck. As you cross each strand over, give it a twist with your thumb so that it points upward behind the next strand to cross over.

Incorporate one strand of yarn.

Tie off the end.

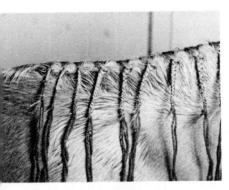  

aid as far back on the withers as you can.

Poke the loop of your braid puller through the base of the braid.

Thread the yarn through the loop . . .

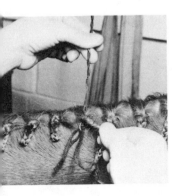  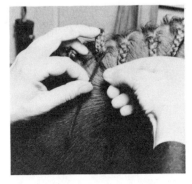

. . . and pull up to double the raid under.

Separate the strands of yarn and . . .

. . . cross them behind the braid.

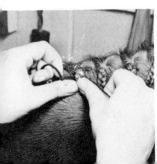 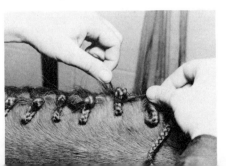 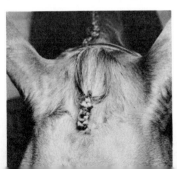

Push up on the braid with your thumb . . .

. . . and tie a surgeon's knot. The extra twist will keep the first tie tight while you make the second tie on top of it.

When you've finished the mane, follow exactly the same procedure for the foretop.

Braiding with Rubber Bands

If you want to braid your horse's mane in a hurry and you don't mind sacrificing something in appearance, you can put the braids up with rubber bands instead of yarn. Most tack stores sell braiding elastics in black, gray, and several shades of brown; these bands blend into the mane much better than the tan, office-style ones.

Part and braid the mane just as you would to put it up with yarn, except that you must braid all the way to the end of the hair. Fold the end of the braid so that the tiny "paintbrush" hairs point upward on the outside of the braid. Wind the rubber band around the little braided knob, doubling the band again and again and keeping it well down toward the end of the braid.

Turn the braid under so that the first elastic is hidden and use a second elastic to secure it. Each time you twist the elastic, lift it up above the previous twist. Let the last loop drop one quarter inch below the rest to help the braid "turn the corner" around the crest and lie flat against the neck.

If you use one elastic instead of two, you can put the mane up faster, but this method is also less secure. Braid the hair all the way down and pinch the end tightly while you double the braid up and secure the whole thing with an elastic. Put the single elastic on just as you did the second elastic in the double-band method, and pull the tiny "paintbrush" to the left, where the next braid can cover it.

To take out a mane put up with elastics, simply take hold of the little knob or the unbraided hair at the end of the braid and pull. The elastic will pop off and you can unbraid the hair with your fingers.

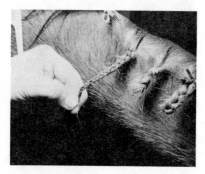

Braid as far down the section as you can.

Fold up the end.

Secure with a small rubber band

Fold the braid under. Wrap a second rubber band several times around the base of the hair.

Push up the braid to form a "corner" and . . .

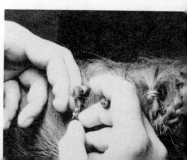

. . . anchor it with the last twist of the rubber band.

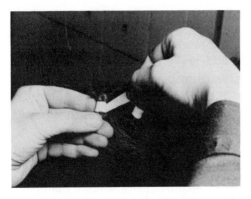

Wrap the tape as close to the base of each braid as you can get it.

Taped braids—flattering when the crest is flexed.

TAPED MANES

Dressage horses and Event horses competing in the dressage phase are usually shown with white tape along the mane. The mane is first braided with yarn or elastics of the same color as the hair, and then each braid is taped. The neat line of white dots along the crest draws attention to the line of the neck; it is especially flattering when the horse flexes his neck.

You can use ordinary adhesive tape, but the plastic tape used for mending and bookbinding is whiter and easier to work with. The tape should be no more than a quarter inch wide. Cut a piece about one and one half inches long and simply wrap it once around the braid as high up as possible. Be sure to stick the end of the tape to itself, not to the hair, or it will come off.

Tape each mane braid and the foretop as well. If your horse has a white mane and the tape doesn't show up, leave it off. Never use colored tape. It will mark you as a newcomer to competition.

TRAINING THE MANE TO LIE OVER

Roger Ruetenik, Quarter Horse judge, show stable owner, and all-around horseman:

We start out by thinning the mane. If a horse has a really cresty mane, we may use thinning shears on the underside; that is, on the side where the mane will lie. Thinning has to be done gradually, a little bit at a time, for a professional-looking job.

After the mane is thinned, we shampoo with a high-quality shampoo and braid the mane while it is still wet. We usually put the braids in at night and take them out very carefully by hand in the morning. You can't just braid a mane and forget it, or the hair will die and break off. After the braids are out, we brush the mane with rainwater and brush it dry. I don't know exactly why, but rainwater seems to leave the hair softer and less brittle than tap water even after it dries. We do a lot of brushing with rainwater to keep the moisture in the mane replenished.

If the mane is an especially difficult one to get to lie down, we may put little fish weights about the size of BBs on some fish line and braid it into each braid. The horse is hardly conscious of them, but the extra weight they provide helps to flatten the mane against the horse's neck.

A few days' repetition of the shampooing, braiding and unbraiding, and brushing with rainwater will give you a healthy mane that lies in a flowing manner.

JOE FERGUSON, of Norristown, Pennsylvania, an expert amateur trainer and conditioner of hunters and jumpers:

I use a wave-setting product to train a mane over. The stuff I use is a gel, heavy-duty-type, and I buy it by the gallon.

First comb the mane over and pull it. With nervous or very sensitive horses, you might try wearing a thin rubber glove, or rubber "fingers," which are made to protect an injury, on your thumb and index finger, and plucking the hairs from underneath by hand instead of using a comb. You must take only a few hairs at a time and perhaps not attempt to do the whole job in a single session.

When it is all pulled and plucked the way you want it, take handfuls of the gel and saturate the mane with it, right into the roots on the neck. Then take a comb and comb out the excess.

After all the excess is combed out, go to the other side (the side opposite the one on which the mane is to lie) and with a stiff mane brush or an ordinary scrub brush, brush the mane over from the roots. Let it dry with the gel in it.

You may have to apply the gel three or four days in a row if the horse is uncomfortable and tries to shake it out. The most difficult type of mane to get to lie down is the one with a particular section that keeps flipping over. But if you keep after it with the gel and brushing, it will come over. After the mane is lying right, take a comb and comb out the stickiness.

I think this method is much simpler than braiding or rubber bands, and you don't have to worry about breaking the hair. You don't even have to keep the horse in while you're doing it. I do it on horses right out of the field.

HOW TO PULL YOUR HORSE'S TAIL

JIMMY HERRING, groom for the F. Eugene Dixon string of Grand Prix jumpers, demonstrates his system for producing a sleek tail for showing unbraided.

 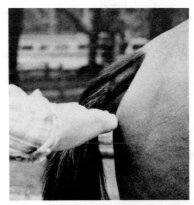 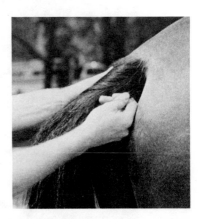

1. Jimmy makes a part from the base of the tail down to the bulge of the quarters. The part begins in the middle of the side, and as it descends the tail it curves smoothly toward the underside.

2. This is where the part should stop.

3. Holding the hairs to the left of the part firmly out of the way with the left hand, he strips away all the hairs to the right of the part, grasping a few at a time between thumb and forefinger and plucking them out by the roots. Hairs too short to grip with the fingers can be removed with pliers.

4. The finished area tapers from top to bottom, covered only by wisps of hair that grow from the upper surface. When both sides are completed, a view of the underside of the tail would show a U-shaped hairless area.

5. To train the hairs to lie smoothly, he wraps the tail in a wet elastic knit tail bandage, starting as close to the top as he can lay the bandage and working in a crisscross pattern. If you use a cotton knit racetrack bandage, you won't have to worry about the bandage tightening as it dries.

6. He secures the bandage with a knot that he tucks under the last lap.

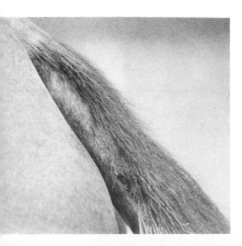  

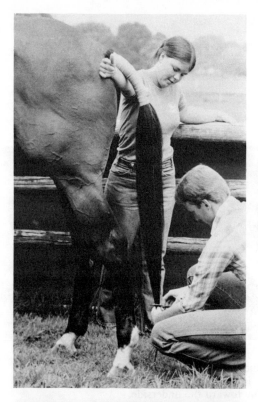

7. While a helper supports the tail with her forearm to stimulate its natural carriage in motion, Jimmy trims the bottom with scissors, angling the blade slightly upward as he cuts from back to front. The aim is to eliminate the wispy ends, leaving the tail as long as possible but full at the bottom and neatly banged.

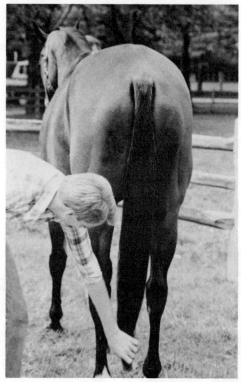

8. The finished job.

BRAIDING THE TAIL

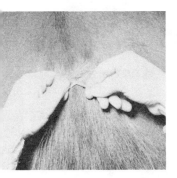  

1. Pick up a small section of hair from the left side of the dock and place it between two small sections from the right.

2. Hold the sections from left and lower right between your right thumb and forefinger. With your left hand, pass the higher strand from the right behind the strand below it.

3. Bring it up between the other two strands. Pinch the strands tightly in your right hand while you part a small section of hair from the left side.

 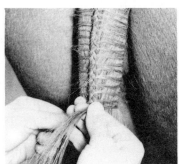 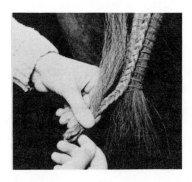

4. Pass the new section from the left under the lower strand originating at the right, add it to the strand you've just braided, and pull it tight.

5. Repeat the procedure with the higher strand originating on the left, again on the right, and so on until you reach the end of the dock. You will always be working with three strands.

6. Continue a simple braid, without adding any more hair, for six to eight inches past the dock, and turn the end up.

7. Twist an elastic around the end to make a little braided knob.

8. Stuff the knob up under the tail braid.

9. Wrap another rubber band around the top of the loop to anchor it, and the tail is finished.

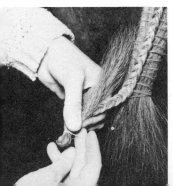  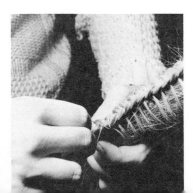

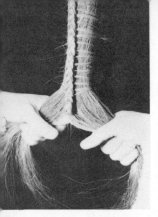   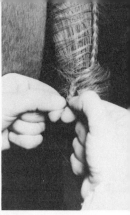

Adding a Mud Knot

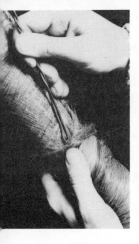 

1. Divide the skirt into two equal sections.
2. Cross the left section up and over the front of the tail. Hold it with your right thumb while you reach behind the tail, and pull it the rest of the way around.
3. Cross the right section up and over the left one. Hold it with your left thumb while you reach behind the tail with your right hand, and pull it around. Repeat the alternating wraps, right and left, up the dock.
4. When you have just enough left to make one more circuit of the tail, braid it together and . . .
5. . . . poke the braid down into the top wrap.
6. This will keep your horse's tail clean until you go into the ring. If you do it neatly, you can show in it too.

French-braiding the Foretop

If your horse has a messy foretop or if you want to add a fancy touch to your braiding job, you may want to do a French braid in the upper foretop. The French braid gathers all the foretop hair into a neat braided line that ends in the mane-style braided loop. If your horse is head-shy or if you are in a hurry, this method may take too long to be practical.

1. Start by bringing a strand of hair from the left side of the foretop between two strands from the right.
2. Bring the upper strand from the right behind the one below it and add a strand from the left, just as you do to French-braid the tail.
3. Continue your French braid until you reach the point where the hairs on the underside of the foretop grow free of the skin. Add any remaining hair to the center strand of the braid.
4. Braid the hair to the end and put it up as you did the mane braids.

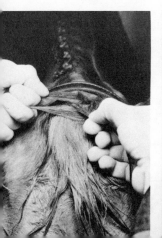 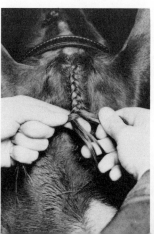 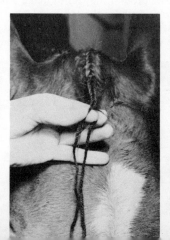 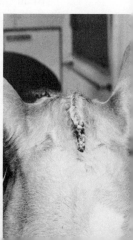

CLIPPING YOUR HORSE

Getting the Most from Your Clippers

Make sure you have all the necessary equipment handy before you start to clip.

You'll need: heavy-duty body clippers (never try to do the job with small trimming clippers), a coffee can full of kerosene for rinsing the clipper blades, light machine oil for lubricating the oiling points, a rag and a small brush for cleaning hair from the blades, and masking tape for marking off areas you wish to leave unclipped, such as stockings or a saddle patch.

Your horse's skin and hair must be thoroughly clean or the clippers will stick. If possible, bathe him the day before you clip, so that his hair is completely dry and clean when you begin. Secure him in cross-ties and use a halter with a removable throatlatch. Just before you start to clip, vacuum the horse or groom him thoroughly with a body brush to eliminate any remaining dirt.

Clipping a horse, even a quiet one, is usually a two-man job. Clipping a nervous one will probably require not only an assistant but also a dose of tranquilizer. Some horsemen use a twitch when clipping a nervous horse, but it has a temporary effect, which may not last long enough to complete the clipping. It may serve merely to confirm the horse's impression that clipping is an unpleasant ordeal.

Professionals divide the horse's body into small sections and clip each section thoroughly, reclipping if necessary, before going on to the next section. In any case, never start with the head. Start with the hindquarters, which are easy to clip and the least ticklish to the horse.

When clipping the chest and flanks, and elsewhere, too, you will run into "whorls," where the hair reverses itself. You will have to turn the clippers in order to keep the blades working against the direction of hair growth. It is easier to clip the flank and jaw areas if you hold the loose skin taut with your fingers as you work. When you clip behind the horse's elbow, have a helper pick up the foreleg and pull it forward in order to stretch and smooth the loose skin and make it easier to clip.

Even if you plan to clip your horse all over, start with a trace clip, expand it to a hunter clip, and finally to a full clip. If your clippers break down or something else interrupts you, your horse will still be presentable, rather than left naked on one side and fuzzy on the other. Schedule your clipping session at least one week ahead of a show, with a touch-up the day before the competition.

Clip in a good light. A trouble light on a long cord is helpful for checking your work. Make sure that your working area is free from drafts, and have a blanket handy to put on your horse after you have finished. You will find the job less ticklish if you wear a nylon windbreaker and a scarf or stocking cap to keep the horse's clipped hair out of yours.

Clippers work by feeding the hair through the comb, or lower blade, into the movable upper blade, which does the cutting. When you handle the clippers, you need to keep two things in mind: The blades must work directly against the direction of hair growth, and they must lie as close to the skin as possible so that they don't leave patches of longer hair. Don't dig the front of the clippers into the horse's skin, though. You might nip him with the sharp cutting edges.

A tension screw on the upper front portion of the clippers adjusts the pressure of the movable upper blade against the lower blade. You can increase the tension by turning the screw clockwise. Don't use any more tension than is necessary to produce a clean cut, or the friction between the blades will cause them to overheat and quickly dull.

By increasing the tension a little at a time as the blades wear down, you will be able to get a fairly clean cut even after the blades have become a bit dull. You can do four or five hunter clips or three or four full clips, before the blades will need resharpening, *if* you clean the horses before you clip them. One dirty, scurfy horse with ground-in manure or matted hair will do in a brand-new set of blades.

A high-pitched, laboring noise from the clippers indicates that the blades are becoming clogged with hair and grease. Clean the blades and the clipper head (the part of the machine that holds the blades) periodically by dipping the running clippers in the kerosene can. Dip only the blades and the lower end of the clipper housing. Don't get the motor near the kerosene! Let the excess kerosene and hair drip down into the can, then shut off the motor and clean the blades with your brush and wipe them off with a rag.

Rinsing the blades frequently in kerosene helps to reduce friction and keeps the blades from heating up. But the blades also need periodic lubrication with light machine oil. Every second or third time you rinse the clippers, put a few drops of oil in the oiling points. In most clippers the oiling points are on top of the clipper housing, in front of and behind the tension screw. They are usually marked "oil here."

You can also buy a lubricating spray, such as Kool-Lube or Spray-Lube, which is sprayed directly onto the blades while the clippers are running. It is useful for clearing hair out of the blades and cooling the clippers, but it is no substitute for rinsing the blades in kerosene.

A final word of warning: Be careful not to drop the clippers. The blades break easily, and even a single broken tooth will leave a line of unclipped hair on your horse.

Introducing Your Horse to the Clippers

Never advance toward the horse, with running clippers extended. And never let the cord dangle in his face. When clipping a horse for the first time, you can start the motor and stand away from the horse, but within view, in order to accustom him to the sound. If the noise frightens him, you can put wads of cotton in his ears. If he still doesn't settle, tranquilize him. Whatever you do, don't fight him.

Let your horse sniff the clippers with the cord still rolled up.

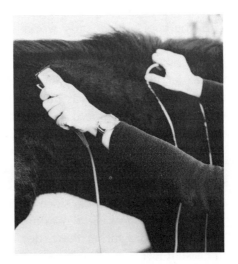

Rub them over his neck.

Uncoil the cord and let it dangle while you rub.

Stroke the horse with the palm of your hand. Turn on the motor and lay the clippers against your hand.

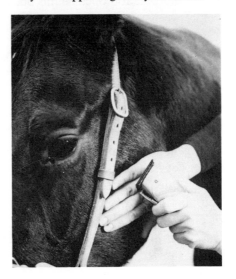

To Clip or Not to Clip?

Are you really sure you need to clip your horse? Clipping requires time, patience, and a certain amount of skill. It also has a few drawbacks. If you remove the horse's natural protection from the elements, you will have to guard against chills by providing him with sheets, blankets, and turn-out rugs. Also, since you cannot turn a clipped horse out as often or as long as you can his hairy stablemates, you will have to ride or longe him regularly to make sure that he gets enough exercise.

If your horse frequently works hard enough to sweat through his winter coat, if he takes longer than ten or fifteen minutes to cool and dry, or if he breaks out in sweaty patches after work, he (and you) will probably find life easier if some of his long hair is clipped off. Most horses engaging in strenuous exercise such as hunting, racing, or eventing during the fall, winter, and early spring need to be clipped. Moreover, if you plan to show during the winter, you will probably have to clip your horse to make him look respectable.

On the other hand, if your horse doesn't work very much during the winter, he will probably be better off if he keeps his winter coat. You can turn him out for long periods, since his long hair will protect him from cold, wet weather, even snow. So if you are a fair-weather horseman who doesn't plan to ride until the spring thaw, don't condemn your horse to a boring winter in his stall just because you hate to see him with a shaggy coat.

If you plan to clip your horse in the fall, wait until his winter coat has grown in; otherwise, you'll have to do the whole chore over again in a few weeks. It is also best not to blanket a horse you plan to clip. If the horse gets used to wearing a blanket when he has a heavy coat, he will need twice as much protection once he has been clipped.

Clipping Styles

If you have decided to clip your horse, you must next decide *how* to clip him.

There are three basic styles of body clips: the full clip, the hunter clip, and the trace clip.

In general, the more hair you clip off, the better your horse will look and the easier he will be to groom and cool out but the less protection he'll have from winter weather. The kind of clip you give your horse depends on what you plan to do with him. An all-purpose horse may even need various styles of clips at various times of year: a hunter clip for the fall hunting season, a trace clip to tide him over the winter, and a full clip to prepare him for the spring shows.

Whatever the style you choose for your horse, remember that clipping can create optical illusions. For example, if you clip a saddle patch slightly smaller than normal, you will make your horse look taller and deeper through the girth. If you cut a straight edge on the front of the saddle patch instead of rounding it, and if you place it slightly to the rear of the withers, you will give the impression of a shorter back and a longer, more sloping shoulder. A horse with short, thick legs usually looks better with his legs fully clipped. And a common head usually looks more refined if it is clipped. If you want to make your horse's forearm and gaskin appear more heavily muscled, leave the stockings higher and fuller than normal. A slightly slanting line at the top of the stocking gives the impression of a wider hind leg, while a steeply slanting line clipped far down makes the leg look longer and slimmer.

So while there are no hard-and-fast rules, and plenty of leeway to allow for personal taste and individual conditions and conformation, these are the traditional clipping styles:

The full clip leaves the entire coat a bit shorter than its summer length; only the mane and tail remain untouched. Because it gives the horse a smooth, shiny appearance all over, the full clip is the most flattering style for show horses. Even if you do not intend to show, you may find it worthwhile to make your last clipping in the spring a full clip. It leaves no long-haired places to shed out. Bear in mind, though, that a full clip removes the horse's natural protection from the cold. A fully clipped horse may need a warmer barn, more blankets, deeper bedding, and even a hood and leg wraps to keep him comfortable.

The hunter clip (page 212) is the best style for horses that are ridden cross-country in mud, water, and snow and need the extra protection of the hair on their legs. This clip leaves furry "stockings" rising to a line even with the belly and a "saddle patch" shaped like a small saddle. The stockings may be clipped with straight, slanted, or rounded tops. If you know your horse doesn't need the protection of a saddle patch, you may decide to omit it, because it gets wet with sweat and prolongs the cooling-out process. A hunter-clipped horse can be turned out in moderately cold weather, but he will need a turn-out rug to keep his body warm.

The trace clip (page 213) is a partial clip whose exact style varies according to the sweating pattern of the horse and the needs of the owner. (The name originated in horse-and-buggy days, when this clip was used to keep a driving horse from lathering under the traces.)

A compromise clip, it removes the long hair from the places that sweat most but leaves a natural blanket of long hair over the back and most of the body to protect the horse when he is being ridden or turned out. If the trace clip is extended high along the neck and sides and up into the flanks, it provides only minimal protection, and the horse should be treated as if he were hunter-clipped. However, a less exaggerated trace clip may leave the horse

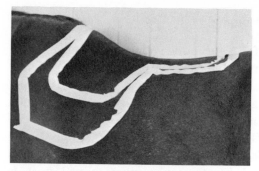

HUNTER CLIP

1. Lay your saddle on your horse's back and outline it with tape. Take the saddle off and make a smaller outline following the same contours. Remove the outer boundary and clip to the smaller one.

2. Outline a V shape at the root of the tail. Remove all the long hair that remains between these boundaries and the tops of the stockings.

3. The hunter clip completed.

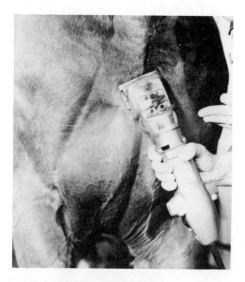

STRIP CLIP

1. Clip the hair from an area one clipper's width on either side of the neck's midline, widening over the chest and including the underside of the belly. Work in long strokes against the direction of the hair, and then . . .

2. . . . turn the clippers sideways to neaten the edge.

3. Finish the neck in a curving line to meet the jaw.

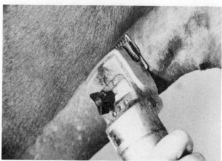

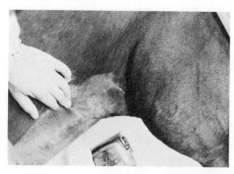

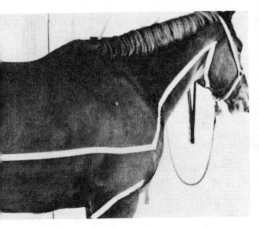

1. With masking tape, mark the boundaries of the area you plan to clip.

2. Follow the line of the muscle around the top of the front leg, then begin the upper boundary about one hand's length above it.

3. End it one hand's length above the stifle.

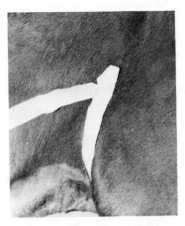

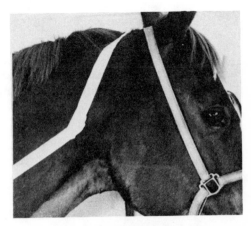

4. Lay out your neckline two hands' width above the midline.

5. If you plan to leave the head unclipped, end at the groove between head and neck.

6. To include the head, end a little sooner and angle upward to meet the mane just behind the ears.

TRACE CLIP

7. The finished trace clip, head included.

with enough protection to be turned out without a rug most of the time and still reduce the heavy sweating associated with a winter coat.

The most conservative of the various trace clips is *the strip clip* (page 212). Starting below the chin, it removes the hair along the gullet and in a strip about eight inches wide down the underside of the neck. The clipped area widens out across the chest and beneath the belly, but it does not extend to the legs. Properly done, a strip clip will not show when you look at the horse from the side. Since it leaves the horse with virtually all of his natural protection from the cold, he probably will not need a blanket.

The standard trace clip starts out as the strip clip does and then extends upward for about ten inches along the sides of the neck and belly. The line of clipped hair looks best if you keep it straight and level. You may end the clip at the flank or clip all the way around the top of the gaskin.

The standard trace clip gives the horse slightly more air conditioning and slightly less insulation than the strip clip. If you wish, you may extend the neckline up to a point about eight inches behind the poll and clip the horse's head. Although clipping the head doesn't have much effect on his body temperature, it does give him a cleaner, more refined appearance.

The trace clip extended around the hindquarters is useful for horses that sweat heavily in the flank area. *A high trace clip* with a "keyhole" (below) at the flank serves well on horses that work hard enough to sweat all over but still need protection over the back and loins. The high trace clip, often seen on racehorses in northern states, reaches twelve inches or more up the horse's sides, with the flank area clipped in a smoothly rounded shape. (You can slant the rear line of the keyhole to emphasize the muscling of the horse's

A high trace clip with "keyhole."

hindquarters.) A horse with a high trace clip will need to be blanketed most of the time.

The blanket clip (below) looks quite neat, but it affords even less protection than a high trace clip. The horse's head and neck are clipped, and the standard trace clip pattern is squared off at the front and extended up the buttock in a straight line, to form a "blanket." If you are giving your horse a blanket clip, be sure to keep all the lines straight and square, or the horse will have a lopsided, moth-eaten appearance.

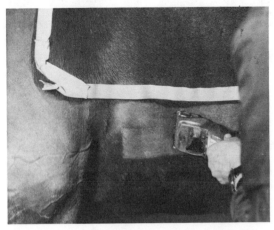

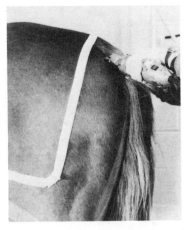

Working from a regular trace clip (not high), alter the front corner to form a right angle. Your new boundary will end just in front of the withers.

Create a rear outline, dropping a straight line down from the root of the tail to form a right angle with the existing boundary.

BLANKET CLIP

Your horse will be left with four full stockings and a rectangular blanket of hair over his back, extending most of the way down his sides.

Trimming the Head

To take the whiskers off the muzzle, stretch the skin and press the back of the blade of your trimming clippers firmly against it with the clippers working against the direction of growth of the whiskers.

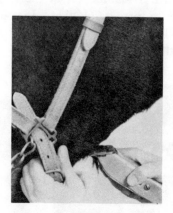

For removing just the long fringes that dangle from the jaws, hold your clippers upside down and run them from throatlatch to chin in the direction the hair grows.

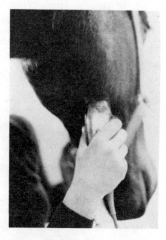

If you prefer to clean off the whole underside of the head, turn your clippers over and work against the growth.

For a bridle path, hold the forelock out of the way and insert the clippers into the mane at what is to be the lower end of the path.

Finish just behind the ears.

A hunter-type bridle path should be no longer than this.

Take hold of an ear and lay the clippers, running, against the back of your hand.

Squeeze the ear shut and run the clippers down the edges to remove the fringe.

If fashion dictates that you clean out the inside of the ear, stuff it with cotton, hold your clippers upside down, and run them from tip to base. Some horsemen prefer to leave the inside hairs for protection against dirt and insects, just trimming the long ends by folding the ear shut and removing the hairs that protrude.

Trimming the Legs

To remove the long hairs that grow from the tendons and fetlocks, run your clippers down the backs of the legs, blades pointing downward.

It may be easier to trim the fetlock and the back of the pastern if you pick up the foot.

Trim the long hairs from the coronary band, clipping against the hair and lifting the clippers away from the foot to form a short, even hairline.

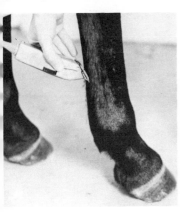

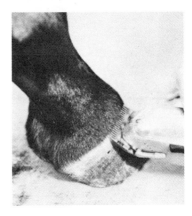

Booting Up

To refine a horse's legs and prevent them from picking up shaving dust. But it also removes protection (from scratches, wet, and cold) that your horse may need.

 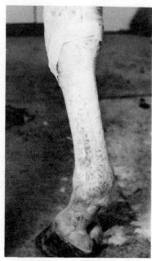 

Use short pieces of adhesive tape to mark boundaries. Clip upward to your boundaries, using a coarse blade or heavy-duty clippers. Lift the head of the blade slightly as you reach the tape, for a blended effect.

Chapter 5

STABLES AND
STABLE MANAGEMENT

AN EXPANDABLE BACKYARD STABLE

When Mr. and Mrs. Daniel Walsh III decided to build a stable behind their home in the Philadelphia suburb of Gladwyn, the important considerations, aside from economy, were efficiency in the working layout and expandability in a structure that would blend with its surroundings on a small woodland lot. The three-stall stable was erected in ten days. Two more stalls and a tack room were added later, using materials purchased from the builder.

The building is a straightforward pole design structure, 36 feet square with a six-foot overhang abutting the south side. The siding is tongue-and-groove, painted a beige-gray to blend with the surrounding woods; the roof is asphalt shingle, and the flooring in the aisle, tack room, and stalls is asphalt.

The 36 × 36-foot main structure consists of five 12 × 12 stalls and a 12 × 12 tack room, flanking a 12-foot center aisle. The three original stalls face south, each with a Dutch door opening to the six-foot overhang. Across the aisle, the two new stalls and tack room open to the interior only. Above the stalls and on elevated platforms built at both ends of the aisle is storage space for about eight tons of hay and straw. The wide center aisle gives plenty of working space and receives generous daylight through a green fiberglass skylight running the length of the roof. Stalls and working areas are roomy, but the simplicity of the layout makes it easy for eleven-year-old Missy Walsh and her mother to do most of the stable chores.

The stalls have sliding doors opening to the center aisle. The three on the south side also have Dutch doors opening to the overhang. In nice weather, horses can be brought out and cross-tied under the overhang for grooming and tacking up. The overhang offers protection from rain and snow, while the upper halves of the Dutch doors remain open to provide ventilation and light. Horses turned out in the adjoining paddock can come under the overhang in bad weather or for shade.

The stalls are constructed of fir planks, tongue-and-groove, to form solid partitions rising to about four and one half feet in front and eight feet between the stalls. Neighboring horses are isolated from each other, but metal grills in the upper portion of the stall fronts and sliding doors give each horse a view of activities in the aisle, while promoting ventilation. Wooden ledges surrounding the grillwork are metal-flashed to prevent chewing. Stall walls that adjoin the building exterior are reinforced with vertical oak planks to a height of about four and one half feet.

Each stall is equipped with a rubber feed tub and feed window in the stall front grill, as well as an automatic water bowl within the horse's reach.

The tack room is a 12 × 12-foot area that could be converted to stall space. It is equipped with wooden bridle and saddle racks and flanked on one side by wooden cabinets and shelves providing storage space for show supplies, grooming equipment, and other stable items. A spacious counter surface above the cabinets provides plenty of working space, including a sink with hot and cold running water for tack cleaning. Feed is stored in the tack room in plastic and galvanized garbage cans.

The original *hay storage* consisted of a platform formed by the roofs of the first three stalls. Later, when the two additional stalls and tack room were added, the storage capacity was increased by building two elevated platforms at either end of the aisle. Now the building is capable of storing about eight tons of hay and bedding on a continuous mezzanine running around all four walls. Hay is loaded through a door under the peak of the roof at the east end of the building. Although there is no access by vehicle to the other end of the building, there is a similar door, for ventilation and architectural balance.

The loft is reached by ladder from below. Bales are simply dropped over the side of the loft.

In addition to the roof skylight, each stall has its own non-protruding *light bulb*. Above the stall fronts, four more bulbs light the aisle, two from each side. Above these, four more fixtures light the hay-storage platforms. Floodlights at ends and corners of the building light the surrounding paddocks and the path from the house. Three fixtures light the overhang. All the barn switches are special heavy-duty outdoor switches, with plunger-type, moisture-proof action.

In addition to the automatic drinking bowls in each stall, there are two frost-free *hydrants,* one in the aisle beside the tack-room door, and one outside the east door. The outdoor hydrant has a double spigot with two hoses, one for outdoor bathing and hosing of legs, and another which fills an outdoor drinking tub. The indoor hydrant is similarly equipped with one hose for stable use and the other reaching a drinking tub in a paddock at the far

The Walsh stable, viewed from the jumping paddock, blends with the woodland setting.

Three stalls open to a six-foot overhang and side paddock. The overhang, equipped with cross-ties, is a handy place to groom or tack up in warm weather. Horses enjoy their view of the outdoors.

The aisle opens both toward the house at this end and toward a large, aproned driveway at the other. A hay-storage mezzanine is above the stalls, with a loading platform at each end. The skylight illuminates working space in the roomy aisle.

Lengths of pipe were rigged up to keep horses out of the building while the door is open. In summer, the horses can escape from flies by standing in the open doorway.

The poles slide freely except when pins are down, fixing them in position.

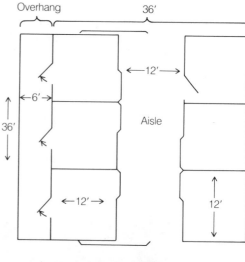

Floor plan of the Walshes' expandable backyard stable.

The chimney-pipe drains were installed as a substitute for conventional drains but have proved desirable in their own right.

end of the building. Under the hydrants, and under a coupling in the tack room, is a unique *drainage* system, dictated by necessity but proving advantageous. Since the floor went down before the plumbing was finished, Mr. Walsh sank eighteen-inch terra cotta chimney pipes in the ground at the foot of each hydrant and filled them with small stones. The drains catch the drips, are used to empty buckets, and also give easy access to the plumbing fittings by simply scooping out the stones.

At each end of the aisle is a twelve and one half-foot *sliding door*. At the west end, which faces the house, the large door encompasses a smaller, hinged, step-through door, so that one can enter the barn unaccompanied by a horse without having to slide the big door open.

To avoid shutting out light and air when horses are turned into the small, adjoining paddocks, a system of sliding iron pipes allows the doors to remain open while keeping horses out of the barn. Two horizontal pipes rest in tubes fixed at one end to the wall beside the door and at the other end to the door itself. The pipes bar the door but slide out of the way to let horses in and out. At the east end, the poles are on the outside of the building, blocking the large doorway. At the other end, the poles are inside, fixed at both ends to the door itself and blocking the small, step-through door.

All *windows* are louvered, operated from within by a crank. The louvers admit air while cutting down drafts and keeping out weather. Each window is protected on the inside by a grill.

The stable and three small *paddocks* occupy a little more than an acre of ground behind the house. An *asphalt apron* at the east end of the stable extends through the front paddock to meet the driveway, making feed and hay deliveries possible in any weather. The unpaved portion of the paddock is equipped with a small course of low schooling fences. A side paddock surrounds the overhang. The portion under the overhang is also paved with asphalt, so that horses don't churn up mud. There is another small paddock on the west side of the building. The paddocks, all post-and-rail fenced, are too small and too shady to provide grazing, but they serve as ample turn-out exercise space for the five-horse barn.

THE LIVE-OVER STABLE

Living with one's horses has been a way of life in Europe for two thousand years. Quebec families have shared their *maisons blocs,* or connected barns, with their livestock since the seventeenth century. In New England, a few connected barns still survive. Now increasing numbers of twentieth-century horsemen are turning to living with their horses as a means of economizing on board rates and rising home-construction costs.

This attractive live-over stable is a good example of a four-stall-stable-and-apartment combination that is easy to operate and economical to build.

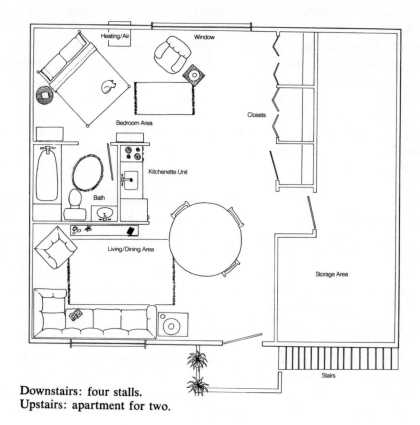

Heating/Air

Window

Closets

Bedroom Area

Kitchenette Unit

Bath

Living/Dining Area

Storage Area

Stairs

Downstairs: four stalls.
Upstairs: apartment for two.

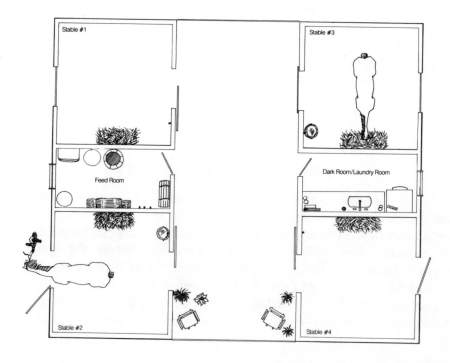

Stable #1

Stable #3

Feed Room

Dark Room/Laundry Room

Stable #2

Stable #4

This 30 × 36-foot barn-and-apartment combination provides under its gambrel roof one thousand square feet of living space.

The stalls open onto a 12-foot-wide center aisle. Plants, easy chairs, and stringent hygiene domesticate the working area.

The hunters enjoy free-choice exercise in two 100 × 75-foot paddocks, adjoining the sides of the barn and enclosed in four-foot fencing.

The great advantage of living with horses is easy accessibility. It is convenient to be able to feed your horse during a heavy snowstorm or at 5 A.M. before a horse show just by walking downstairs! You also know immediately when you have a sick horse. You develop a greater understanding of your horses' needs and personalities by living under the same roof with them.

Most early connected barns stood side by side with the residence, probably because of the noise factor: While good insulation cuts down noise, it is true that one can still hear horses kicking and doors sliding from upstairs. Some people claim such noises are soothing, or at least reassuring.

The biggest problem is flies. Elaborate fly control at one combined barn and residence involves the spreading of manure on a twenty-acre field, in addition to the use of fly baits and sprays. Even then, there is no substitute for stringent sanitation. Paddocks and stalls must be picked out two or three times a day to control flies, and the manure pile should be as far away from the building as possible.

Fire is a potential danger in a wooden combination barn and residence. Insurance rates soar when hay is stored in the barn or closer to it than thirty feet. Most barn residents build a separate hay shed, which brings the fire and liability insurance rates down to those of non-concrete stables without living quarters.

Concrete construction has certain disadvantages: All hardware must be installed with a masonry drill. Cutting holes through the slabs after completion is very costly. Much trouble can be avoided by putting chasings in the slabs during pouring, in order to provide for electrical wiring and plumbing.

Nevertheless, where zoning permits, this is an economical arrangement. In fact, visitors often remark that once they're upstairs, they don't even know they're in a barn.

EFFICIENCY AND ECONOMY

This handsome, sturdy four-stall stable was built in 1960 by Susan Thayer Norris, of Chester Spring, Pennsylvania, for only four thousand dollars. Although it would probably cost much more today, it would still be an attractive buy.

The building is economical in every respect, handy to work in and easy to maintain. The layout is so compact that one person can do all the stable work for four horses—clean the stalls, feed, hay, and water—in under an hour. Two coats of exterior paint and periodic addition of clay to the stall floors had been the only maintenance expenses as of May of 1973, when these pictures were taken.

The construction of the two-story stable, barn-red with white trim, is

Front and side views of the stable. The three-foot overhang and the loft design are unique features, making room for storage of a year's supply of hay and straw.

board-and-batten on cinder-block footings, with an asphalt-shingle roof. It faces south. Every corner downstairs has a use. Against the wall to the left of the entrance is a frost-free hydrant. Across the aisle is a ladder to the loft. A custom-built feed bin stands against the wall of the far-left stall. Opposite is storage space for pitchfork, broom, and shovel. Tack is stored in the house, but it would be a simple matter to vary the plan to three stalls, with the fourth becoming a combination feed and tack room.

The stall doors, four feet wide, oak with iron grills in the upper half, slide open on overhead tracks. Flush against the stall walls, they save aisle space. The disadvantage of adjoining stall doors is that, when open, neighboring horses can reach each other over the stall guards. For this reason, only one stall door on either side of the aisle can be open at a time.

Since each stall occupies a corner of the building, each has two windows protected by iron bars on the inside. In summer, with windows and aisle doors open, the stable catches northern breezes and stays comfortably cool. Shut up in winter, when temperatures drop below freezing, four horses maintain the temperature at 40 to 45 degrees. Because it is so small and solidly built, the stable tends, if anything, to be on the warm side, and seldom are all the windows and doors kept shut.

An efficient and economical stable floor plan.

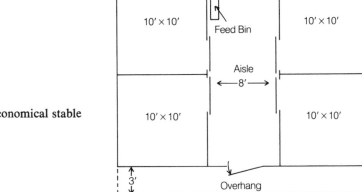

Warm in winter, cool in summer, this economical five-stall stable has a tough, horse-proof interior, a paneled tack room, a wash stall, overhead hay storage, and an efficient, work-saving layout.

EASY-CARE STABLE

When one woman plans to look after five horses, she needs a stable that practically runs itself. Ease of operation, plus economy and summer/winter comfort for the occupants were the main considerations when Janet Stoltz designed her attractive and unusually durable stable in the Pickering Hunt country of Pennsylvania.

The building consists of five oak stalls, pine-paneled tack room, wash stall, and feed-storage area (the latter two convertible to additional stalls), overhead hay storage, and center aisle.

Perched high near the top of a hill, on well-drained soil, the stable catches prevailing breezes and stays remarkably free from flies. In winter, when the windows are closed and the ten-foot door at the southern end of the aisle is open, sunshine warms the building.

Feed and hay deliveries are made via a gravel drive that runs through the front paddock.

Board-and-batten was chosen over tongue-and-groove construction for economy, and the horses don't chew the hemlock battens as they might pine. The stable is painted pewter-gray/blue with white trim. A charming feature is the window boxes on the south wall, facing the road, which are

An interior view showing upper stall doors open. The tack-room door is at the left foreground, and the principal feed-storage area is out of sight at right.

planted with geraniums during the warm months. The boxes are designed to allow the sliding aisle doors to slip behind them until fully open, whereupon they serve as door stops.

The design of the building is simple: a center aisle with double sliding doors at each end, flanked on one side by three stalls and a feed-storage area, and on the other side by a wash stall, two stalls, and a tack room.

The overall dimensions are 34 × 40 feet, with stalls, wash stall, and feed storage each 10 × 12 feet, a 10-foot aisle, and 10 × 9-foot tack room.

The Dutch doors of the stalls are made of solid oak below and iron pipe in the upper half, which is usually left open when horses are in their stalls, so that they can watch what is going on in the aisle. The sliding windows in each stall, 34 × 26 inches, are large enough for a horse to put his head through, which also helps to prevent boredom.

The two stalls on the tack-room side are separated by a removable partition and can easily be transformed into a foaling stall. There are no lights in the stalls, but four overhead lights in the aisle operate from switches at both ends.

The overhead loft, which can store ten to twelve tons of hay and straw, is reached through a trapdoor by ladder from the wash stall. Another trapdoor, halfway down the aisle, serves as a central hay drop. In warm weather, the loft doors and trapdoors are opened and the heat from the horses goes up and out.

Beside the tack-room door there is a built-in feed-storage bin with two compartments, each holding between four hundred and five hundred pounds of feed. A second double feed bin, in the feed-storage area, holds ear corn in one compartment, the other serving as a safety storage bin for pitchforks and stable tools. "We've stored tools in the food bin," says Mrs. Stoltz, "ever since a horse got loose one night and stepped on a pitchfork. Another safe place I've found is in a barrel with sand in it."

The wash stall, equipped with hydrant and drain, is a handy feature that can always be converted into another stall if needed. The little tack room is paneled in knotty pine and carpeted.

Finally, two floodlights, mounted near the peak of the roof and operated from either house or stable, light the way from the house at night.

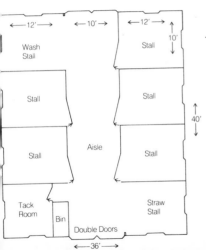

An easy-care stable.

Bridle brackets in the pine-paneled tack room add a loving touch.

EXPANDING YOUR STALL SPACE

It is practically a law of physics that, just as gas expands to fill an available space, a horseman never has fewer horses than he has stalls. The contrary is more often the case: too many horses and no place to put them!

However, extra stall space can often be found by using a little ingenuity, a small investment in materials, and a few days of labor. For example:

In an Existing Outbuilding

You may be desperate enough to give up some garage space or tool-shed space for extra stabling. At Fox Hollow Farm, in Pennsylvania, Major Jeremy Beale converted a poured-concrete garage into a roomy, three-stall stable.

The building is rectangular, the front end taken up by a pair of sliding doors. The first stall was built in the right front corner, so that when the doors are pushed to the left, one wall of the stall opens to the outside. Later, two more stalls were added at the back, leaving an L-shaped aisle, roomy enough to permit some storage of tools and grain as well as providing plenty of working space.

The width of the building is 20 feet, permitting stall widths of only 10 feet each. Because the lumber for the partition between the stalls was most economically purchased in the standard, 12-foot length, the two rear stall doors slant back toward the partition between them, adding a couple of

There was room in this garage at Fox Hollow Farm for three airy stalls. When doors are pushed to the left, front stall opens to the outside.

Three new stalls in an unused garage.

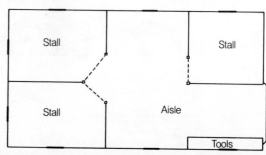

Raymond Burr added two extra stalls in this garage wing of his show stable.

extra feet in length to each stall. The result is an irregular shape 10 feet wide, 12 feet long on one side, and 14 feet long on the other. Webbing stall guards provide a simple, inexpensive substitute for stall doors. A low board nailed across the bottom of each doorway retains bedding in the stalls, which are equipped with usual amenities: automatic waterer, feed tub, and sliding windows.

Trainer Raymond Burr added stabling in a new garage, part of a recently built, ten-stall complex for show horses on his Foxwood Farm, in Pennsylvania. It took two men less than two days to erect two solidly built 12 × 12-foot stalls.

Uprights were dug into the ground and anchored in concrete. The partition between stalls is fir, and the kickboards are redwood for strength. All the wood is creosoted in order to prevent chewing. The sliding stall doors and iron grillwork were salvaged from a nearby stable that was being dismantled. The grillwork used around three sides protects windows, admits light and ventilation, and separates horses above the dividing partition. The stall boards are slightly spaced to the height of the grillwork, to make the lumber go farther. But at the rear of each stall, where lumber is used instead of grill, the upper boards are close together in order to prevent chewing. Each stall is equipped with a removable feed tub, water bucket, mineral-block holder, and an individually operated light. The door to the hay and bedding storage area is at the other side of the garage.

Sliding doors and grillwork were salvaged from an old stable. Two men completed the work in less than two days.

The David Trumpers added this small board-and-batten lean-to to an existing garage to provide shelter for family ponies.

Stabling consists of two open stalls which, when gates are open, double as a run-in area. Feed/tack room at left, small box stall at right.

Against an Existing Building

To solve a housing problem for children's ponies, the David Trumper family erected a simple shed against an existing garage. The board-and-batten structure with tin roof consists of a central run-in area, flanked by an enclosed box stall at one end and a small tack room at the other. The run-in portion is divided by a wooden partition, each half with its own gate opening to the paddock, so that either or both may be closed to form small stalls. The combined feed and tack room, on the left, has built-in saddle and bridle racks plus a corner shelf for supplies. At the other end of the run-in, a Dutch door opens onto the box stall. Windows in box stall and tack room slide on interior tracks, a space-saving feature. The dividing partition of the run-in area is set back from the front partition, leaving a narrow space to permit a person to slip from one stall to the other without going outside, but not so wide that a pony can slip through. When not in use, the opening is barred with two chains.

Every farm has its share of extra stall space. It takes more imagination than work or money to make it a reality. But remember: Don't build more stalls than you want horses. The law still applies: There is no such thing as an empty stall!

The center partition is set back from the front fence to allow children to slip through from stall to stall without going outside. Chains keep ponies where they belong.

Pony stabling against an existing garage.

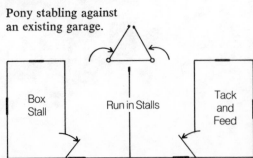

Built-in convertibility.

BUILT-IN CONVERTIBILITY

An ingenious scheme for quick convertibility was designed by Paul and Ann McEnroe for their North Carolina stables. The south wall of the ground floor consists of three sliding doors mounted on overhead tracks. With the side doors open, the end stalls become airy boxes. The end partitions themselves can be removed, converting the building to a three-bay garage or a combination garage-barn-workshop. With all the stall partitions removed, the McEnroes can use a loader to strip all but one stall of its bedding.

PASTURE WALK-THROUGH

Do you get tired of opening and closing the pasture gate when you are not accompanied by a horse? Why not do as Joan Koponen, of Fairbanks, Alaska, did, and build yourself a "people walk-through."

Choose a convenient spot where the fence meets the barn, or beside the gate, and make a gap in the fence about sixteen inches wide (perhaps a bit more if you are on the chubby side). You can slip right through it.

If your horse tries to follow you, plant a post twenty-two inches inside the fence so that it forms a triangle with the two posts framing the gap. You can easily walk around the posts, but a horse, even a small pony, knows that he cannot curve his body through the passage. It works!

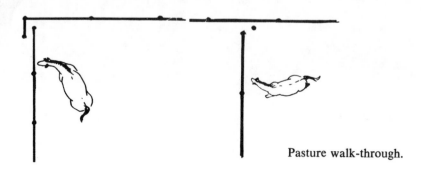

Pasture walk-through.

COMPACT TACK STORAGE

Here is an inexpensive way to keep your tack accessible and clean in a small, portable tack room, as Mrs. R. D. Harmon does, in Tucson, Arizona.

Purchase a metal utility wardrobe, available at large discount stores for a modest price. It will have at least one shelf on top, with a garment bar directly underneath. Use the shelf for storage of small items such as liniments, medications, and wraps.

Using number 10 gauge wire, form as many S hooks as needed and slip them over the garment bar. They can be used to hang bridles, halters, and martingales. In the bottom space, you can store blankets, pads, and towels.

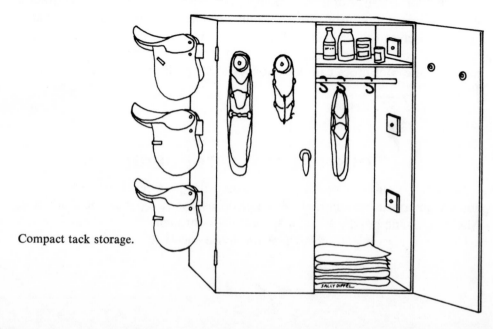

Compact tack storage.

Cut half-inch pieces of plywood to fit the interior side walls. Buy metal saddle brackets and bolt them to the sides of the cabinet, through the plywood. There should be room for three English saddles on each side.

Even the fronts of the doors can be utilized, by bolting small cans (such as tuna fish or cat-food cans) to them, for hanging frequently used bridles and halters.

A SUPER-SIMPLE SADDLE RACK

All you need for each rack is a 20-inch piece of 4 × 4 with sanded edges, one screw eye, and one J hook.

Install the screw eye in the wall. Nail the J hook onto the 4 × 4 so that the curved end protrudes ½ inch from the end.

Your rack is now ready. Hook the J hook into the screw eye from the bottom. This will hold the 4 × 4 at a right angle to the wall. When the rack is not in use, hook it from the top and it will hang flat against the wall, taking up practically no space at all.

Ilona Ujhelyi, of Woodbine, New Jersey, recommends installing an extra screw eye on the side of your van and taking the 4 × 4 with you when you go to a show. She also finds it useful to have another screw eye next to the fireplace, for cleaning saddles in the winter.

A variation of the same saddle-rack system is shown in this tack room, attractively paneled in 4 × 8-foot plywood sheets. The saddles are hung on homemade racks consisting of short 4 × 4s covered with scrap carpet. The racks hang from the wall by double-end snaps and lie out of the way when not in use. Next to them, bridles hang from homemade half-moons of wood screwed onto a horizontal board.

A super-simple saddle rack.

PRACTICAL DETAILS
IN AND AROUND THE STABLE

In Raymond Burr's Pennsylvania stable, the Dutch-style doors are open most of the time, while full-length screens provide ventilation and visibility.

Doors are white with red trim on the outside. Inside, the lower half is painted red in order to conceal soil.

Sturdy, safe paddock-and-pasture fencing is made of post and square mesh wire topped by a treated 2 × 6. The wire is nailed halfway up the inside of the board to discourage fence chewing.

Two 10 × 12-foot stalls share a fluorescent lighting fixture. Water is supplied to each stall by plastic pipe that slopes overhead to permit draining in winter.

A gift from a client, this antique candy jar comes in handy for storing sugar.

A blackboard in the feed room records special diets. Above it, on a high shelf, feed supplements are stored out of reach of rodents.

A well-equipped wash room. The floor is scored cement to prevent slipping. A shower-type water regulator on the wall adjusts for hot or cold water from the hose. The water heater is situated behind the wall, in the tack-room closet. Radiant heaters, each operated by a separate switch, are used for drying horses as well as for warming the work area on cold days.

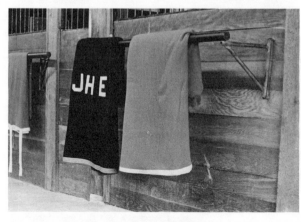

These blanket racks are made of three-inch pipe and hinges that permit each rack to swing flat against the wall when not in use.

A FIRE-PREVENTION CHECKLIST FOR YOUR STABLE

Unless you can answer yes to each of the following questions, there is room for improvement in your stable fire-prevention program.

—Are your barn and stable yard free from debris such as loose piles of hay, scrap lumber, and oily rags? Loosely piled hay burns more quickly than baled hay.

—Is your gas pump at least twenty-five to fifty feet away from the barn?

—Is your hay stored away from your barn, in a separate area, with the minimum required hay and bedding material brought into the stable a couple of times a week?

—Do you have several fire extinguishers in the barn, and are persons who frequent your stable trained in their use?

—Are farm machinery and automobiles kept in a separate garage, away from the stable? Gasoline leaks on loose hay are a frequent cause of stable fires.

—Are NO SMOKING signs posted and enforced in your barn?

—Is your barn wiring in conduit so that rodents cannot chew through it?

—Are your wiring and lighting inspected periodically by a local fire inspector?

—Are the lights in your stable (and especially those in the stalls) enclosed in heavy wire or unbreakable glass cages?

—Is the roof of your stable made of noninflammable tin or asphalt? If it is wooden, has the wood been treated with a chemical to retard burning?

—Do you personally verify that the hay you buy is well cured, in order to avoid spontaneous combustion?

—Is manure removed from the barn immediately after it is collected from the stalls? Manure heaps also invite spontaneous combustion.

—Have you rehearsed fire drills with those who use the barn? Have you worked out the quickest way to clear animals from the building?

—Is the grass around your barn closely mowed during dry seasons as a precaution against grass fires?

—Are portable heaters operated only when someone is present to keep an eye on them?

—Is your barn free from gasoline or kerosene lighting sources?

—Are insecticides, gasoline, and other combustible fluids stored in tight containers and in minimum quantities?

—Are all lightning rods, antennas, and wire fences properly grounded?

—Are the stable aisles kept free from clutter, to give permanent access to each stall and to the exits?

BEDDING, THAT NECESSARY EVIL

One of the least-charming aspects of caring for horses is the matter of stall bedding. No matter how conscientiously you bed your horse's stall on Monday, on Tuesday you're right back where you started. Bedding is hard to get and even harder to get rid of. It is bulky to store, awkward to handle, and often dusty to work with. Each training session, each feeding, each grooming improves your horse a little. But with bedding you can only maintain the status quo. You put it in and throw it out and your horse is none the better for it.

But he would be badly off indeed if he were deprived of proper bedding. A soft, dry bed protects his feet from thrush, cushions his legs and feet from the hard floor, and encourages him to lie down and rest. Granted that a stable can't be run effectively without bedding, the next question is, What kinds of bedding and what methods of stall care are best for your particular situation?

What Makes Good Bedding?

The first function of stall bedding is to keep the stall dry. The more absorbent the bedding, the less you have to use and the more you save on both material and labor.

Bedding should be free from dust, which causes and aggravates respiratory problems in horses. Dust collecting on horses' coats is a nuisance in a show or sales barn, where it is important for them always to look their best. Dusty bedding is disagreeable to work with and messes up the entire stable.

Disposability is a vital consideration. How do you plan to get rid of your soiled bedding? Most of the firms that supply compost to mushroom growers will accept only straw.

If you have a relatively small manure pile, you may be able to pass it on to neighbors as garden fertilizer. If you plan to spread it on your own fields, remember that sawdust and shavings tend to raise the acid level of the soil. You may have to pay somebody to take it away.

Bedding should be unpalatable to horses, but hay discarded as unfit for feeding is a poor choice. If it's not good enough to feed, it's not good enough to bed with. Many horses even eat straw, resulting in big roughage bellies.

Bedding should be easy to handle. Bales and bags are generally easier to manage than bulk, but very large bales may be too heavy for some people.

People to whom appearance is important are usually straw fanciers. They accept certain disadvantages for the satisfaction of seeing their horses knee-deep in a shiny, golden bed.

Cost sometimes overrides all other factors. If a product is plentiful and cheap, it may not matter so much if it is not the most absorbent, most convenient, or even the most dust-free. It may still be the most practical.

Straw outsells all other stall bedding. It makes a pretty bed, it is the only material mushroom growers buy, and it is traditional. But there are drawbacks: Straw is relatively expensive. The best buys are found at harvest time, in June and July.

In tests, conducted at the University of Maryland, comparing straw, shavings, sawdust, and ground corn cobs, straw was found to be the least absorbent of the four.

The dust content of straw varies considerably, depending on the variety and on the conditions of harvesting and curing. Some is clean, some is very dusty.

Straw is unsuitable for horses that tend to eat their bedding, since it is one of the most palatable of bedding materials.

The three popular varieties of straw are wheat, oat, and barley. Wheat straw is most prevalent, while barley is quite rare. Wheat and oat straw are dark yellow. Barley straw is pale. Oat straw tends to be dusty and can be most easily distinguished from wheat straw by seeking out the occasional head of grain. Barley straw is the least palatable of the three and also the least dusty. It has a soft, fluffy texture.

Shavings and sawdust. In the University of Maryland studies, sawdust ranked second in absorbency to corn cobs, with shavings close behind. When both products were purchased in bulk, sawdust, surprisingly, was found to be less dusty than shavings. It seems that the planing process for making shavings also produces a fine wood dust. The particles of sawdust, on the other hand, are larger than dust, and when cut from fresh wood, as is generally the case, sawdust contains sufficient moisture to settle any dust that may be present.

The brightest, cleanest shavings come in convenient, thirty-five-pound paper bales containing a minimum of dust. Unfortunately, these bales are not always readily available and are expensive.

Shavings are also packed in plastic bags, smaller than the paper bales but containing a high proportion of sawdust. They are hardest to come by in winter, when transportation is difficult.

Sawdust can be bought in bulk quite cheaply if you collect it yourself from the lumber mill. Delivery charges add a lot to the cost.

Horses will not eat sawdust or shavings. In case of fire, they ignite more slowly than straw, but disposal is more difficult. Mushroom growers will not accept manure with a sawdust or shavings base.

Stazdry is the trade name of a bedding material made from the residue of sugar cane. Very low in dust, it is recommended for horses with heaves and other respiratory problems. It is also claimed to be less inflammable than straw or shavings.

Sold in highly compressed ninety-pound bales, it is hard to handle and to break up.

It is most plentiful, thus least expensive, shortly after the sugarcane harvest, around the middle of November.

Horses will not eat Stazdry, nor will mushroom growers accept it.

Ground corn cobs proved to be the most absorbent bedding but also the dustiest and the most drying to horses' hooves. However, on farms where corn is shelled, the availability of cobs might make them economically practical.

Peanut hulls are packaged in sixty-pound bales, which are awkward for some people to handle. They are absorbent but tend to be quite dusty.

Peat moss is highly absorbent, moist enough to hold down dust, and it makes a lovely, soft bed. It is a rather unattractive dark earth color, which makes the droppings hard to spot. Sold in very heavy bales of about six cubic feet, it is difficult to find in quality suitable for the stable. Most garden suppliers store it outdoors, where, once rained upon, it absorbs too much moisture to be used as bedding.

Deep Litter

There are two basic ways to bed a stall. The traditional method is to remove all the droppings and damp material daily, sifting through to the bottom of the stall, then add considerable new bedding. The other method, infinitely quicker and in many respects more efficient, is "deep litter."

Deep litter means that you start out with a thick layer of bedding, perhaps three times as deep as you would normally use. Every day, you carefully remove the droppings, preferably at frequent intervals throughout the day. You never touch a wet spot, and you add fresh bedding when necessary.

To "do" a stall in deep litter takes no more than five minutes. You remove only the soiled bedding that adheres to the droppings, which means that very little new bedding needs to be added, and your manure pile grows very slowly.

Clay stalls last longer in deep litter, because there is no digging to the bottom. Hard-surfaced stalls in deep litter have a thick cushion that protects the horses' legs. If you are faithful in adding fresh bedding, there is no odor. The deep litter will generate a certain amount of heat, which will help keep your barn warm in winter.

You may want to clean to the bottom of your stalls once or twice a year, but there is never any real need unless the bedding is so deep that you need more ceiling room, or unless your barn becomes too warm in the summer.

A Bedding Tip

If you bed your horses in straw or shavings, you might follow the advice of Judy Barbour, of Elon, North Carolina, and combine the two for the best of both worlds. She puts down a base of shavings and scatters a third of a bale of straw on top. The straw keeps the shavings from scattering in the aisle, and the shavings reduce the cost of bedding—a definite plus since straw has become so expensive.

1. Dispose of manure and wet straw. A flick of your wrist drops the heavy material to the wheelbarrow, while the clean straw stays on the fork.

2. Pile the straw you save near the stall door. First clear the soiled bedding away from underneath.

3. If you feed hay on the floor and there are leftovers scattered around the stall, sweep the hay corner clean and pile salvageable hay there.

STALL CLEANING TECHNIQUE

A system that saves on bedding, while producing a professional-looking stall.

4. Rake up the remnants of bedding you can't pick up with your fork.

5. Sweep the corner under the feed tub, so that the grain doesn't accumulate and mold. Sprinkle lime over the damp spots. Remove water and feed tubs for cleaning. From time to time, when your schedule permits, leave the stall this way to air for a few hours. Put feed and water buckets in the sun.

6. Redistribute the straw from your pile. Working from left to right, lay forkfuls side by side to form a row across the back of your stall. Now start a new row, in front of the first, working from right to left. Lay each forkful well up against the previous ones, so that depressions don't form between them. Work your way back toward the doorway, row by row, forming an even bed. Since your straw pile is within reach of the door, you won't have to tramp back and forth over the new bed to reach it.

7. Where your original straw pile stood, start another pile consisting of brand-new bedding you plan to add to the stall. Shake it into the pile by hand, so that it separates thoroughly.

8. Repeat, with the new straw, the procedure just completed, laying it out in rows, forkful by forkful, to make a bright covering over the base. Work from the doorway, tossing the straw off your fork so that it maintains its loft.

9. Sweep back into the stall any bits of bedding that have straggled out to the aisle. Form the edge of the bed into a neat boundary a few inches back from the threshold. Replace water and feed tubs.

10. The finished product. A fluffy, uniform bed . . .

11. . . . with a clearing under the feed tub that allows the horse to retrieve dropped grain . . .

12. . . . and a clear space around the hay.

STABLE INSECT CONTROL

There are highly effective commercial insect-control programs for stables, but some people, such as Judy Barbour (the practical horsewoman who mixes her bedding), consider them costly and possibly dangerous. She controls flies with many tubes of old-fashioned sticky flypaper and prevents the paper from tearing as it is unrolled by warming it first in her hands or in the sun.

To control mosquitoes, she installed a special birdhouse to attract purple martins to the stableyard, and the mosquito population dropped dramatically. Once attracted, the purple martins return year after year.

Barn swallows are among her other allies. They nest in the beams and are very tame; it is fun to watch the parent birds swoop in with insects for their brood.

Free-ranging chickens, turkeys, and guinea hens have proved to be efficient in holding down ground insects and ticks.

MONEY-SAVING STABLE MANAGEMENT

HOLLY HUGO-VIDAL, rider, trainer, and judge, now lives in California. But at the time she gave these ideas on stable management, she was helping her then husband, Victor Hugo-Vidal, run Cedar Lodge Farm, in Stamford, Connecticut, which consistently produces top contenders in the hunter, jumper, and junior divisions.

At Cedar Lodge, we do not make a conscious effort to save pennies, but in order to remain in business, any business, it is necessary to hold expenses down.

Some people think they are saving money by using a medium grade of feed. Here we feel that the best is the cheapest, because the horses get more out of the feed and are not likely to waste it. Of course, being able to buy by the ton, as we do, instead of by the bag, results in savings. We are also fortunate in being able to grow all of our own hay (enough to feed thirty horses on a year-round basis). Since we control the ground on which it is grown, we can be sure the proper additives have been used and that our hay is nutritionally complete. In effect, we are getting top-quality hay at cost.

We bed on shavings, which we also buy loose in bulk, which is less costly than bags or bales.

In the labor department, we are again fortunate in having two working students as part of our help, who work in exchange for boarding their horses and riding lessons. Several other girls come in the afternoons after school to help with the work and clean tack in exchange for rides. Both arrangements have proved to be money savers.

We don't charge people every time we perform a small service such as trimming or bandaging a horse (both of which are small recurring "hidden" expenses that some stables use to increase their income); these are included in our basic charge for board. What we do is to divide the total cost of the supplies, which are bought in large quantities for stable use (such as sheet cotton by the bale) among the boarders, which saves on overall stable expenses.

A washer and dryer have proved to be a good investment. We now wash everything ourselves: bandages, rub rags, sheets, etc. Clean sheets and towels last longer.

Having the tack cleaned daily is another cost saver in the long run, because tack that is well cared for lasts much longer. Also, any flaws are discovered early, before an entire piece of tack is ruined.

Despite the fact that we do not look for the cheap way of doing things, our policy of buying quality, taking care of it so it will last forever (almost), has resulted in substantial economy over the years—enough so that we have never had to make a sudden or giant escalation of our charges and are still able to deliver first-class service for prices that are competitive within our classification.

> MICHAEL KELLEY, owner of Hickory Hill Farm, in Genesee, New York, and cofounder of the Genesee Valley Hunt, is a professional horsewoman who specializes in teaching cross-country riding with the ultimate goal of fox hunting. She is also the author of many equestrian books and articles.

The stable we operate in the Genesee Valley, in New York State, is devoted entirely to fox-hunting horses and the people who ride them. We require horses that can take an enormous amount of work and look well during most of the season. This can be an expensive operation unless the owner stays right on top of it at all times.

In my opinion, the best way to save money is to watch the feeding ration carefully—not monthly, but weekly. We believe in feeding the best-quality hay we can possibly find (ours is second-cut alfalfa), although it often takes time to locate this type and quality. As far as grain is concerned, we have found that mixing a pellet feed such as Purina Checkers with whole or crushed oats (depending on the horse's age) produces a good, nutritive ration that keeps our horses in good flesh. We feed this ration three times a day and feel that in doing so we waste less and therefore realize another saving. Ideally, the best way to save money with grain is to have your ration mixed and bagged to your own specifications, so that every horse is getting the same ratio of the components of the mix and every measure contains the same balance. It is impossible to do this when you have to take two quarts from one bag, one quart from another, and two half-quarts from two other sources. Furthermore, accurate measurement is poor with this method, and waste is unavoidable.

We believe that the best way to control costs is to keep an eye on every phase of the operation at all times, so that no condition is allowed to get out of hand and create unforeseen expenses. For example, checking our horses on a daily basis for any injury that may have occurred during the day's hunting has saved many a visit from the vet, because the problem was not permitted to develop to the point where veterinary assistance was necessary.

Little economies, such as washing horses' backs with plain salt and water instead of expensive body washes, will help cut costs. Using old crankcase oil for hoof dressing, and old Turkish towels in place of sheet cotton under bandages (especially for soaking), are other ways.

We use the best felt saddle pads available and keep them clean with a curry and brush after each use. We use washable nylon girths instead of leather, which is more time-consuming to care for. Anything that saves time also saves money! We buy the best equipment we can, and then take care to maintain it and repair it when necessary, so that it will last a long time. There are other little things one can do that help, such as cutting the saddle-soap bar in half, as it often breaks in the middle and much of it is wasted.

Because this is a one-person operation with ten horses, I muck my stalls every other day and bed them well in between times. I figure that in this way I save on time and straw, both of which add up to money. Availability has a lot to do with your choice of bedding, but where it is possible to get straw that has not been chopped into little pieces in the combine process, or crimped and flattened (which reduces the absorbency and requires more to make an adequate bed), you are getting the most for your money.

We use baling twine instead of tape to secure mud tails for the hunt field, and also use it in making cross-ties so that if a horse breaks them there is no real loss.

We trace-clip our horses instead of clipping them all over or in the classic hunter style, because we do not have to blanket them so heavily this way (a saving on blanket purchases); but we do cover them, which keeps them relatively clean and reduces the labor involved in grooming each horse (a time saver).

Putting a half teaspoon of plain table salt in the horses' feed once daily is preferable to using bricks (unless you have an exceptional holder) because of the waste usually involved.

We have an awful lot of trouble with scratches in this area, due to the mud and heavy rains, and I have found that Desitin works very well (we bandage over it if the case warrants) in preference to more expensive ointments that must be purchased through a vet.

General preventive maintenance of equipment and tools (such as keeping the vacuum cleaner emptied and sending clipper blades to be sharpened before they are completely worn out) are other ways to save.

By and large, I think that in a small operation such as this one, the best savings are on feed and equipment, while smaller economies add up to big ones only in the long run.

BARBARA VAN TUYL, rider, trainer, breeder, riding-club manager, dealer, horse-show organizer, and equestrian author, is experienced in almost every phase of Thoroughbred horse sports.

Over the years, I have picked up many economy tips from knowledgeable horsemen and horsewomen. All of them agree that buying the best-quality feed you can afford is cheapest in the long run. Keep all grains in covered containers such as galvanized garbage cans, tin-lined bins, or heavy-duty cylindrical cardboard packing boxes such as those in which moving companies pack china and bakeries receive flour.

It has often been said that "worming is the cheapest feed." Horses that are wormed regularly definitely thrive on a lesser quantity than those which have to nourish a host of parasites in addition to themselves. Keeping a horse's teeth in good condition with routine visits once a year from the "tooth man" helps him get the most from his feed by ensuring proper mastication.

Turning horses out whenever and wherever possible is a way to save on bedding. It also helps to bank the edges of the stall during the day with slightly used bedding, which will dry sufficiently to be pulled back down for the night.

Metal watering troughs and buckets often get bent out of shape and spring leaks at the seams long before they have outlived their usefulness. A small tube of metal mender applied to a clean, dry surface and smoothed with your fingers can postpone the purchase of replacements.

Burlap bags, cut into handy sizes and washed, make superior grooming cloth and in a pinch can substitute for practically all grooming tools except a hoof pick. Dry burlap plus a little elbow grease will remove even caked manure from a horse's coat; dampened, it will pick up dust and dirt raised by a curry or by a dry piece of burlap, and a quick swipe over the dampish hair with the dry piece again will polish the coat to a high sheen.

Inexpensive loose-weave thermal bed blankets make fine coolers at a fraction of the cost of ready-made saddlery ones, although you may have to sew two together for a large horse.

Old sheets beyond repair should be washed and saved to patch others; the surcingles and closing parts should be saved as replacement pieces too.

Sheet cotton is a big expense in stables that bandage frequently for treatment and shipping. Old bed pads cut to size make excellent quilted leg wraps that are washable and reusable. They can also be cut into large rectangles and used as saddle pads or underneath a regular saddle pad to reduce wear and tear. Old woolen bed blankets can also be cut into long strips for use as leg bandages.

Saving all small pieces of saddle soap and periodically melting them down and pouring them into any useful form is another thrifty practice.

KEEPING STABLE RECORDS

There are health records, there are breeding records, and in commercial establishments, there are billing records. A good record-keeping system can make a major dollar difference in the profit picture of a large stable, significantly affect the in-foal rate on a breeding farm, and help the single horse owner give better care to his horse for less money.

When did your horse receive his last tetanus toxoid booster? In an emergency, your vet will probably ask that question. And if you don't know the answer, he may administer an unnecessary injection of tetanus antitoxin. What product was used when your horse was last wormed? Since your object is to provide broad-spectrum protection against worms, how can you be sure of using a different worming product this time if you can't remember what product was used last? For that matter, do you know when your horse was last wormed?

Health records should do two things: 1) remind you of work done, and 2) warn you of work due. For an operation consisting of one or a handful of horses, the best health record is a sturdy calendar with plenty of blank space for each day.

First, plot your health-maintenance program for the coming year. Decide how many times you'll worm, at what intervals, and with what products. Plan frequency of foot care, and the immunizations you wish your horses to receive. Choose a time for a visit from the horse dentist.

Standardize your intervals. For example, if you decide to worm your horses every two months, plan on doing it the first of the month. Pick an easy day to remember and stick to it. Schedule your annual immunizations on a day that coincides with a tube worming, and combine the two treatments in one farm call.

Do the same with foot care. If you trim or reset once a month, make it the same day each month. It will help you to remember when your horse is due as well as when he was done last. It will help your blacksmith to plan his own schedule too.

If you have more than one horse, put them all on the same schedule, even if you have to do it gradually. You can design a single worming and immunization program that will suit almost all classes of horses. For example, in a breeding program, in which young horses need trimming every four weeks, and broodmares ideally every six weeks, you may find it practical to let the mares go for eight weeks, thus simplifying the schedule and cutting down on blacksmith visits.

When your health-maintenance program is set, mark the due dates on your calendar. If there is usually a long delay between the time you call your blacksmith, say, and the day he comes, you might write in a reminder to phone him a week ahead of time. As each phase of the program is completed, inscribe it on the calendar as in a diary, including the trade names of products used. This information will give you the opportunity in the future to use the same favored products and to avoid unsatisfactory ones.

In addition to health maintenance, use your calendar to record illness, injury, and treatment. Particularly during a long illness (although you never can tell which are going to be long), it is very helpful to have a daily record of temperature and medication to refer to. In some difficult diagnoses, a history is extremely helpful. (He was lame about a month ago, but was it the left front or the right front?) If a problem crops up similar to one you recall having treated successfully six months ago, you should be able to look back over your records for the exact procedure and medication.

Use your calendar to record commercial transactions. When the feed man comes, note the day and the quantity delivered. Do the same with hay and bedding deliveries. Soon you'll be able to calculate how long a given quantity will last. If you anticipate your needs for next year, you can probably save money by ordering early and in bulk. Track the progress of a load of straw, then try a load of shavings. See which bedding lasts longer and works out most economically for you.

Use your calendar to keep a record of farm maintenance and equipment repairs. If you lime and fertilize your pasture, make a note of the kind and amount of fertilizer as a guide for the following year. Write in equipment-servicing due dates so that you'll be reminded when it's time to service the tractor or to inspect the trailer. If you sell your manure, record dates of pickup and quantities. When payment arrives, you can check its accuracy.

Finally, use your calendar to keep track of coming show dates.

This is what the calendar of a small private stable might look like:

Notes on a stable calendar.

TUESDAY	WEDNESDAY	THURSDAY	
1 Worming, Immunizations Due	**2**	**3** Taffy, Elk, Folly Tubed with Dyrex TF, Tetanus, Flu, E+W, Encephalitis boosters.	**4**
8 Call blacksmith	**9** Broadview meadows schooling show 8 A.M.	**10** Trailer inspection due	**11**
15 ELK: Reset all Round RAMBLER: new shoes in front, reset behind FOLLY: trim	**16** Feed delivery 200 lbs. sweet feed 100 lbs. oats 4 salt bricks 1/2 ton Alfalfa-Timothy hay	**17** Folly- off feed Listless, temperature 104.4. Dr. Brown examined, Rx 25cc Pen/day and stall	**18**
22 FOLLY: temp. 100.3	**23**	**24** Green Ridge Show Breeding classes.	**25**
29	**30**		

THRIFTY OWNER, CAPITALIST HORSE

Why not open an extra savings account at your regular bank, as Bea Hocker, of Havertown, Pennsylvania, suggests? Designate it as being for your horse only. Deposit in it a small sum every month or out of every paycheck. In a matter of months you will have accumulated a fair amount of money with interest as a bonus. This is a relatively painless way to save for unexpected emergency bills, new equipment, or special training.

HOW TO CHOOSE A BOARDING STABLE

If it's your first horse, or if you've never been involved in caring for horses, it is difficult to judge whether the boarding stable you've chosen or are about to choose is capable of providing the quality of care that your horse needs. You can visit the stable and look around, but unless you know what to look for you may overlook significant evidence. You can also ask questions, of course, but unless you know what questions to ask, you may not know how to evaluate the answers.

Here is a mental checklist that should reveal all you need to know about the quality of care your horse is likely to receive:

AT FIRST GLANCE

Is the driveway in sufficiently good repair to permit safe transport of horses in all weather conditions?

This is especially important if you plan to show, hunt, or engage in any activity requiring frequent ins and outs with trailer or van.

Is the fencing safe?

Paddock fencing should be strong and in good repair. No portion should be barbed wire. Page wire fencing must be of sufficiently tight weave to ensure that hooves stay on the pasture side, and it must be stretched tightly across the posts, with no sag at the bottom in which a horse could catch a shoe.

Are the paddocks adequate for the number of horses?

Often space is at a premium, which means too many horses on too little grass, and for the sake of a convenient nearby location, you may have to settle for "exercise" paddocks. But all paddocks should show signs of sensible management. If they are nothing but dust in summer, they will be deep mud in winter, making exercise not only difficult but also dangerous. Small paddocks should be free from accumulated droppings. Where large numbers of horses graze confined areas, droppings must be picked up frequently to minimize parasite contamination.

Are the grounds surrounding stable and paddocks reasonably neat and uncluttered?

Aside from aesthetics, the important consideration here is whether a horse that breaks loose would be in danger of tangling with a scrapped car or an abandoned coil of barbed wire. Tidy grounds are also a reflection of the general attitude of the caretakers.

IN THE STABLE

Do the majority of horses have hay in front of them?

One or two may be without hay for some good reason, but in general, horses, as grazing animals, need something to nibble during their long hours of confinement.

Do the majority have water?

Water is cheap. A row of empty buckets is a sign of negligence.

Is the major portion of the stall bedding dry?

The stall may not be immaculate, depending on how your arrival coincides with the stall cleaning schedule. But it should never give the impression of more than twenty-four hours of inattention.

Is the stall construction sturdy, safe, and in good condition?

Stall partitions must have the strength of two-inch planking or better, with no sharp projections and no openings in which a foot might catch. The stall floor should be reasonably level, without sudden step-downs. Some wood chewing is inevitable. One badly chewed stall probably reflects only on its occupant. But when the whole stable looks as if it has been ravaged by a band of termites, the chances are that its inhabitants are confined for too many hours of the day with too little hay.

AROUND THE STABLE

Is the feed suitably stored?

This means in mouse-proof containers with tight lids and, most important for your horse's health, raised well above concrete floors and away from damp walls, in order to avoid mold.

Is the hay of acceptable quality?

Pick up a flake and pull it apart. If clouds of dust fly up, your horse may fill his lungs with it. Smell the hay. It should smell sweet. A sharp, unpleasant odor means mold. Moldy hay is not only dusty but sometimes contains toxins that cause colic and even death.

Is there appropriate supervision by competent personnel?

If you have progressed this far in your inspection without receiving an offer of assistance from a responsible adult, the answer is no. The volunteer help of horse-loving kids is a valuable resource when properly directed. But a mature, knowledgeable person should coordinate their efforts.

Some boarding stables keep their charges down by cutting corners here and there; others dress up the package with fancy facilities such as an indoor school, a Grand Prix course, prime location, or a famous instructor. But the basic principles of humane horse care are covered by the above questions. Few horse owners would knowingly settle for less, although many do just that, because they are unaware of their horses' needs and unfamiliar with the details of proper horse management. Owning horses is a luxury not only in terms of financial commitment, but also in terms of time and care.

(By the way, this same checklist can be used to ensure that your own stable management is what it should be.)

Chapter 6

SOLUTIONS TO COMMON HORSE PROBLEMS

CATCHING THE UNCATCHABLE

The people who have no trouble catching horses are those who go out in the field with some other purpose in mind. They intend to dig a ditch, for example, and from nowhere come the horses galloping over the brow of the hill, surrounding the equipment, bringing work to a halt. No amount of shooing and arm waving can counteract the curiosity of these loving pets. Now's your chance to lay your hands on one.

Another surefire scheme is to send someone into the pasture who has a genuine fear of horses. Few horses could resist the opportunity to dash over, and back your decoy against the nearest fence or wall.

There are two approaches to the problem of catching a horse. One is to make him think he really wants to be caught; the other is to let him know that there is no alternative. When it's you alone against the horse, your only option is the former. You have to develop a technique that makes the horse think it is he who is catching you.

If your horse is hard to catch, leave his halter on when you turn him out. Make sure that the halter fits snugly enough so that the horse cannot put a front foot through the noseband. And use a leather halter (not rope or nylon), which will break if the horse gets hung on a fence post. Now the trick is to condition the horse so that he is really glad to see you. Don't be too quick to rescue him from the first fly of the day. Let him suffer a little. Let him get a little hungry, even a little thirsty if necessary. Bring all the other horses in. Have a cup of coffee. Then stroll out slowly, aimlessly, to the pasture and see if you don't find a totally reformed character anxiously hanging his head over the gate.

When the blacksmith arrives at an inconvenient moment and you have to catch a horse you know isn't ready to come in, take a bucket of feed out to the field with you. There's nothing wrong in bribery as long as you turn it to your own advantage. Don't chase the horse around for twenty minutes and then trudge back to the barn for a bribe. The horse might reason that he earns his snack by running you around first.

When you know he's hard to catch, make a habit of arriving at the field with a bucket of feed. If he hangs back, set the bucket down and move back a few steps. The moment to lay a hand on his halter is when his nose is buried in the bucket. Let him have a bit more now and then on the way back to the barn. Pretty soon he'll be meeting you at the gate, and once the reflex is well established, an empty bucket may do just as well.

On days when you have a helper, you can forget the psychology and bribery if there is a fence in sight. Your horse is at your mercy. Two people can almost always make a horse believe he's cornered. The trick is concentration. If there are other horses in the field, decide together which one you are going to catch and stick to that one, even if another should come within your grasp. Select a spot against the fence, preferably a corner. Now both of you close in on the horse slowly from either side, driving him toward the chosen spot. As he feels his boundaries shrink, he'll whirl around to escape. If your attention is on him, and only him, you'll be able to block his path. Make up your mind that he's not going to get past you; he'll make a dodge or two and then wait to be caught. He'll know he hasn't a chance of winning.

But the best cure of all is prevention. Don't give your horse good reason to avoid being caught. Foals that are caught only in order to be given shots or to have their feet trimmed grow up to be expert escape artists. Horses that are caught only to be put to work have to be pretty dumb to keep falling into the same trap. Vary your routine: Catch your horse, give him a carrot or a pat, and then let him go. See if he doesn't follow you all the way back to the gate!

THE QUESTION OF CRIBBING

The Question: Are cribbing and windsucking learned by horses from each other? I have just bought a horse that has the problem, and all of my friends warn that if I let him stay with the other horses (we have three more) they will start doing the same thing, despite the fact that they have never cribbed before.

An answer from WALTER HUGHES, prominent Quarter Horse trainer and judge, of Monrovia, Maryland:

You bet they will! If you have one horse in the barn that is cribbing or windsucking, you'll have more if you aren't careful. I'd suggest that you get a cribbing strap and put it on the horse right away. Or you can use a two-inch-wide belt, if you can get it tight enough. If neither of these methods stops the horse from cribbing or sucking wind, then I would isolate him from the other animals in the barn. If it is impossible to do this, I would seriously consider getting rid of him, because all he is going to do is to cause you trouble.

HOW TO RESTRAIN A HORSE

JOHN SMITH, owner/manager of the Barnesville Thoroughbred Farm, is an exceptionally versatile horseman, having shown hunters and jumpers, ridden steeplechase and point-to-point races, hunted, ridden Quarter Horse races as a licensed jockey, and bred, trained, and raced Thoroughbreds:

Because I am not a big person to begin with, and because I don't believe in shoving when a gentle nudge will do, I prefer not to have to fight with any horse for any reason. Whenever possible, I will kid a horse out of an argument or resistance. However, when a horse must be held quietly (for treatment by a veterinarian, for example), I always look for the least amount of restraint that will accomplish what I want.

A twitch is the most common piece of equipment used to take a horse's mind off what's happening to him. If I merely need to divert a horse that doesn't really want to fight about what I'm doing (such as working on his legs), I find the metal squeeze-type twitches are the perfect solution. I don't like the "one-man," screw-on type, because I think they flatten the horse's lip too much and are often more irritating than useful.

Sometimes a horse that will not respond to a twitch will respect a chain drawn across his upper gums. This can cut up a horse's mouth if the hand on the shank is heavy, so I'm always aware of how I hold the shank and only pull against it as much as is required.

I have a pet device that has worked very well for me. I put a web or leather surcingle on the horse and a racetrack-type yoke (a leather strap encircling the horse's neck, attached to another strap passing between his forelegs and slipping over the surcingle underneath his belly). To this I attach a tie-down (a short leather strap with a snap at each end) and snap the other end onto the halter ring underneath the horse's chin. With this rig, a horse cannot get away from you no matter what he does. When I use this device I don't need anything else, and I've found that it works remarkably well on horses that want to throw their heads with a twitch, rear when you walk them, or do just about anything else. I've used it to do everything from pulling manes and clipping bodies to restraining horses for the vet. The first time a horse feels it take hold, he may spook a bit and run backwards, but once he knows it's there, he won't try a second time.

If a horse is really tough and continues to resist handling, I'm not at all averse to having the vet tranquilize him. I think that in the long run it saves wear and tear on everyone concerned, and on the horse most of all.

DR. WILLIAM HEFFNER, a University of Virginia graduate with a D.V.M. from Cornell, is a licensed racetrack veterinarian in Charles Town, West Virginia, a farmer, a Thoroughbred breeder, and an active fox hunter as well as Honorary Whipper-in for the New Market Hounds.

I think that any discussion of restraint should start with the old adage "Patience is a virtue." Patience often makes restraint work, while impatience often destroys all possibility of restraint.

One should always be quiet, gentle, and firm with foals. I put one arm under the neck and hold the far side of the head with the other hand. I grasp the tail very close to the body and push it straight over the back. I use this method even when passing a stomach tube.

In restraining an animal of any age, distraction such as letting the horse play with the end of the shank, or scratching its muzzle, will often suffice. Frequently when I'm working on legs, all I need is someone to hold the opposite leg. If further restraint is necessary, various methods can be used, depending on the severity required. The restrainer should be on the same side of the horse as the worker, whether the latter is grooming, trimming, or working.

The single most useful restraint tool is a chain-end shank. The best ones have 30-inch to 36-inch chains, permitting a variety of uses. Placed over the nose or under the chin, a chain offers a great deal of control over an unruly animal. If even more is necessary, it can be passed through the horse's mouth like a bit. The vast majority of stallions are handled this way, especially during breeding. If something stronger is needed, the shank can be placed over the horse's gum beneath his upper lip. Horses that object violently to twitches often succumb to this method.

An important consideration is the positioning of the horse. Personally, I like to have him near his stall wall and not shoved back into a corner. When you make an animal feel trapped, you turn a pussycat into a tiger. So whenever possible, I prefer to let the horse have some feeling of movement or freedom.

And a word of warning: If you are the holder of a restrained animal, do not lighten the restraint until you are absolutely certain that it is no longer needed. You could get your horse, your co-worker, or yourself into serious trouble by releasing prematurely.

GINNY MARSHALL, a Canadian-born free-lance exercise girl and pony girl who has the reputation around the tracks of being particularly adept at handling rough and fractious racehorses:

When you are a girl and not a very big one at that, and you want to work around horses, particularly at the racetrack, it doesn't take too long for you to learn that there's more than one way to get something done.

For example, you often have a horse that's feeling way above himself and wants to buck and play while he's walking the shed. You absolutely cannot allow him to jump about, because sooner or later he may kick the wall or, worse, another horse. He may also wrench a leg, step on himself, or (I hate even to think of it) get loose. When conventional methods of arranging the shank don't seem to do the job, I will sometimes run it through his mouth, although I don't find this too much more effective than over his nose (with the exception of horses that just like to chew on the chain). But my surefire solution is to thread it through the near ring, under the horse's upper lip across his gum (or the lower gum will do just as well), then on through the right side ring, and snap it onto either the higher or the lower ring just as you'd do if you were running it over the nose. It may sound a little rough and lots of people think that horses will not walk this way, but I don't usually have to take any hold of it at all and still the horses walk along like perfect ladies or gentlemen. A horse may test it by bouncing against it once, but after that he usually backs off completely and I can take the lightest contact, just enough to keep it from slipping off, and have complete control. This method is super for holding horses for the vet as well, although vets often prefer to use a twitch.

I guess just about everyone uses twitches of some sort, and I am no exception. However, I prefer the rope-end ones, because I think they're the least likely to slip. If the twitch has some length, it gives a small person added leverage and a chance of staying out from under the horse's feet. I've also found that at the odd times when I might have needed a twitch and not had one handy, a piece of baling string or clothesline tied into a loop about the size of a conventional twitch loop, with a double-end snap on it, is a fair improvisation. By looping the rope on the horse's lip and twisting the snap, you can tighten it pretty well, and then with the other end of the snap you can fix it to the halter. It won't hold a real toughie, but it's a lot better than nothing.

Sometimes I have to work on a horse alone. If he's halfheartedly fighting about it, I put a surcingle around his belly as you would a girth and attach the loop end of a longe line (or a draw line) to it between the horse's front legs, like a standing martingale. Then I run it through the center halter ring (if it will fit) or simply through the halter under the horse's chin. I hold on to the other end. By pulling my end of the line, I get a draw-line or pulley effect that pulls the horse's head down. When he stands still and behaves himself, I ease off. I can feel if he's about to act up and am usually ready for him. After a little while, I can be quite light with it. With a really tough horse, I put on a chifney bit first and snap it onto the halter. Then I run the longe line out through the bottom of the chifney (the part encircling the horse's chin), and that way I get a direct pull on his mouth.

Mainly, I try to get along with the horses I handle. But when it is necessary to hold them for their own good, these methods are the ones with which I've had the most luck.

HOW TO USE A TWITCH

The use of a *long-handled twitch* is *a two-man job*. You'll need a helper to hold the twitch while you work on the horse.

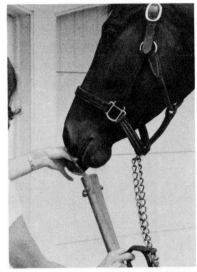

1. Hold the twitch in your right hand and slip the thumb and middle finger of your left hand through the loop. The other fingers, outside the loop, hold it forward on your hand.

2. Pull the horse's upper lip out and slip the loop over it. Be sure to keep a firm hold on the twitch handle so that it won't hit you in the face if the horse jerks his head up.

3. Twist the loop tight enough so that the horse can't work free.

4. Stand to one side where the horse won't hit you if he rears or strikes out, and hold the twitch firmly in both hands while your helper works on the horse.

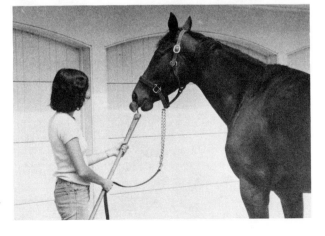

If you don't have a helper, you can use an aluminum *one-man twitch* to hold your horse still. This is the method preferred by most vets.

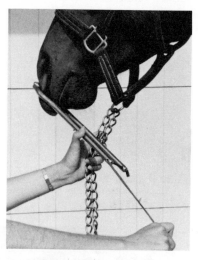

1. Put your hand through the twitch and grasp the horse's upper lip.

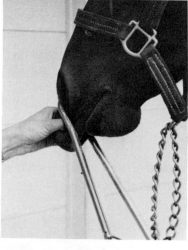

2. Slide the twitch forward and . . .

3. . . . pull down on the rope to tighten it.

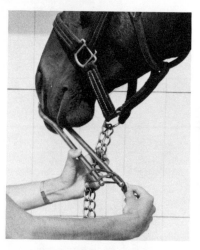

4. Wrap the rope twice around the bottom of the twitch and . . .

5. . . . pull it beneath the lowest wrap to keep the loops from sliding off the end of the twitch.

6. Clip the snap to the center ring of the halter.

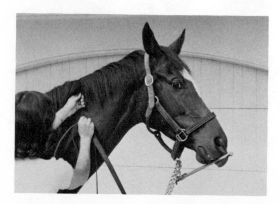

7. The twitch stays put without a helper while you go to work.

1. *If you have neither a helper nor a twitch,* you can make a one-man twitch that will serve in a pinch simply by stringing a loop of baling twine through one end of a snap. Slip the twine over the horse's nose and twist to tighten it.

2. Clip the snap to the side ring of the halter. Remember: If you leave any kind of twitch on too long, it will numb the horse's nose and lose its effectiveness. Remove the twitch every fifteen minutes or so and give your horse a rest.

RESTRAINING A HORSE WITHOUT A TWITCH

There are a number of effective and humane methods you can use to keep your horse still while he's being trimmed, inoculated, tubed, or bandaged. It will take you only a few minutes to master them all. You can experiment with them until you find the one that works best with your horse.

    1. Pressing down with one hand on the sensitive cartilage at the end of the nose encourages most horses to keep the head still.

    2. Squeezing with your fingers to close one nostril reduces the horse's air supply and makes him even more willing to stand still. Be sure not to hold both nostrils shut, though. Your horse cannot breathe through his mouth, so he will have to fight you to keep from suffocating.

    3. Holding one ear also convinces some horses to keep the head still. This technique is especially useful when you're trying to trim the muzzle, since using a twitch or holding the bridge of the nose would interfere with the clippers.

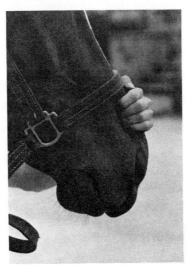
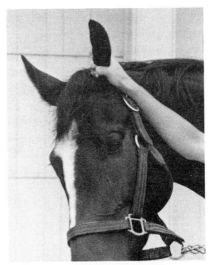

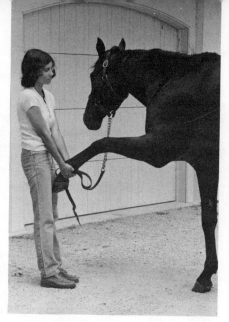

4. A "shoulder wrap" discourages the horse from walking forward or striking out with his foot. Pick up a fold of skin over the bulge where the horse's neck joins his body and roll your knuckles forward so that they rest against the neck. You can make an even more effective shoulder wrap by rolling the skin forward with both hands.

5. Picking up one front foot will help keep the other three feet on the ground while someone bandages or treats them. But if you pick the foot up in the usual manner, with the knee bent, your horse may lean on you. Instead, interlock your fingers behind his fetlock and pull his leg forward. His forearm should be horizontal. If someone is working around his hindquarters, you may want to hold his leg a little higher to put more of his weight on his back legs.

6. If your horse still refuses to stand still, try putting a chain shank across his nose. Because the chain is thinner than the noseband of the halter, it concentrates the pressure on a smaller area, and its ridges also make it more severe. Put the chain through the lower left ring of the halter. Wrap it once around the noseband of the halter to keep it from slipping down, and run it through the lower right ring of the halter. The mildest arrangement is to clip the end of the chain back to its base. When you pull down on the shank, the chain transfers the pressure to the bridge of the horse's nose.

7. If you need a little more control, you can clip the chain to the center ring of the halter so that it will tighten around the horse's nose when you pull.

8. If your horse's halter has a sliding center ring, don't attach the chain there. It will pull the ring out of position instead of tightening across the horse's nose.

9. Instead, pull the chain up and attach it to the top ring of the halter on the right side.

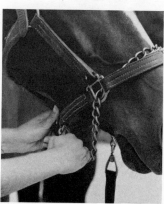

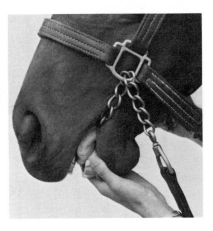

10. Some horses rear as soon as they feel the pressure of a chain across the nose. If your horse is one of these, you may be able to get a little extra control without upsetting him by running the chain under his chin and attaching it to the lower ring on the right side.

11. If your horse still refuses to stand still, run the chain under his chin, through the lower right ring, and up to the top ring on the right side. Then let some slack into the chain and pull it forward through the horse's mouth.

12. This arrangement is very severe, so be sure not to jerk on the shank.

13. If all else fails, pull the chain across the horse's gum. Start with it through his mouth, as before. Then pull it forward and slip it over his upper gum . . .

14. . . . so that it rests at the point where the gum meets the upper lip.

15. You will have to keep a slight pressure on the chain all the time to prevent your horse from dislodging it.

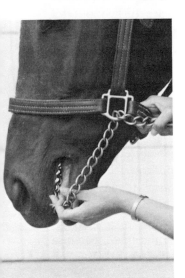

HOW TO HANDLE A HORSE THAT BITES

DR. RON QUERRY, former director of the Equestrian Center, at Lake Erie College:

I think people teach horses to bite by feeding them tidbits from their hands and letting them mouth jackets and pockets. All our students are girls, and they spoil their horses, with the result that the animals develop some very bad habits.

Of course, there's a big difference between an occasional playful nip that's really more lips than teeth, and a vicious bite that draws blood. I get rid of a really confirmed, malicious biter.

While I was in graduate school and shoeing horses, there were a number of horses at the racetrack that were terrible biters when given the chance. The solution was simple. While they were being shod, they wore a muzzle. Period.

Generally a slap on the nose and an end to hand-fed tidbits are enough to correct a horse that is a little nippy. In my situation, though, it is hard to get the girls to smack their horses.

Recently I saw an interesting article in an old horse-training book. A surefire way to cure horses of biting was claimed to be by firing a revolver whenever the horse made a move to bite. The loud noise allegedly solved the problem.

EDDIE BYWATERS was manager-trainer of Waverly Farm, in Warrenton, Virginia, during the era when Waverly virtually dominated the Conformation Hunter Division:

Biting is a natural instinct. When a group of horses are turned out together, you'll often see two of them going around nipping at each other. I prefer not to turn horses out together, because it encourages nipping. They soon forget the difference between biting another horse and biting a person.

Another thing that sometimes encourages nipping is tightening a girth too tightly or too quickly. Tighten the girth gently. Keep the horse's head turned to the outside, and discipline him if he tries to bite you.

The best kind of discipline is to take a crop or a whip and really punish the horse in the shoulder or flank area every time he tries to bite you. Holler at him at the same time so that he associates the two and you'll be able to correct him later by voice alone. Of course, it's a lot easier to correct the habit in a young horse than when it has become an established vice. It can be very difficult, if not impossible, to reform a chronic biter.

I don't like to slap the horse's muzzle or hit him around the head, because that makes him head-shy. Also, he simply learns to nip you and then jump back.

JOE KING is co-manager, with his wife, of Waldemar Farm, in Ocala, Florida, where they are responsible for some 160 Thoroughbreds, including the two-time Leading Sire in North America, What A Pleasure:

We've never really had a problem with biting here, perhaps because of the way we handle our horses. Colts are inclined to nip—that's just natural to them—so from the time they are very small we scold them whenever they make a move to nip.

Slap the colt with the end of the shank, or, if he's loose in the stall, peck him on the nose with your hand. Of course, you have to use judgment about hitting him around the head, as this can make him head-shy.

Some colts will continue to try to bite if given the opportunity, no matter what you do, so remain alert and don't turn your back on them.

All stallions should be considered potential biters. Again, it's just instinct. When handling a stallion, you must be sure that you're in control at all times. If you're dealing with a vicious stallion, you have to be even more careful and perhaps use two men and two shanks to control him.

At the racetrack, we sometimes muzzle colts to prevent them from biting the lead pony or the pony rider. Of course, it's partly the responsibility of the pony rider to avoid being bitten and to keep the pony under control.

Aside from these situations, which can be anticipated, the only other biting problems we've encountered here have resulted from people feeding horses sugar and other goodies from the hand. Sugar is terrible. When the horse expects it and you don't have any, he will want to bite you for sure.

HOW TO PUT WEIGHT ON A THIN HORSE

THOMAS D. BROKKEN, D.V.M., graduate of the University of Minnesota School of Veterinary Medicine and a veterinary surgical residency at the University of Saskatchewan, in Canada, is a partner in an important equine practice in Miami, Florida:

I think you can put weight on any horse if it is healthy and if it is managed properly. However, special conditions arise when a horse has gone through the stress of losing a lot of weight, whether from a disease, poor management, or parasite infestation.

If I were presented with a seriously underweight horse, the first thing I would do would be to examine him for any signs of infection and treat as required. Then I would go through the routine of checking the horse's teeth and checking the management. An important thing, especially with Thoroughbreds, is to watch for cribbing and wind sucking. Even though the owner may not say that the horse cribs, I would observe the horse carefully and take precautionary measures, because cribbing can prevent weight gain.

When the animal is eating and drinking adequate amounts, I would recommend deworming with five to ten times the normal dose of thiabendazole via the stomach tube. This should be done regardless of the fecal counts. In twenty-one days I would worm the horse with a normal dose, and then keep him on a regular monthly deworming program for one year.

I would put the thin horse on a timothy-and-alfalfa or straight timothy-type hay, free choice, and a low-protein grain ration, either a mixture of bran and oats or straight oats, with about half a pound of soybean oil meal added per day. A too-high-protein diet is not advantageous, particularly for a debilitated horse. The grain shouldn't exceed 12 percent protein for the first month. Good hay is very important, and if I could only feed one or the other, I would certainly feed hay.

I would start by feeding four times a day, and then if the horse was doing well in three or four weeks, drop back to twice a day. I'd start with about one and one half pounds of feed per one hundred pounds of body weight, and every week increase the feed by 25 percent, so that at the end of a month the horse is eating twice as much. I think the important thing is to feed very often, rather than large amounts once or twice a day. Horses get into trouble with grain because of overzealous appetite. Loading up the stomach and small intestine with a large quantity of carbohydrate leads to digestive upsets and laminitis.

A seriously debilitated horse will probably not gain any weight during the first two weeks or a month, until his metabolism has adjusted to his diet, but then he should gain approximately two to three pounds a day if fed properly and not asked to do too much exercise. With a really starved horse, I would keep him in confinement for sixty days, with maybe just a little hand-walking for exercise.

Water is very important. Ideally, a horse should have unlimited access to fresh, clean water. The normal horse should drink about a gallon of water per 100 pounds of body weight, something in the area of eight to twelve gallons a day. Keep in mind that the standard water bucket holds only about three gallons, so it needs to be filled frequently.

How much weight a horse should carry is difficult to determine, because of the variables of conformation and age. But, at minimum acceptable weight, you should be able to see the last three ribs, no more. Sometimes with old horses, however, you can never get the ribs well covered, because they lack adequate muscle.

Poor management and care of a horse by a person with inadequate knowledge of the equine field usually results in poor nutrition and consequently an underweight animal.

These thin horses are more prone to disease and thus to added stress. The most important single treatment of the thin animal, if it is basically healthy, usually involves moving it to a new owner. That is my best treatment, along with proper education of the client.

Sandy Vaughan trains Quarter Horses at Westenhook Farm, in Southbury, Connecticut, home of numerous champions and World Champions and a pioneer in promoting the Quarter Horse as a hunter and jumper:

Weight isn't just a matter of putting on fifty pounds of fat. Our halter horses can't be flabby. With the conformation of the Quarter Horse, you have to worry about the throatlatch being small and clean, the neck being very long and thin. When you put weight on a Quarter Horse, it seems the first place it goes is right to the neck, and that's the last place it comes off. Fattening the Quarter Horse requires a combination of feed with exercise to tone muscle, and sometimes sweating to reduce heavy areas.

For a horse to be fit and properly turned out, you have to groom him from the inside. If a thin horse came to the farm, the first thing I'd do would be to have a stool sample checked for parasites and have a blood workup done, to see just what physical shape the horse is in. Anemia can take a horse apart, while nobody knows what's wrong with him. And it's terribly important to make sure the animal is parasite-free. We worm our horses every two months. Of course, it's also important to check teeth in order to ensure that the horse is chewing his grain properly and digesting it thoroughly.

Once you know the horse is free from parasites and that his blood picture is normal, you work on feeding him. You increase the grain slowly because of the danger of founder and colic and so on. With a thin horse, the stomach has shrunk and has to expand gradually to a capacity that will accept the increase. I wouldn't increase any faster than one to two quarts a week.

You should also consult the former owner to get an idea of the horse's eating habits, what he's been fed, and how much. If the horse is not cleaning up his feed, he may be normally just a slow eater. I have horses that take all day to clean up their morning feed.

Consistency in the feeding schedule is important, feeding every day at the same time. And I believe it's a must to have a salt block in the stall and free access to water. The more water horses drink the better.

We have always held that 16 percent protein in the grain ration is the maximum you can feed without harming the horse. We've had people feed adult horses up to 22 percent protein and take the hair right off.

A mixture of oats and sweet feed is good for putting weight on. We feed triple-cleaned crimped oats, which I like very much, but I think the crimped oats have a tendency to add steam to a horse that is already hot. Sweet feed will put weight on faster than oats. I'm not high on feeding a lot of supplements, but I do put a handful of dry bran in the feed each meal. If I've got a horse that has undergone unusual stress, either isn't feeling well or has been worked very hard, I'll mix up a mash for him.

You can't put weight on with grain alone. It takes roughage, too. Horses need hay. I like alfalfa, but if mishandled it can be very dangerous. Alfalfa hay is higher in protein than other hays, and one flake twice a day will do, but that isn't much hay. The horse gobbles it down in half an hour and then he just stands there all day, doing nothing or chewing the barn down. I don't like clover hay at all, because you have to be too careful about mold and dust. The best is a good timothy-and-alfalfa mix. You don't have to worry about how much you feed: You get the protein content of the alfalfa and the bulk from the timothy.

One of the causes of weight loss is mental frustration, worrying. A nervous horse is a lot harder to put weight on than a quiet horse. The quiet horse stands around like a feeder cow, nothing upsets him, so his food is digested thoroughly and is assimilated. With a nervous horse, the feed goes right through him. That's why it is important to keep a horse you are trying to put weight on quiet, and keep his exercise quiet too. You can either pony him or work him in a round pen, or give him quiet riding. If not in work, he should at least be turned out. Horses are like children in that they need time to relax and let down. If a horse is kept quiet, you can probably put fifty to one hundred pounds on him in a month or two with no difficulty. A nervous horse might need ninety days or longer to gain the same amount of weight.

LEG BLEMISHES AND
WHAT CAN BE DONE ABOUT THEM

DELMAR TWYMAN, of Woodbrook Farm, in Montpelier Station, Virginia, breeds and shows conformation horses:

Wind-puffs, bogs, capped hocks, thoroughpins, and splints all respond pretty well to a good blister, as long as you catch the injury when it's fresh. If you let things set, they're the devil to reduce.

Large fillings and curbs pretty well end the horse's conformation career. A blister will put him in shape for the working division, but the on-the-line classes are out.

Capped Hock   Splint

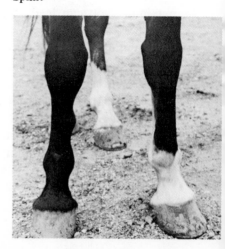

Reducine is the best blister I've found. It's effective but not caustic enough to drive the horse crazy.

If I have a horse that pops a little splint, first I hose the leg to cool it down. When the inflammation disappears, I begin treatment. I shave the splint area, scrub it with a stiff brush, and dry it thoroughly.

Reducine is thick, tarry-looking stuff. I use a corn cob to apply it, really rubbing it in for three or four minutes each day for ten to twelve days.

Track people wrap the leg to get a stronger effect, but I leave it open to the air. I keep the horse in his stall to hold the swelling down and keep the leg dry. I don't want the blister to run down the leg.

By the end of the period of treatment, the leg has swelled and the skin has scurfed. I clean up the leg and leave it alone while it heals. In about five weeks, the hair will have grown back and the horse can return to work.

Soft-tissue swellings are very common in show horses. A high-protein diet puts a nice coat and good flesh on a young horse, but it also puts fluid in his ankles and hocks. He may wolf down twelve quarts of grain a day, bury his nose in alfalfa, and miss his paddock time because he's standing around in a van or a stall. You can often eliminate small ankle fillings, bogs, and thoroughpins simply by adjusting the horse's diet and increasing his exercise.

At the sight of a puffy hock, some horsemen reach for a needle to tap the fluid. Not me. Any time a needle goes in, infection may go with it. From a small puffy area I could move up to a major infection impairing soundness.

If a colt comes up with a capped hock, first I find out why and eliminate the cause. For example, if he stands up against the wall of his stall, I pad the wall. Otherwise he'll only do it again.

The minute I see a suspicious hock, I drag out the hose. If you don't start on a cap right away, you'll have it for life. I hose it twice a day for fifteen to twenty minutes until the inflammation is gone. When the hock is cool, I blister with Reducine, following the same procedure I use for splints.

Bog spavins, thoroughpins, and windgalls all get the same treatment. I hose until cool, then blister with Reducine. If the swelling is really minor,

Bog Spavin   Wind-puff   Curb

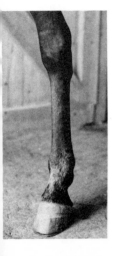
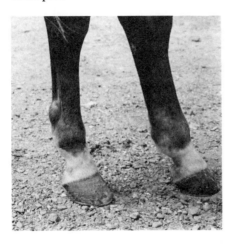

the hosing alone sometimes takes care of it. But usually the blister is surer. It tightens the tissues so that the fluid doesn't creep back in.

Some trainers keep their horses in standing bandages all the time to hold wind-puffs down. But a horse that lives in wraps comes to depend on them for support. Pretty soon the tissues lose their ability to tighten and the horse can't do without the wraps.

Occasionally I sweat a leg to treat a minor filling. I rub the leg with a glycerine-and-alcohol mixture, cover it with Saran Wrap to hold the heat, and protect the whole thing with cottons and bandages. But I'm always a little leery of what I'm going to find when I take the bandages off. Four or five days of sweating can put a wavy pattern on a leg.

RICHARD TAYLOR breeds conformation hunters and Thoroughbred racehorse prospects at his Rivendell Stud, in Virginia:

A conformation horse has to be clean-legged. Enlarged ankles and big knees won't make it. Even a large splint means a quick career change. An older conformation horse may be able to get by with a little tendon bump or two, but any kind of bony enlargement more severe than a little splint puts his younger brothers right out of the in-hand classes for yearlings and two-year-olds. However, unless you wrap a horse in cotton batting he's going to turn up with the odd bump. What to do?

Hosing does nothing. The results are not worth the time. A sweat is the safest, easiest way to deal with such soft-tissue swellings as wind-puffs and filled ankles. A sweat also works well on the little knee swellings the older conformation horse picks up hitting a fence.

Since most of these fillings have nothing to do with unsoundness and we're reducing them for cosmetic purposes only, I wait until four or five days before the show to do anything. If the horse lives in bandages, pretty soon the bandages don't produce results. If I use a sweat only when I need it, it remains an effective treatment.

Any mild liniment will do: rubbing alcohol, Vetrolin, Absorbine. I've also used Furacin successfully. I apply it liberally, encase the leg in a plastic wrap, and cover it with cottons and a bandage. I remove the sweat for exercise and replace it when the horse returns to his stall.

When I take this horse to a show, he stays in his shipping bandages until two or three hours before a class. Then his wraps come off and I wash, dry, and brush out his legs so that there are no wavy lines or rough hair to hint that he's been in bandages.

Capped hocks and bogs need something stronger. My most successful remedy is a massage with a moderate-strength preparation such as Iodex or Icthamol. I massage several times a day and keep it up. If the cap or bog doesn't respond after several days of this, I'll blister.

The degree of success is directly related to the severity of the injury.

Short-term remedies such as tapping the joint and injecting a steroid give immediate results: no fluid. But they can also produce serious infections. Blisters are safe.

Irish Reducine is my favorite moderate blister. I get good results and an excellent hair return. In thirty days the hair is back, and it comes in normally—with no pigmentation problem.

I scrub the Reducine on with a toothbrush for fourteen days. The area scurfs and swells. Turning the horse out for light exercise keeps some of the swelling down, but if you're supersensitive and stop treatment at the first sign of swelling, you won't get a good result.

After fourteen days I ease off for two or three days and wait for the irritation to subside. Then I massage with a mild ointment like lanolin and Furacin and assess the results. One treatment usually does the job.

Bony enlargements are harder to reduce. I can hide a small splint if it's right below the knee. An iodine-based ointment rubbed into the splint area produces a mild irritation, enough to fill the surrounding area slightly and conceal the splint.

If the splint is between the knee and the ankle, it's pretty difficult to hide. Once it's cool, I'll try to reduce it with a severe blister such as M.A.C. solution. Since there's a chance of infection when you use a strong blister, I do it under veterinary supervision. I equip the horse with a cradle so he won't chew his leg, put him on complete rest, and paint the stuff on for ten days. Then I wait.

It takes about sixty days for the hair to grow back and I know whether I have a success or a flop. Leg paint can produce pigmentation problems. I can end up with sprinklings of white hair, or the hair may grow in wavy. The splint is gone, but the horse is still out of on-the-line classes. It's chancy.

If your conformation prospect comes in with a puffy leg, hope it's a soft-tissue swelling. A wind-puff may be chronic, but it's a lot easier to reduce than a splint.

KENNY WINCHELL was breeder/trainer of Freshet Farm, in Pennsylvania, home of many outstanding conformation hunters:

Wind-puffs are manageable, capped hocks are troublesome, and bogs are impossible. If your prize two-year-old turns up with a bog spavin, you'd better have God on your side, because not much else will work.

If you catch a swelling early, you have a much better chance of reducing it than if it's big or if it has had a chance to set.

Thorosweat works pretty well on wind-puffs. A minor wind-puff needs only a light sweat. I rub on the Thorosweat and cover it with cottons and a bandage. For a large wind-puff, I put a layer of plastic wrap under the cottons to hold the heat in.

I also cut back on the groceries. Overfeeding blows up hocks and ankles fast.

Thorosweat will take the average ankle down overnight. The next day, I unwrap the leg and exercise the horse. If the swelling isn't down, I repeat the procedure. I wrap it up again. Every day, I remove the wrap just long enough to exercise the horse. The rest of the time, he stays in his stall. If the skin starts to scurf, I give it a rest for a while.

If a colt of mine has a freshly capped hock and it's just a minor one, I hose it four to six times a day or bathe it in an Epsom salt solution. When it's dry, I rub it with DMSO. As long as I'm making progress, I keep it up. A week's treatment usually reduces a minor cap substantially. But if the leg starts to scurf before I see improvement, I stop and do a blister.

A severely capped hock is bound to require a blister. But since I have to cool it out before I can apply the blister, I start out with the Epsom-salt-and-DMSO routine until the heat and inflammation subside. Then I clip the hair and slap on the Reducine. For the next week, I rub in Reducine every day with a stiff brush. I lay off a week and then repeat the procedure.

Once I have a good scurf, I stop and let the hair grow back. In about five weeks I reassess the hock and start the Reducine routine again if there is still swelling.

I like Reducine for blistering, because it's mild and yet it works. It doesn't burn, so I don't have to use a cradle. When a colt gets hung up in his cradle, you usually end up with a worse problem than a puffy hock.

Nothing reduces a full-blown bucked shin well enough to put you back into the conformation division. But if you catch the shin early enough, you can take it down with Reducine, or you can inject an iodine blister under the skin. They work equally well, and they take about the same amount of time to heal. The internal blister usually doesn't take the hair off.

Yearlings come up with baby splints all the time. I use a lot of Dr. Wright's Splint Medicine. It's easy to work with, because you apply it only once instead of daily.

I prepare the leg in the same way as for a Reducine blister, and I rub in the medicine hard with a toothbrush for five minutes, working in the direction of hair growth so that the new hair will grow in normally. I grease the leg underneath the splint to protect it should the medicine drip down. And then I leave the horse alone.

It certainly is a lot less trouble than the method we used in the old days: rubbing olive oil into the splint with a deer bone.

In ten to fourteen days the swelling in the leg will have subsided enough for me to see what I have. In most cases a new splint may need another application or two. From the end of treatment the hair is back within about five weeks.

You can't do much firing with a conformation horse. You might get by with one needle hole, which is sometimes sufficient for a very small splint. Any more holes than that are just too noticeable.

That's why curbs are so hard to treat. A true curb which affects the horse's soundness is going to require a leg-paint blister and firing. In a couple of months you'll have a strong leg but not one that will pass inspection in the conformation division.

IF YOUR HORSE SHIES, FIRST FIND OUT WHY

By Elaine Sedito, with the assistance of Dr. Lionel Ruben, equine eye specialist at New Bolton Center, and Dr. Alexander Delahunta, Chairman of Veterinary Clinics at Cornell University.

Your horse is entered in his first show. You've picked up points in earlier classes. Now, as you enter the ring, the championship seems to be within your reach—until your horse spies a grooming towel fluttering on the rail. Before you can say, "We blew it," he shies halfway across the ring and the championship is down the drain.

A bad break. Why did your horse shy, when the other horses in the ring didn't? Could you have prevented him from shying, or minimized it once it began?

It's sometimes hard to believe that a horse isn't being paranoid or even malicious when he shies. But those are human, not equine, traits. For a horse, shying is a natural reflex, the vestige of a basic survival mechanism.

In the wild, the horses that lived long enough to reproduce were the ones that ran away at the slightest sign of trouble. Those that stuck around (only to find out, for example, that a faint rustle in the bushes was caused by a lion) did not fare so well. Over millions of years, the fright/flight response became ingrained in the horse through natural selection. It's still there, in the form of shying.

The fright/flight trigger can be pressed by any of the horse's senses. A horse might shy when he hears a strange noise, like a car backfiring or the crunch of dry leaves underfoot, or when he feels a low branch brush against his hindquarters. However, horses are primarily visual creatures, with the largest eyes of any animals except the whale and the ostrich, and their range of vision is extraordinary, from straight ahead to nearly directly behind. So, more often than not, fright/flight is set off by a stimulus through the horse's eyes, as in the case of your show horse and the fluttering towel.

With an imaginary slow-motion instant replay of that incident, we can watch the chain reaction set off inside your horse's body.

The image of the towel entered his eye through the pupil and was picked up by the cells that line the rear of the eye to form the retina. These cells flashed the message to the brain through the optic nerve. The message entered at the brain stem, or medulla, the part of the brain concerned with unconscious body functions. Whether or not it traveled farther—into the cerebellum or the cerebrum, the parts of the brain that handle progressively more conscious responses—is anybody's guess. In any event, the towel was perceived as a threat. It had undergone a subtle change when it began to move, and in the wild such subtleties can mean death.

In a flash, the adrenal medulla, the part of the adrenal gland that deals with danger, was signaled to release epinephrine into the bloodstream. This hormone sounded an alarm throughout the horse's body. His heart rate shot up. His eyes widened, and he gulped air. Blood rushed to his muscles to help provide them with an extra burst of energy. Meanwhile, orders streamed out from the brain to the muscles and they went into action. The entire reaction, from initial sight to final bolt, took less time than it takes to say "suddenly."

The horse is not alone in responding to danger in this way. Fright/flight is common to all prey animals: gazelles and other antelopes, for example, as well as cattle. Even a dog, basically a predator, will shy if taken by surprise. But we don't think of shying as a problem with these animals. Our relationships with them are different. We do not ride them.

People are not immune to fright/flight either. In a strange place, we'll spook when a door slams or jump when something moves within our peripheral vision. But, largely through social restraint, we've overcome the flight part of the response. We focus on whatever made us jump and decide whether or not it is dangerous before we turn and run.

Your horse has to cope with a problem that you have been spared and with which you may find it difficult to sympathize. His eyes report a world that is different from the one you see. When you look at an object, the separate images seen by each eye are superimposed to form a single impression. You have one field of vision. The horse, with his widely spaced eyes, has two overlapping but separate fields. His right eye reports to the left side of his brain; his left eye, to the right.

He also lacks something that you possess: a part of the brain called the corpus callosum, which links the brain's two sides—in short, which lets your right hand know what your left hand is doing. So some shying that may seem totally unjustified to you is actually the result of the normal functioning of your horse's vision. He sees everything afresh with each eye. He shies at a bucket by the side of the ring, gets over his fright, and then shies again when he changes direction and sees the same bucket through his other eye. As far as he's concerned, he has never seen it before.

When you train your horse, you're asking him to do as you do: overcome an instinctive response with learned behavior. With a foal, the only instinct that counters fright/flight is the one that prompts him to stay with his dam. So you expect a foal to shy at his first car, his first bicycle, his first flock of birds or drainage ditch. You also expect that in time he will learn that these things are harmless. By training, you hope to teach him to suppress the flight part of the response, even when he is frightened by a new sight or sound.

Your horse sees everything afresh with each eye. He shied from a frightening object on his right (first three photos) and now it's on his left (photo opposite). As far as he is concerned, he's never seen it before.

The response is never completely overcome. Even a well-trained horse will startle, if not shy, at times. And there are times, the first gusty days of spring for example, when the most steadfast of horses is more alert to everything around him and quicker to respond by shying.

Why some horses shy more than others. For some horses, shying is a continual problem. For them, the twentieth or two hundredth bicycle is every bit as terrifying as the first. A few horses seem to learn to control fright/flight and then, as six- or ten- or twelve-year-olds, suddenly begin to spook at every bush and tree. Why do some horses shy more than others? The causes can be divided into two main categories: medical and behavioral.

Shying may be a symptom of a medical problem. Theoretically, anything that interferes with the horse's vision can cause him to shy. He'll be taken by surprise if he suddenly gets a sound cue from an object or person that he does not see, and he'll be alarmed if the images he does see are so indistinct that they cannot be identified.

A few horses are *nearsighted.* They cannot distinguish an object (a trash can by the side of the road, for example) until they are almost on top of it. When they do see it, they are startled. But there is a gamut of disorders that can produce poor vision.

One of the most serious and most common is *periodic ophthalmia,* or *moon blindness,* an inflammation inside the eye itself. It plays havoc with all the structures of the eye but often seems to strike hardest at the iris (which controls the amount of light that enters the eye) and the lens (which focuses the eye). As a result, the horse may become very sensitive to light, and images will be blurry or indistinct. This is an on-again, off-again problem that can eventually lead to complete loss of sight in the affected eye.

A *cataract* is an opacity, a cloudy spot, in the lens. It, too, will interfere with the quality of the image that the eye reports to the brain, so that the horse is surprised by objects he is unable to distinguish. A severe scar left by an injury to the cornea (the outer covering of the eye) may block light. The images may be indistinct or partially blocked out and unrecognizable to the horse.

Retinal degeneration is less common than the other disorders. The light-sensitive cells of the retina begin to die off because of inflammation or some other degenerative process. The result: blind spots or, if enough cells die, total blindness. If the horse develops blind spots, objects pop in and out of his vision in an alarming way.

Some cases of retinal degeneration are revealed by a difference between the horse's daytime and nighttime behavior. During the day, the horse's pupil narrows to admit only a thin beam of bright light. If this beam falls on a blind spot, the horse cannot see and may shy. At night, however, the pupil dilates and lets in a wide beam of dim light. The healthy retinal cells around the blind spot fill in for the cells that have died and the horse's vision improves.

There are conditions that affect only the rods, the retinal cells that are sensitive to dim light and operate only at night; or only the cones, the cells that respond to the bright light of day. So a horse that shies only during the day or only at night may have a vision problem caused by retinal degeneration.

Vitreous floaters are commonly blamed when an older horse begins to shy, but this may be little more than a medical myth. Vitreous floaters are strands and clumps of protein that form in the vitreous body, the area of fluid that composes 70 percent of the eye. They often appear in horses over six years of age, apparently as part of the aging process. The floaters can jiggle around. Theoretically, they could cast a shadow on the retina which the horse might interpret as a moving object. But while a great many horses have vitreous floaters, only some of them shy. And many horses that do not have floaters are as jumpy as a ten-year-old child who has just seen *Dracula* for the first time.

How much shying is caused by medical conditions and how much by behavioral problems is a moot question. Because an increase in shying is the first sign of so many vision problems, it should always be considered a signal for an eye examination, particularly if the horse seems to shy consistently at objects on one side. The fact that your horse's eyes may look perfectly normal to you is no reason for not calling the vet. Most eye problems cannot be seen until the vet dilates the pupil and peers inside with an ophthalmascope. When poor vision has been ruled out, however, it is time to look for behavioral causes.

Your horse may be unhappy . . . or not very bright. Sometimes shying is a form of what psychologists call "displacement activity." In other words, shying is a symptom of another problem. Something as simple as a saddle sore can set a horse on edge, and this extra nervousness will show up as spookiness.

When a normally calm horse begins to shy, one thing to look for is a change in his schedule or surroundings. Horses are creatures of habit and are easily upset by changes. Perhaps you're riding in the morning now, when you used to ride in the afternoon. The horse's familiar world may look strange to him at a different time of day. Or familiar objects may have been moved: A tractor that the horse passed daily without blinking an eye when it was parked beside his barn may turn into a terrifying monster if it is moved in front of the barn. A change in feed or feeding time, or a new and incompatible pasture mate can upset the horse—make him nervous and more apt to shy. Such things are trivial to you, of course. But horses, for survival, are tuned in to trivialities.

Beyond this, some horses just seem to be spookier than others. Certain horses are hypersensitive; they pick up more stimuli and react more quickly than other horses do. Some horses are selectively bred for this trait. The Thoroughbred, for example, is bred to make a fast getaway from the starting gate, so it should not be surprising that he is quick to respond to other stimuli as well. However, hypersensitivity can turn up in individual horses of any breed.

Furthermore, there are differences in intelligence among horses, just as among people. Some horses may need to see twenty or thirty bicycles before they learn not to run away from them. It's even possible (though purely speculative) that some horses have a learning disability, similar to the dyslexia that prevents some children from learning how to read. To such a horse, each bicycle would be as fresh and frightening as the first one.

The rider's role. It is a mistake to attribute human traits to horses. As far as paranoia goes, forget it. Shying is a normal, not a psychotic, reaction by the horse. And you can rule out maliciousness, too. Your horse doesn't make a conscious decision to shy. Fright/flight is much more basic and in many cases is a purely involuntary response. In others, memory of a previous bad experience may play a part. A confirmed shier may well turn out to be a horse whose basic fright/flight response has been reinforced by maltreatment or misguided training methods.

A hypothetical case in point:

You are riding your horse down the road when a scrap of paper blows across his path. You quickly take close contact with the reins, because you suspect he'll shy. Sure enough, he does. You yell, "Whoa," haul him to a quick halt, and then give him a few sharp slaps with your stick just to teach him a lesson. A lesson is learned indeed, but it is not the one you had in mind. First, when you tensed up, your horse was convinced by your reaction that there was something alarming about that paper. Second, he learned that responding to your "Whoa" earned him a beating. It's quite possible that the next time a piece of paper blows across his path he won't shy. He'll bolt and keep on going. Punishment is obviously of no help with a spooky horse.

Is shying therefore an incurable problem, something so basic to the horse's nature that riders simply must learn to live with it? Not necessarily. Not, at least, if the problem is dealt with early enough.

Shying is easiest to combat when it first starts in *a young horse*. The key to the solution is exposure. Take the horse out and let him see as many different things as possible: cars, dogs, ditches, motorcycles, whatever. There's nothing new in this. Xenophon, in Greece of the fourth century B.C., advised that young horses be led through the marketplace so that they would become accustomed to strange sights and sounds. But it's easy in this day and age to concentrate on ring work and overlook this vital part of your horse's training.

Your own reaction to potentially threatening objects is crucial, because the young horse will take his cue from you. Don't stop to show the horse every rock and ditch along the road. Ignore them and keep going. Chances are your horse will ignore them too. And don't tense up when a motorcycle roars toward you; you'd be telling your horse that there's something to worry about. Wait for him to make the decision himself.

If your horse should shy, don't punish him. Bring him back quickly and gently, talk to him and pet him. The idea is to build the young horse's confidence in you, as his trainer, and in his own ability to deal with the strange world around him. Gradually, as he gains confidence, he becomes "socialized" and learns to suppress the flight instinct, because you have asked him to.

Much the same tactics are in order with *an older horse* that shies. If you can pinpoint the underlying cause of the problem, and if it turns out to be a change of schedule or environment, you can probably put a stop to it.

With *a confirmed shier,* results are not so easily obtained. Whether or not a horse can be retrained is an open question. The answer probably depends as much on the individual horse and rider as it does on any particular training method.

It is important, however, not to typecast your horse. If you assume that he will always shy at cars, he probably will, because he will pick up your own nervousness every time one comes near. Handle the situation the same way you would with a green horse: Be prepared, but be relaxed.

HOW EXPERT RIDERS DEAL WITH SHYING

CAROL SASLOW, Associate Professor of Psychology at Oregon State University, breeds and trains national award-winning Morgans:

Age is the key in dealing with shying. We rarely have trouble with horses after they are three years old, because we start working on the problem early. I take lots of walks with young foals, long before they can be ridden, to get them used to new sights and sounds. When a foal shies at something strange, I comfort him and bring him back to whatever it was that frightened him. This builds his confidence.

I deal with shying in older horses in the same way: by hiking with the horse. Horses are most responsive when they can see their trainer. Walking next to the horse gives me an advantage too. I can see his eyes open wide and his nostrils dilate when he begins to feel alarmed, and I can catch the response before it gets out of hand. I lead him past the frightening object, comforting him as we go.

Catching the response early is important when you're riding a horse that shies. When I come to a potentially frightening object, I try to guess which side the horse will shy toward. Then I transfer my crop to that side and get ready to correct his movement with my leg. I talk to him and perhaps use a half halt to let him know that I'm around and in charge. You want to allow a slight movement, so that the horse has the feeling that he's moving away from the frightening object. But correct him quickly and pat him to reward him for responding to your correction.

MELANIE SMITH is one of the brightest stars of the Grand Prix circuit and of the U. S. Equestrian Team:

A lot of spooky horses improve as they gain experience at shows. But some horses shy no matter what you do and probably always will. There's no cure for this. You simply have to cope with it. You have to learn to think one step ahead of the horse and recognize places where he might spook.

If I see that a jumper course includes a spooky-looking rolltop or combination, I'll plan my entrance circle to bring the horse right past that jump. As we go by it, I'll cluck, just to give the horse the idea that when we pass that way again he's to go forward—and over the fence.

If I think the horse will spook at something near the rail or at the end of the ring, I'll plan to cut my corners a little closer than usual.

How I handle shying depends a lot on the individual horse. Some horses, particularly cold-blooded, less sensitive ones, respond to discipline with the stick or spur. But a whipping only makes matters worse with so sensitive a horse as a Thoroughbred. You're better off patting him and easing him past whatever is frightening him.

GUNNAR OSTERGAARD, a champion dressage rider in his native Denmark, has become one of the leading dressage riders, trainers, judges, and coaches in America, where he trains the dressage horses at F. Eugene Dixon's Erdenheim Farm, in Lafayette Hill, Pennsylvania, and also runs his own farm, in Bucks County:

The obedient dressage horse that is under the rider's aids and is on the bit will not shy. The best way to deal with shying is to sit deep, use your legs, and bring your horse under the aids. It's important that the horse realize he should be paying attention to you, not to some object along the road.

When a horse I'm riding shies, I might ignore the incident the first time or let the horse take a closer look at whatever is frightening him. But, the second time, I correct him. Very often I use the shoulder-in, turning the horse's forehand away from the object as we pass it. This forces him to pay closer attention to me. I don't choke him with the reins, but I attract his attention by driving him forward with seat, legs, and perhaps a touch of the whip.

If I'm riding a green horse that is not completely under the influence of my aids, I might spend more time showing him the object. First I walk by it and then, when the horse is relaxed, trot and canter by. But I don't pat him for half an hour when he shies. I concentrate on riding him forward so that I can start to bring him on the bit.

If you think of shying as being caused by a medical problem, you will always be able to find an excuse for your horse's behavior. I think most shying has an emotional cause. Some horses, if allowed to go too far with it, turn shying into a game. So it's important to correct shying quickly in a firm but friendly way. An experienced rider can feel the horse tense up and can correct him before he actually shies.

JEANNA FISKE, a professional horse trainer and veterinarian who has conducted many research projects, at Texas A&M University, devoted to the study of the horse's behavior and learning ability.

You can retrain an older horse who shies, as long as the horse does not have a medical problem. But you must do it on two levels, dealing first with the problem at hand, the object the horse is shying away from, and secondly with the underlying emotional cause.

For the first phase, I have had success with a planned program of desensitization. I find an object the horse is shying away from—dog, paper, car, or whatever—and set up a situation on my terms. I put the object in the center of a field or ring, then ride the horse at a walk in a large circle around it. I stay on the rail until the horse is calm, then gradually spiral in toward the object. If he gets nervous, we return to the rail and begin again. I never press the horse. It can take two hours to reach the center of the ring. When the horse will stand relaxed next to the object, I reward him by getting off and taking him back to the barn.

This system works equally well with horses that are afraid of noises. I have an assistant stand in the center of the ring and bang two trash-can lids together. Horses can generalize this sound to include engine noises, gunfire, and similar sounds.

Unless the underlying problem is dealt with, the horse will shy again, perhaps at a different object. I keep a diary of everything I do with each horse, so that if I've inadvertently upset him by a change in his environment I can track it down and rectify it.

In most confirmed shiers that I've seen, it doesn't take long to spot the cause. They've been conditioned by their riders to shy. Coming up to an object like an open culvert, the rider "gets ready," tightens the reins, and tenses up. The horse, particularly a hypersensitive, emotional type, feels this and actually shies away from the rider as much as he does from the culvert. I always try to relax rein contact when approaching such an object.

In retraining a confirmed shier, I've found that punishment invariably does more harm than good. Punishing fear produces a neurotic horse. His fear of one object becomes generalized to include his trainer and, in fact, everything around him.

RODNEY JENKINS, owner of Hill Top Stable, in Orange, Virginia, has trained and ridden some of the most famous Grand Prix jumpers and hunters in the world, including Idle Dice (with which he won the American Gold Cup two years in a row), Icey Paws, Prime Time, Touch the Sun (winner of two consecutive Horse of the Year titles), San Felipe, and Riot Free:

Most of the shiers I've seen fall into one of four categories. The biggest one is that of horses with vision problems, so eyesight is always the first thing to check. Then there are horses who shy at noises—whistling or crowd noises—at shows. If I'm riding a horse like this in a show, I'll stuff his ears with cotton.

Green horses very often shy away from the rail. I use my inside rein and leg to turn the horse's head and neck away from the fence and focus his attention elsewhere.

Most horses get over shying as they put on mileage, but each one is different. Some are simply "evergreen" and always have to look at everything. There isn't much you can do about this except keep taking the horse to show after show and hope that the problem will lessen.

Punishment gets you nowhere. You can punish a horse for not listening to your aids but not for shying. You don't whip a child for being afraid of the dark.

LOADING THE DIFFICULT HORSE

by CLAIRE WARREN

The horse you love so much that you hope to keep him till death do you part suddenly becomes a hated burden when you discover that you couldn't get rid of him even if you wanted to. He won't load onto a horse trailer. Nothing is more exasperating than a horse that won't load. People who are besotted with their horses have been known to weep, curse, and finally beat the beast because he wouldn't go onto his trailer.

If you own a difficult loader, you know that no method works all the time for all horses. The following procedure combines all of the techniques that work most often. I hope it works for you. First, you must:

Know your horse. Before you even attempt to load your horse, you must understand his temperament and know what kind of discipline is most effective with him. Most horses really believe that humans are smarter and stronger than they are. Although these horses may resist or fight, they will obey if you employ the method of discipline they respect. Other horses require a different approach. If punishment is too severe, these horses will

PATENT PENDING?

not concede but will continue to fight, heedless of injury. These horses respond best to perseverance.

Because horses are creatures of habit, perseverance (not patience) is the
rule in trailer loading. We don't want the horse to get in the habit of standing around the trailer, refusing to load. So if you have given one method of
loading a fair trial and it has failed, switch to another method. Don't let
your horse return to the barn until he has been loaded.

Be prepared. Before you lead your horse from the barn, make sure you
have plenty of time and are determined to get him on the trailer. Have an
assistant nearby. The trailer should be parked on a level and attractive spot.
The trailer and the lowered loading ramp should be level and firm so that
they won't wobble when the horse loads. Make the inside of the trailer as inviting as possible. Pull any partitions to the side and secure them. Open
windows and doors if your horse is liable to be frightened by the dark interior. And place a bucket of oats inside the trailer so that the horse will have
an instant reward. Ensure that all the equipment you might need is handy.
Then, and only then, go and get your horse.

Leading. Even if he can normally be led around by his forelock and
remain quietly tied for hours with a piece of baling twine, your horse can
turn into an obstinate devil when it comes to being led onto a trailer. There
are many ways to make a horse lead well, and all work on the choke-chain
principle used in dog obedience: one hard pull and a quick release to bring
the point home without injury. You must never give a sustained pull, because it might injure the horse and also because the horse may discover that
he is stronger than you are.

Most successful methods of leading employ of a lead shank with a chain.
In order of increasing severity, you can attach the chain to the halter so that
the chain is 1) under the nose, 2) over the nose, 3) completely around the
nose, or 4) under the horse's upper lip. Another method is to use a conven-

tional lead rope or lariat and devise a choke halter that tightens only when the horse fights, and that can be released quickly.

All these methods can be dangerous unless you use care and hold your temper. If your horse rears backward, follow him, giving short jerks on the lead shank until he stops fighting. If your horse doesn't fight but still refuses to move, you can try a few jerks on the lead shank. If that doesn't work, do not pull, no matter how mad you are, but get:

Assistance from behind. Your horse should now be standing at the foot of the loading ramp, ready and willing to follow you anywhere except into that hated trailer. The assistant behind the horse must be a knowledgeable horse person who knows how and when to get out of the way. Knowing your horse, you should be able to decide whether the assistant should punish (solid whacks) or simply persuade (constant, nagging taps). This determines what your assistant should use: a broom, a whip, or a two-by-four. If your horse is liable to kick, use a long broom or whip or board, and be sure that your assistant is agile.

Should your horse still refuse to get on the trailer, or if he gets on only to leap back out again, you can try backing him in. If this doesn't work, keep your temper under control and try:

The channel method. With you in front and the assistant behind, the only place your horse can go is to the side, so now your purpose is to block off that escape route. You can do it with an arrangement of jumps and such, by parking the trailer in a natural alleyway, or by the use of long ropes. The ropes should be attached to either side of the trailer and worked by two more assistants. When the horse is standing at the foot of the loading ramp, the two assistants cross their ropes behind the horse while assistant number one continues his tapping or whipping.

If this doesn't work, you do have a difficult horse! He is probably standing there, a quivering mass of jelly, prepared to die rather than give in. Don't despair. You can try something even more severe, such as:

Starvation. A lot of non-loaders give in graciously if they are very hungry. This means that you will have to do what I said you shouldn't do: give up for today. Besides, if you haven't gotten him on the trailer by now, continual efforts would only tend to reinforce his non-loading behavior pattern, so you might as well take him back to the barn. But don't give him any grain. Preferably, let him see other horses eating. A confirmed trailer hater will interpret this as deserved punishment and should not tear the barn down. (But you'd better hang around to make sure.) You may give the horse hay to keep him alive. Don't attempt to load him again until he has been grainless for several days. Then, equipped with a bucket of his favorite food plus your three assistants, you are ready to try again.

Get your horse to the same point where you left off. For example, you might have a chain around his nose for leading, an assistant tapping on his rump with a broom, and two other assistants holding side ropes crossed tightly against his hindquarters. Now hold your grain bucket temptingly about a foot in front of his mouth. Slowly back into the trailer, as he (theoretically) follows you.

If he doesn't, and while he is still hungry, you can try:

Blindfolding. This is a dangerous method, because if the horse bumps his head or falls off the loading ramp while blindfolded, you may as well give up trying to get him on a trailer ever. Nevertheless, with some horses, blindfolding works beautifully. Whether you try blindfolding or not depends on what you know of your horse and how desperate you are. In any case, be sure that the blindfold is secure and won't slip off no matter what.

On the trailer. Let's hope and assume that your horse is at last on the trailer. The very first thing to do is to reward him with his favorite food, while your assistants raise and fasten the loading ramp so that your horse can't leave. Stay on the trailer with him for at least half an hour, feeding and petting him. Your work is far from over. You must now break the habit of refusal to load.

After this first half hour in the trailer, unload and reload your horse several times, making him stay in the trailer at least five minutes each time. Then load and unload him once a day, preferably just after his work and before you feed him. You want to establish routine obedience, just as in your riding. When he is finally obedient in loading, you must consider the problem of:

Hauling a difficult horse. With every horse you haul, but most especially with a horse that is a difficult loader, you must try to make his ride as pleasant as possible. Once again, you must know your horse. Does he need strict confinement to make sure he doesn't climb over the breast bar? Or does he need extra room, because he cannot find his balance? Drive carefully, slowly, and try to avoid unfamiliar roads. If you turn your trailer over on the Expressway, you really can't expect your horse to load willingly.

Good luck!

SHIPPING YOUR HORSE

By professional shipper MICHAEL GRADY, whose clients include
the United States Equestrian Team; as told to Lenore Scallan.

When your business is shipping horses and you log thousands of horse-miles every month, you soon develop a repertoire of tricks to make your life easier. As it turns out, those things which make your life easier when you're at the wheel of a horse van are the same things that make your passengers comfortable and keep them safe en route. These techniques will help you ensure the safe arrival of your horse when you ship commercially, and most of these tips will be useful to you if you use your own, private van or trailer.

Well in advance. Find out the health requirements of the destination to which you are shipping. If your horse is traveling across state lines, you may need a negative Coggins certificate and a health certificate. More-complicated documents are required for horses leaving the country, often requiring the signature of a federally accredited veterinarian (whose names are available through your state department of agriculture.)

Have your veterinarian help you assemble all the necessary papers and put your horse's documents in an envelope marked with his name, color, and markings, so that the vet meeting the plane at its destination will be able to identify your horse immediately.

Give the commercial vanning company plenty of advance notice. Some people think that shipping a horse is like hailing a cab. A week's notice is fine for shipping within the country by van or by air, as long as the health documents are in order. Bookings for overseas flights should be made six weeks in advance, in order to provide sufficient time for the more complex formalities involved.

When money is no object, you can ship your horse faster than if you have to seek the cheapest possible route. The cost for each horse is usually based on the number of horses on the van. Van drivers with empty space are often reluctant to deviate from their route in order to pick up one extra horse. Frequently, the owner of the horses already on board specifically requests the driver not to stop en route.

It is easier to find space on a van if you ship in the same direction and at the same time as many other horsemen. For example, there should be no problem if you go to South Carolina in the winter or north to Lake Placid, Chagrin, or Devon in the summer.

Just before. If the trip is to exceed three hours, you should take precautions so that the horse's digestive system continues to function smoothly. Horses are prone to constipation during long trips. Use a small amount of oil in a bran mash for four or five nights before you leave, and ship with good-quality hay, preferably alfalfa, which will keep the horse loose. Most constipation problems are caused by dehydration. After I've been on the road for about forty-five minutes, I stop and fill water buckets for the horses to have in front of them the rest of the way. I wait the forty-five minutes to give the horses a chance to settle down and also to avoid frightening them if the water should splash while I'm negotiating rough back roads.

I pull into the first rest stop on the Interstate and turn the motor off for twenty minutes before hanging the water buckets. The horses don't like to drink for the first time while the van is still vibrating, but once they begin to drink they will continue for the rest of the journey. I fill the buckets only two thirds full in order to avoid splashing.

Preparing the horse for shipping. The safest way to ship is without shoes or bandages but with the van well padded to prevent injuries. I believe in bandages only when they are properly applied and do not make the horse uncomfortable.

I don't advocate commercial hock and knee protectors. They tend to get very hot and encourage the horse to kick. Often, so-called "protectors," such as head bumpers, only add stress to a situation, especially if the horse has not been vanned before. A head bumper may even be dangerous. If it gets hot and the horse manages to rub it off, he will also rub his halter off.

The fit of the shipping halter is very important. The noseband should fall at least two fingers' width below the cheekbone and be roomy enough so that the horse can munch his hay in comfort. But it must fit snugly enough so that there is no chance of its slipping off the horse's head. A halterless horse is in a dangerous condition. You have no control at all. Sheepskin is a nice addition to a shipping halter in order to protect the head from rubbing.

I don't like to tranquilize unless I have to. The motion of the van will usually relax the horse before he can get upset, but if I anticipate a problem, I do tranquilize. If a horse is overtranquilized, two things can happen: He can come out of the tranquilizer suddenly and panic; or he can become so relaxed that he loses control of his legs and falls down. I also tranquilize horses that are shipping by air, except for broodmares and horses scheduled to race in the immediate future. I give two and one half cubic centimeters of the tranquilizer at the farm where I pick up, about six hours before the flight's departure time. This permits me to observe the horse's reaction on the way to the airport. If the amount is too much, most of it will have worn off before the flight; if too little, I'll give another half cubic centimeter before takeoff and a half before landing. If there are stopovers during the journey, I give one half cubic centimeter before each takeoff.

If you are vanning a horse, try withholding hay from him for several hours beforehand instead of resorting to a tranquilizer. He may find the hay net in the van so preoccupying that he will forget to fret.

Preparing the van. A good commercial shipper should arrive with a properly prepared stall. But this is no reason for not checking his arrangements and perhaps making a few adjustments of your own.

Leg bandages for shipping should extend from just below the knee to over the coronet band, for complete protection. Use at least six layers of cotton so that the bandages can be wrapped snugly without injuring the horse's legs. Fasten with masking tape or pins, putting the fastenings on the outside to prevent the horse from rubbing them off.

First prepare the van. The opening between ramp and van floor is a dangerous trap for a horse's foot. If you do much shipping, a good investment is your own coco-mat rug to cover ramp and opening. The mat provides secure footing even in wet weather. Make sure the mat is long enough to extend a couple of feet into the van, or, during unloading, a horse may kick it down the ramp ahead of him and stumble. For a first-time loader, you can camouflage the whole approach with a familiar material like straw. Leave the opposite van door open to make a more inviting scene, but be sure you put the bar across the opening.

I like to bed my stalls four inches deep in straw. The deep bed encourages the horse to urinate en route. At the rear of the stall, I bank the straw deeply against the wall to protect the horse's hind legs from injury against the rear wall. If I know I have a kicker, I provide extra padding by dropping a feed sack filled with sponge rubber eight to ten inches thick behind the horse so that he can lean against it like a pillow. I secure it outside of the stall so that he can't catch his legs in the strings. The banking and padding encourage him to stand toward the front of the stall. If the driver has to make a sudden stop, the horse is safe. Instead of scrambling forward, even to his knees, he comes right up against the breast bar.

In some vans, the two upright poles that support the stall dividers are placed together when three stalls are converted into two. Believe it or not, it is possible for a horse to get his foot caught in the narrow gap between these bars, especially youngsters, which tend to be boisterous anyway. If there is no other horse next to yours, and if one of the bars is removable, ask the driver to take it down.

Check that the windows are open or closed, whichever is appropriate to the weather conditions. Remember that horses generate a tremendous amount of heat in a closed van. Consult with the driver regarding any change of clothing your horse may require en route. A horse shipped from New York with two blankets and closed windows should not arrive in Florida with two blankets and closed windows.

Loading procedure. If you ship horses with any regularity, you would do well to keep your own coco mats on hand for laying over the van ramp and the approach as well when the footing is questionable. These mats don't reverberate and they cannot slip. Be sure that the mat is long enough to cover the gap between the ramp and the lip of the van with a foot or two to spare and that it covers the approach to the ramp at the other end. I once had an eight-day-old foal catch his foot between the ramp and the lip. We were lucky. I grabbed the ankle joint and kept it straight while we pulled the leg out.

For a first-timer or a horse you know is frightened of loading, open the doors on the far side of the van from the ramp and put a guard across. Cover the van floor, the matting, and a few feet of ground at the approach to the ramp with straw or shavings. The horse will think he's walking on his familiar bedding. He sees the light at the far end of the van and doesn't feel trapped.

During the loading procedure, have all the help handy you're likely to need, but stay relaxed. Use a chain shank with a sixteen-inch chain. Run it through the ring under the horse's nose and double it back on itself. Now you can hold your right hand up near the horse's head for good control without having to hold onto the chain part of the shank. Don't run your chain over the horse's nose unless he's so difficult that you have to. If he breaks loose or if the shank happens to fall slack, there will be a loop of chain in which he can catch his foot or which can hit him in the face.

When you're a stranger to the horse, as I usually am, stand for a minute holding the shank and let the horse smell your clothes and hair. You want him to identify you as someone he can trust. Be sure you have his attention. He shouldn't be gazing off into space. Stay relaxed and so will he.

If he starts to load and then flies backward out of the van, let him go. Don't try to restrain him. He'll only fight you, throw his head in the air, and maybe hit his head on the roof of the van.

Use a little grain to encourage him. If he still refuses to cooperate, you'll have to put the chain over his nose. Run it through the near ring, through

The *wrong* way to tie a horse on a van. His head is too high; he can't clear mucous from his air passages. On a long trip he'll arrive badly congested. With the chains snapped to these rings on the noseband, he's bound to rub his nose.

the far ring, and hook it to the upper ring on the far side. This arrangement gives you good control and prevents the chain from rubbing the horse's nose. Stand facing the horse with your shoulders parallel to his. Snatch him back and keep him backing in a straight line. If he swings his quarters to one side, turn the rest of him in that direction. Just keep him straight. When he's going back straight, stop and remove the chain from his nose. Pull on the shank. If he doesn't immediately walk forward, snatch him back again. The idea is to make walking forward more attractive than backing up.

When he moves forward willingly, remove the chain from his nose and try loading him. If he absolutely refuses to load forward, back him in and then spin him around. You must keep the horse straight whether he goes on forward or backward. If you keep control of his head and station a helper on either side of the ramp, the horse will have no inclination to swing out. This is where the extra help comes in. Remember to relax. Don't anticipate problems.

Once inside. The horse should be tied on both sides of his head. The chains should attach up high on the sides of the halter, so that the halter won't rub his nose. He should have enough freedom to reach for hay and water and to lower his head to permit his air passages to drain. If you leave a horse on a short shank for a long time, his sinus cavities fill up. Don't leave so much loose chain that he can catch his throatlatch in it or that it can hit him in the face.

Always tie the loose end of the chain out of the way. It's common sense. Don't leave anything hanging loose to cause trouble. Hang hay nets between horses to keep their heads apart. Keep the nets full so the horse cannot catch his foot in dangling string. I attach hay nets with double-ended snaps to avoid dangling rope ends. To keep the hay net from swinging, snap a lead shank to the bottom of the net, stretch the shank across the aisle, and tie it

A properly tied horse. The chains are attached to the higher rings. The horse has much more freedom of movement. Another tie chain has been used to hang the water bucket securely within his reach. Hay is tied to the right.

to the bar on the other side. If the hay net comes untied at the top, it will fall away from the horses. When two rows of horses face each other across the aisle, use the shank to tie opposite hay nets to each other.

When you're shipping weanlings or yearlings, be sure someone rides in back with them. Babies do not like to be left alone. You also need an attendant if you ship stallions and mares in the same van. If you ship them together, remember to put the stallion or colt on first. Rub Vicks VapoRub in his nose to keep him from smelling the mares, and use the rear stalls with the breast bar in place. Use a hood or hang a blanket in front of him if necessary. Once he's secure, load the mares or fillies. Always unload the mares first. Never try to load or unload a stallion beside a mare. You can kill yourself that way.

Use a double stall whenever possible. I ship in double stalls 90 percent of the time, to make the horse more comfortable. I use a box stall for a first-time shipper and leave him loose until he has settled down. At some time during the journey I try to tie him up. I also use box stalls for mares with foals or for one or more weanlings. Keeping the colts and fillies separate, I put two weanlings loose in each box stall and throw hay down on the floor for them.

Costs. Commercial shipping is priced by the mile. The charge for each horse is based on the number of horses in the van and whether the van is coming back loaded or empty.

A box stall costs three times as much as a single stall, and I charge one and a half times the cost of a single stall for a double. The charge for an attendant is also based on distance and the number of horses in his care.

Vanning charges vary throughout the country. The East Coast is more expensive than the Midwest and the West Coast, because of the number of toll roads.

SOURCES OF SELECTIONS
EDITED FOR THIS BOOK

Chapter 1

The Riding Horse Breeds (December 1977)
Conformation in Action (November 1975 through March 1976)
How the Experts Judge a Horse's Way of Moving (November 1979)
Look Before You Ride! (July 1976)
Precautions the Pros Take
How to Test a Horse for Soundness (March 1980)
Pre-purchase Vet Checks (July 1975)
What Unsoundnesses Are Acceptable? (July 1978)
The Question of Thoroughbred Unsoundness
The Question of Weight-carrying Ability

Chapter 2

What Your Horse Needs and How to Select It (October 1975)
What the Well-dressed Horse Should Wear . . . and Why (August 1974)
How to Put on Your Horse's Blanket (September 1979)
The Art of Blanketing (October 1978)
Leg Bandages (January, February 1977)
A Question about Tail Wraps (February 1977)
Leg Bandages: A Question, an Answer, and an Idea (February 1977)
When, How, and Why Should a Horse Wear Leg Bandages? (February 1979)
All About Saddles (June 1974)
Favorite Saddles of Famous Riders (November 1978)
All About Saddle Pads (October 1979)
Fitting Your Horse's Halter (August 1978)
Should Horses Wear Halters in the Stable? (August 1979)
How to Make an Emergency Halter (1971)
Speaking of Martingales (February 1976)
Buying a Bridle (March 1972)
All About Bits (February 1973)
Favored Bits of Famous Riders (September 1975)
Tacking Up

Chapter 3

Identifying Your Pasture (April 1979)
Pasture Psychology (June 1976)
In or Out for Fitness? (July 1979)
The Nutrients in One Pound of Feed (October 1978)
Daily Nutritional Requirements for Horses (October 1978)
Balancing Your Horse's Diet (June 1978)
How to Buy Hay (October 1978)
When Things Go Wrong with Hay (October 1975)
Where to Buy Hay (October 1978)
False Fears About Feeding Hay (October 1978)
How to Feed Hay (July 1974)
All About Grain (June 1978)
All About Commercial Feed (August 1978)
All About Vitamin-Mineral Supplements (June 1979)
What You Should Know About Vitamins (June 1979)
What You Should Know About Minerals (June 1979)
Which Ones to Worry About (June 1979)
The Risk of Deficiencies in a Standard Diet (June 1979)
Mind Your P's (June 1979)
Megadosing (June 1979)
Feeding Horses on a Budget (June 1974)
Feeding Grass (June 1977)
Hot Meals for Horses (January 1974)

Chapter 4

The Importance of Grooming (1980)
Grooming the Good Old-fashioned Way (January 1973)
How to Make Your Own Grooming Wisp (January 1973)
Grooming Techniques, by Susan Harris (1980)
How the Experts Groom Their Horses (August 1976)
Pulling the Mane (1980)
Braiding the Mane (1980)
Braiding with Rubber Bands (1980)
Taped Manes (1980)
Training the Mane to Lie Over (July 1973)
How to Pull Your Horse's Tail (October 1979)
Braiding the Tail (1980)
Adding a Mud Knot (1980)
French-braiding the Foretop (1980)
Getting the Most from Your Clippers (1980)
Introducing Your Horse to the Clippers (1980)
To Clip or Not to Clip? (1980)
Clipping Styles (1980)

Chapter 5

An Expandable Backyard Stable (December 1973)
The Live-over Stable (January 1978)
Efficiency and Economy (May 1973)
Easy-care Stable (April 1974)
Expanding Your Stall Space (June 1974)
Built-in Convertibility (May 1979)
Pasture Walk-through (July 1978)
Compact Tack Storage (December 1978)
A Super-simple Saddle Rack (February 1979)
Practical Details In and Around the Stable (July 1973, May 1978, August 1978, October 1978, June 1976)
A Fire-prevention Checklist for Your Stable (December 1973)
Bedding, That Necessary Evil (October 1973)
A Bedding Tip (October 1973)
Stall Cleaning Technique (May 1979)
Stable Insect Control (June 1973)
Money-saving Stable Management (March 1975)
Keeping Stable Records (October 1977)
Thrifty Owner, Capitalist Horse (October 1977)
How to Choose a Boarding Stable (August 1976)

Chapter 6

Catching the Uncatchable (September 1975)
The Question of Cribbing (September 1975)
How to Restrain a Horse (August 1975)
How to Use a Twitch (June 1981)
Restraining a Horse Without a Twitch (August 1975)
How to Handle a Horse That Bites
How to Put Weight on a Thin Horse (March 1977)
Leg Blemishes (July 1974)
If Your Horse Shies . . . (March 1979)
How Expert Riders Deal with Shying (March 1979)
Loading the Difficult Horse (February 1975)
Shipping Your Horse (November 1977)

THE EXPERTS

RICHARD ABBOTT, lawyer

MARY BACON, riding instructor, dressage judge, Combined Training competitor, and jockey

THOMAS D. BROKKEN, D.V.M., veterinarian

BUDDY BROWN, Grand Prix star, member of the U.S.E.T. Jumping Team

BONNIE BYRNES, trainer of gaited and harness horses

EDDIE BYWATERS, stable manager and trainer

JANET CARTER, hunter and jumper trainer

TAD COFFIN, Olympic Three-Day Event Individual Gold Medal winner

ALEXANDER DELAHUNTA, D.V.M., Chairman of Veterinary Clinics at Cornell University

RAY DUNPHY, stable manager

JOE FERGUSON, hunter and jumper trainer

JEANNA FISKE, trainer and researcher in equine psychology

MICHAEL GRADY, professional horse shipper

LENDON GRAY, dressage competitor

ROBERT HALL, former British Dressage Team coach, founder of the Fulmer School of Equitation

CLINTON HANKS, former president of Smith-Worthington saddlemakers

SUSAN HARRIS, horsewoman and equestrian author

KAREN HEALEY, equitation, hunter and jumper instructor

WILLIAM HEFFNER, D.V.M., racetrack veterinarian

JOSEPH HEISSAN, D.V.M., veterinarian

JIMMY HERRING, Grand Prix jumper groom

PATTY HEUCKEROTH, show rider and trainer

DAVID HOPPER, horse dealer

WALTER HUGHES, Quarter Horse trainer and judge

HOLLY HUGO-VIDAL, hunter/jumper trainer, rider, and judge

RODNEY JENKINS, Grand Prix show jumping star

STOREY JENKS, International Three-Day Event rider

MICHAEL KELLEY, professional horsewoman and author

JOE KING, co-manager of Waldemar Farm, Ocala, Florida

CARL KNEE, hunter/jumper trainer and instructor

STEPHANIE LLOYD, breeding-farm owner

ALEXANDER MACKAY-SMITH, breeder, equestrian author

MATTHEW MACKAY-SMITH, D.V.M., veterinarian, Endurance rider, and judge

WINKY MACKAY-SMITH, Endurance rider

TOMMY MANION, Quarter Horse trainer

JOHN MANNING, director of riding, Stoneleigh-Burnham School

GINNY MARSHALL, exercise girl and pony girl

EDITH MASTER, Olympic dressage rider, trainer, instructor, and judge

RALPH MCILVAIN, racing-stable manager

MARIE MOORE, racehorse owner and breeder

DOROTHY MORKIS, Olympic dressage rider

WILLIAM MOYER, D.V.M., veterinarian, University of Pennsylvania

RONNIE MUTCH, instructor, trainer, U.S.E.T. rider, judge

BARBARA NEWTON, Combined Training competitor

GUNNAR OSTERGAARD, dressage rider, trainer, coach

BETH PERKINS, Three-Day Event rider

RON QUERRY, D.V.M., former director of Equestrian Center at Lake Erie College

JUDY RICHTER, trainer, instructor, 1974 Horsewoman of the Year

STANLEY ROSENFELD, Assistant Manager of Miller's, New York City

LIONEL RUBEN, D.V.M., equine eye specialist, University of Pennsylvania

ROGER RUETENIK, Quarter Horse judge, show horse owner

CAROL SASLOW, Morgan breeder, University Psychology professor

ELAINE SEDITO, professional journalist

DONNA SMITH, equestrian journalist

JOHN SMITH, Thoroughbred breeder and trainer, former Quarter Horse jockey, steeplechase rider

MELANIE SMITH, Grand Prix show jumping star, Horsewoman of the Year 1978, World Cup Champion in 1982

RICHARD TAYLOR, conformation hunter and racehorse breeder

CAROL HOFMANN THOMPSON, hunter/jumper rider, trainer, instructor, and former member of the U.S.E.T. Jumping Team

BERNIE TRAURIG, professional show jumping rider and Grand Prix star

DELMAR TWYMAN, conformation hunter breeder and trainer

WILLIAM TYZNIK, D.V.M., veterinarian, equine nutrition authority

BARBARA VAN TUYL, professional horsewoman and author

SANDY VAUGHAN, Quarter Horse trainer

CLAIRE WARREN, horsewoman and journalist

WENDY WATERS, head groom for Rodney Jenkins's Hill Top Stable

MICHAEL WETTACH, steeplechase rider, trainer, and breeder

KENNY WINCHELL, conformation hunter breeder and trainer

JIM WOFFORD, Olympic Three-Day Event rider, director of the U.S.E.T., U.S.C.T.A., and A.H.S.A.

FRANK WRIGHT, racehorse trainer and television racing analyst

Note: More-detailed biographical data about this star-studded panel of experts accompany the preceding articles. But it should perhaps be pointed out that some of the conditions that are true as this book is being prepared are bound to have changed by the time it reaches your hands.

The horse world moves fast. Horsemen move from one part of the country to another with amazing frequency, considering the complications involved. Trainers, instructors, coaches, and riders move from one stable to another, since eminent experts such as these are constantly solicited to change their present activity or position. Furthermore, it is almost certain that a horse will retire or disappear before his rider does, the horse's lifespan being so much shorter than our own, so it is not unlikely that some of the famous horse-and-rider partnerships cited here will have since been supplanted by others.

Nevertheless, this information was exact at a certain "point in time" and should be accepted as such—with perhaps a p.s. to add: "et cetera."